'This inspiring, practical boo[k] businesses to thrive in unce[rtain] examples. I highly recommen[d]

Steve Smith, *Founder, Poundland*

'Steven has shown impressive skill and success as a judge for many companies at Nachural's Signature Awards, which takes place in Britain's most vibrant cities: London, Manchester, Leicester, Wolverhampton, and Birmingham. Additionally, he is a regular contributor to the *Business Influencer Magazine*. His rich first-hand experience provides valuable insights into what helps successful companies survive and flourish. This book shares a fascinating and unique view of some of the top British companies, illustrating how they navigate challenges and economic changes, all while remaining beloved fixtures on our High Streets for many years. It comes highly recommended!'

Ninder Johal DL, *CEO of Nachural, Founder of the Signature Awards and Editor-in-chief of* The Business Influencer

'*Chasing Permanence* is an inspiring and insightful guide for entrepreneurs seeking to build enduring businesses. Through personal narratives and practical wisdom, the author delves into what makes some companies thrive while others falter, offering a unique perspective on the challenges facing our High Streets today.

In the same way, my book, *The Unfair Advantage*, explores how entrepreneurs can leverage their unique strengths to succeed, *Chasing Permanence* provides a roadmap for creating lasting impact. The book explores vital factors for SME and High Street success, including the importance of the entrepreneur's mindset, scalability, and systems thinking. It also highlights the crucial roles of community and collaboration in achieving long-term viability.

This heartfelt and practical resource combines personal stories with robust business strategies, showing how our High Streets can be sustainably and successfully rejuvenated.'

Ash Ali, *Co-founder, Uhubs and author of* The Unfair Advantage *(2021 British Business Book of the Year)*

'*Chasing Permanence* by Steven Adjei is a timely and insightful exploration of High Street businesses' challenges and opportunities today. As record-breaking numbers of businesses close, this book delves deep into the reasons behind the closures and offers actionable strategies to help reverse the trend.

Steven's research, real-life interviews, and extensive experience reveal how fostering community and collaboration, and the power of mentoring can lead to thriving businesses. An essential read for any SME looking to survive and flourish in today's volatile retail sector.

A must-read for anyone in retail, business leaders, policymakers, and anyone passionate about the future of saving our High Streets.'

Chelsey Baker, *Founder of National Mentoring Day, top UK pitching expert, BAFTA award-winning mentor, international keynote speaker, and 2022 Influential Woman of the Year*

'Steven Adjei is a great storyteller. He seduces you to join his exploits and quests. The reward: you learn how companies persist on our High Street. It's a book you should definitely read.'

Professor Christian Stadler, *Professor in Strategy at Warwick Business School and bestselling author of* Enduring Success *and* Open Strategy, *2021 Strategy Book of the Year*

'*Chasing Permanence* by Steven Adjei offers such thought-provoking insights that it can truly shift our perspective on the High Street. I especially appreciate how he weaves in values throughout his work. Get ready to feel touched, moved, and inspired!'

Dr Mandeep Rai, *Sunday Times bestselling author of* The Values Compass, *2023 Business Influencer of the Year, former BBC World Service journalist, and authority on Global Values*

'Steven Adjei's *Chasing Permanence* is a powerful and timely exploration of the challenges High Street businesses face, particularly those led by ethnic minority entrepreneurs. Drawing on two decades of experience, Adjei provides real-world strategies and a compelling narrative highlighting these businesses' critical role in sustaining local economies. This book is a must-read for anyone invested in the future of the UK's High Streets and offers invaluable insights on resilience, community, and sustainable success.'

Sanjiv Patel, *Award-winning Thought Leader, TEDx speaker, visiting lecturer on entrepreneurship at Warwick Business School, and host of the* Just Another Lens *podcast*

'*Chasing Permanence* is a timely and essential guide for SMEs navigating the challenges of today's beleaguered High Streets. As our local economies face unprecedented strain, with thousands of businesses shutting each quarter, this book offers a lifeline by focusing on what businesses can do to survive and thrive.'

Obi James, *Inclusive Leadership expert, CEO of Obi James Consultancy, and #1 bestselling author of* Let Go Leadership

'When I met Steven, I was impressed by his passion for our High Streets. His book *Chasing Permanence* draws on a decade of extensive research, personal experience, and insightful interviews with successful High Street businesses.

What sets *Chasing Permanence* apart is its emphasis on the power of collaboration and community engagement and the unique role that High Street businesses play in combatting issues like loneliness and mental health across societies. In a landscape dominated by reports that lay blame at the feet of the government and can create a sense of helplessness, this book empowers High Street businesses to take control of their future.'

Steve Hughes, *Chief Executive Officer, Plymouth City Centre Company*

'Entrepreneurs from ethnic minority backgrounds are indispensable to the vitality of the United Kingdom's High Streets. However, like other business owners, they encounter significant challenges jeopardising their sustainability. Steven Adjei's timely publication, *Chasing Permanence*, provides hope and inspiration. This work critically addresses the urgent challenges confronting small enterprises on Britain's High Streets with keen insight. Adjei's two decades of practical experience collaborating with High Street businesses contribute authenticity and pragmatism to his analysis. Furthermore, his engaging methodology makes intricate business concepts comprehensible to diverse audiences.

Importantly, this book reinforces the vital role of vibrant High Streets in UK communities' social and economic fabric. Adjei offers a much-needed roadmap for revitalising these crucial spaces by providing practical frameworks for collaboration, community-building, and competitiveness.'

Professor Monder Ram, *Professor of Small Businesses and Director for Research in Ethnic Minority Entrepreneurship (CREME), Aston Business School*

'Most business books move you forward, but few move you inside. With *Chasing Permanence*, Steven Adjei has accomplished a rare feat: reconciling the needs of people with the organisational need to perform. Written with purpose and warmth, this is a gem of a book I cannot recommend highly enough.'

Emmanuel Gobillot, *Global speaker, leadership consultant, author of bestselling books,* This Is Not a Leadership Book, The Connected Leader *and host of* The Word is Leadership *podcast*

'My friend Steven Adjei has done it again! After the riveting read of *Pay The Price*, *Chasing Permanence* is not just a book – it's a blueprint for long-term success. Whether you're struggling to keep your doors open or seeking ways to secure your business's future, this book is vital for any business owner looking to understand the secrets behind the successes of thriving High Streets.'

Jabo Butera, *CEO of Diversity Business Incubator, Executive member of the Devon Business Chamber, award-winning speaker, mentor and consultant*

'Steven N. Adjei's second book, *Chasing Permanence*, is a brilliant mosaic of story-telling, personal experience, solid research and brilliant writing. His exposé on our uncertain High Streets and his belief in its future is thought-provoking and inspiring. A book definitely worth reading for anyone in leadership and everyone interested in the future of our High Streets.'

Brandie Deignan, *Chief Executive Officer, Pier Health NHS, NED, Basketball England, Wales Golf, and author of the #1 international bestseller,* The Agnostic Leadership Playbook

'As an enthusiastic patron of the High Street and a business academic, I possess a profound understanding of the significant challenges confronting our High Streets. *Chasing Permanence* provides a thought-provoking perspective on this crucial subject, integrating Steven's extensive experience with the High Street, rigorous academic research, and engaging narratives. I highly recommend it.'

Dr Mojisola Olugbode, *Lecturer in accounting and finance at Plymouth Business School and expert in gender diversity in corporate governance and social performance*

Chasing Permanence

The UK's High Streets are at a tipping point: 13,500 businesses close each year, mirroring trends in the US and parts of Europe.

Nevertheless, some shining exceptions continue to thrive. This book explores these success stories and demonstrates how High Street businesses can prosper. While many reports cite external influences, this book focuses on how High Street businesses can drive their own lasting success. True Permanence may seem an unreachable ideal, yet this book outlines seven mindsets, five determinants, and four strategies necessary for a lasting, ethical, and sustainable business.

Owners, managers, policymakers, researchers, entrepreneurs, and employees and customers of brick-and-mortar businesses will discover insights and models for a strategy that leverages community and fosters long-term success.

Steven N. Adjei is a multi-award-winning community pharmacist, author, and business consultant. His debut book, *Pay The Price*, won four prestigious awards and is a #1 international bestseller. Steven serves as a judge for some of the UK's most prestigious business awards and has 20 years of experience working with some of the most iconic businesses on the High Street. He holds an MBA from Warwick Business School and serves as a Governor at Plymouth Marjon University.

Chasing Permanence

How Businesses on our High Streets Can Adapt and Thrive

Steven N. Adjei

NEW YORK AND LONDON

Designed cover image: Louis Chadwick

First published 2026
by Routledge
605 Third Avenue, New York, NY 10158

and by Routledge
4 Park Square, Milton Park, Abingdon, Oxon, OX14 4RN

Routledge is an imprint of the Taylor & Francis Group, an informa business

© 2026 Steven N. Adjei

The right of Steven N. Adjei to be identified as author of this work has been asserted in accordance with sections 77 and 78 of the Copyright, Designs and Patents Act 1988.

All rights reserved. No part of this book may be reprinted or reproduced or utilised in any form or by any electronic, mechanical, or other means, now known or hereafter invented, including photocopying and recording, or in any information storage or retrieval system, without permission in writing from the publishers.

For Product Safety Concerns and Information please contact our EU representative GPSR@taylorandfrancis.com. Taylor & Francis Verlag GmbH, Kaufingerstraße 24, 80331 München, Germany.

Trademark notice: Product or corporate names may be trademarks or registered trademarks, and are used only for identification and explanation without intent to infringe.

ISBN: 9781032942261 (hbk)
ISBN: 9781032902265 (pbk)
ISBN: 9781003569527 (ebk)

DOI: 10.4324/9781003569527

Typeset in Galliard
by Newgen Publishing UK

My wife: *Deladem Afia Adjei*
I will never deserve your unwavering love, enduring patience, and dedicated partnership.
May our union chase Permanence, even beyond death.

My dad: *Nana Nyantakyi Amponsem II*
You embody the very essence of Permanence.
My brother Michael and I – we salute you.

Britain's greatest management guru: Charles Handy. 1932–2024.
An example of a leader who chased Permanence.
He passed away just as I finished this book. His insights into culture and organisations were groundbreaking, and I quote him extensively throughout this work.
May his soul rest in peace.

Contents

Foreword by Dr Max McKeown   *xiii*
First Word   *xiv*
Leaders   *xxxiv*

PART I
The Seven Mindsets of Permanence   1
Introduction: The Seven Mindsets

1 Resilience: Weathering the Knocks   3

2 Identity: Who Am I?   6

3 Transcendence: Life Beyond Me   8

4 Openness: Knowledge Beyond Me   15

5 Diligence: Doing the Work   18

6 Principle of the Pie: Enough to Share   22

7 Principle of the Trail: Balancing Competence and Compassion   24

PART II
The Operation of Permanence   27
Introduction to the Five Determinants

8 The First Determinant: Tangibility   29

9 The Second Determinant: Affordability	60
10 The Third Determinant: Human Capital	72
11 The Fourth Determinant: Risk and Resilience	111
12 The Fifth Determinant: Strategy	129

PART III
The Systems of Permanence — 147
Introduction: Systems of Permanence: Balancing Mindset with the Determinants

13 The Three Kinds of Scalability	149
14 Systems Thinking: Hard Realism or Logical Fallacy?	165
15 The Final Determinant: The Importance of Local and Federal Government	188
Epilogue: The Transformation of Our High Streets	*195*
Acknowledgements	*197*
Appendix: Further Reading	*199*
Index	*201*

Foreword

SuperAdaptability is the valuable difference between adapting to cope and adapting to win.

The High Street isn't dead – it's transforming. What's at risk isn't just the loss of bricks and mortar but the disappearance of shared spaces where we live out our daily stories. To save it, we need more than survival tactics – we need SuperAdaptability.

The RUN Loop is at the heart of SuperAdaptability: Recognise, Understand, and make Necessary adaptations.

First, we must recognise the signals of change – the shifting needs of communities, the rise of digital convenience, and the economic forces reshaping our choices. Then we must understand what those changes mean. Not all threats are fatal; not all opportunities are obvious. Finally, we commit to the necessary adaptations – bold, sometimes uncomfortable decisions that move the High Street beyond survival and toward something stronger: transcendence.

A thriving High Street isn't a return to the past. It's a leap toward a better version of what it can be. That demands more than incremental fixes. It calls for imaginative redesign – spaces that become hubs of connection, creativity, and belonging.

When we apply the RUN Loop, we stop reacting to decline and start shaping a future where the High Street remains vital and vibrant.

Steven's book, *Chasing Permanence*, is a passionate call to action. A guide for leaders, entrepreneurs, and communities ready to lead that change.

Dr Max McKeown
Author of *The Innovation Book, The Strategy Book* and *SuperAdaptability*, April 2025
London, England

First Word

July 1972, Oxford Street, London

On a warm but windy morning in Leyton, East London, a woman was alone with her 3-month-old child in a cold, bland council flat, sobbing aloud, tears running down her young, dark face.

She stood in front of the mirror in her cramped bedroom, trying on the cheap make-up she had purchased from a charity shop in preparation for this moment.

But it was hard.

In those days make-up wasn't made for people like her.

But that wasn't her main issue.

It was the little boy, her only child, lying in his crib, blissfully unaware of his fate in the next 30 minutes.

She had travelled to England from Ghana, West Africa, to be with her husband.

After about an hour, when she was finally able to hold back the tears, she touched up her makeup, grabbed the pram, and scooped the boy into her arms, along with the baby bag and the hand-me-down handbag a friend had given her just a week earlier.

Gingerly opening the door, the cold wind hit her right in the face.

She was on her way, just three doors down to the childminder.

Arriving, she knocked, but the lack of response further added to the tension and anxiety she felt.

Finally, she gathered courage and rang the bell.

An older Jamaican woman with three kids of her own waved her in.

'It's a bit cold, isn't it?" the older woman said as a greeting.

The woman quietly nodded externally but disagreed vehemently internally. She was freezing.

The nanny promised to take care of the boy, as she had a hundred times before.

She had kind eyes, thin lips, and a wrinkled face that told millions of stories. But the kind eyes were able to reassure this young woman somehow that her first son would be just fine.

But that didn't stop the noise.

Her crying resumed, painful tears running down her newly made-up face. The shrilling cries of her son as she closed the door behind her rang in her ears like an echo chamber, making the 15-minute walk to the Leyton Underground station seem three times longer than it was.

The guilt she felt was almost unbearable.

She muttered some incomprehensible words in Akan, her native tongue, cursing the cold, merciless weather. Part of her anger was directed towards her husband, who had convinced her to leave her relative comfort in Ghana for this apparent cold-hearted place.

Still in tears, she made her way to Leyton Underground Station and took the Central Line to Oxford Circus. There, she reported for her first formal job interview since leaving her native Ghana.

By the time she arrived at the massive, imposing building, she had managed to dry her tears, partly ready for the next challenge – to be one of the first black African women to interview for a job in one of the UK's most prestigious shops on Oxford Street.

By the time her name was called (with the normal mispronunciation of her surname, Ade-ji instead of Adjei) she had managed to calm herself down somewhat, externally, at least.

The interview was rigorous.

She answered the questions as best as she could, straining her ears to catch the unfamiliar accent and the speed with which the questions were lobbed at her like cricket balls from the three serious-looking white men in suits sitting across the table.

She had to take an aptitude test, and a smiling woman met her at another door and ushered her to the exit.

She went back home, but all was not well.

She could still hear her son crying as she approached the flat to pick him up.

She was convinced that her bad luck would continue – like the dozens of jobs she had applied for, this one would pass her by.

So imagine her surprise a couple of weeks later when, unusually, the postman dropped an envelope through the door addressed to her.

It was good news!

She had successfully passed the interview and was eager to tell her husband when he got home that night.

The next day, despite the usual wailing sounds of her son and the usual guilt that plagued her, her step was a little lighter, her chest a little less panicky and her mood a little brighter as she arrived for her first full day at work.

Rigorous training process completed, she felt a swell of pride as she stood behind the sales counter on her first full day working as a full employee at one of England's most iconic stores – Selfridges, Oxford Street.

She held this position with unwavering pride until, four years later in 1977, she and her husband voluntarily decided to return to their native Ghana.

I was that baby, and that woman was my mother.

16 July 2001, Manor Park, East London

It was a cold morning, and here I was, sleeping with rats.

I had just emigrated from Ghana, West Africa, 28 years after my parents had taken me back. I had been searching for a job for months while studying to qualify as a registered pharmacist in the UK.

I remember waking up in the morning in East London, not far from where I was born, watching as giant, indestructible rats scuppered across my carpet in an apology for a house I had to share with four other residents from different backgrounds. All efforts to rid the flat of those rats had proven fruitless – my landlord was not interested despite our pleas.

So in the end, I gave up and just watched them in horror every night.

One morning, with the nightmare of rats still flashing across my mind, I took the Underground to a massive Superdrug complex that had opened on Oxford Circus, just across the road from the very store where my mother had worked 30 years previously.

I remember that interview day as though it was yesterday. There were lots of other people waiting to be interviewed and with my heavy accent, anxious face, trembling, and sweaty hands, I thought I would never get the job. I waited for weeks without any phone calls or letters and resigned myself to the fact that this was another failed mission to acquire some gainful employment.

I needed the money badly – I was sick of having London rats as co-tenants.

I decided to ring Superdrug.

Happily, I had got the job – they just forgot to inform me. I proudly reported to work the following week in my Superdrug polo shirt, brand-new trousers, and cheap shoes which I had purchased from the market in Hackney a few days prior.

Fast forward twenty years. I was now an entrepreneur, award-winning pharmacist, and bestselling author with a family living in a lovely house in Plymouth, South West England.

We decided to recount our steps back to my first job in 2000.

The Selfridges department store my mother worked in was still standing, but the Superdrug shop I worked in was gone. I took a picture by the side of Selfridges and texted it to my mother and she texted back, excited beyond measure.

Fifty years on, she still remembered with pride the tips from the wealthy Arabs, the friends she had made, the caring nature of her manager, and the discipline, customer service and camaraderie she enjoyed while working there.

The only shop now remaining on that busy street in central London since my mother had worked there in the 1970s (and even since I worked there in the 2000s) was the same Selfridges.

I began to wonder what was different about Selfridges? How had it endured (and even thrived) through those six decades when my mother worked there and now?

I put that question in the back of my mind for two decades.

One day, 12 years later and 6000 miles away, it came flooding back with a rude awakening.

It was the same day I finally began to believe in ghosts.

2 June 2012, Accra, Ghana

After the two-hour drive from Accra, the capital of Ghana, to Sogakope, my wife's hometown in the east of the country, we were full of anticipation. It was the first time my kids had set foot in sunny Ghana, and it was the first time we were meeting her family.

Tradesmen lined the street; you could hear the honking of horns, the bleats of sheep and goats, the laughter of children, the piercing heat of the sun, and youths on locally-made motorcycles driving illegally, shouting at the top of their voices.

The town was bustling, alive and on the brink of something big.

As we trudged into my wife's village, we were greeted by chickens, sheep, goats, children, and adults – a cacophony of noise and the sweet aroma of freshly baked bread from the huge wood-fired ovens.

As in a typical African town, entrepreneurs were everywhere – from fishermen to stall owners, second-hand clothing sellers to bakers.

The town was alive, and so were my in-laws.

To say they were excited to see their grandchildren and son-in-law for the first time was an understatement.

3 May 2021, Sogakope, Ghana

Nine years later, we repeated the same trip. My kids were now teenagers – their ages may have changed, but their anticipation had not.

Sogakope was like a completely different town: the houses were boarded up, the roads were dilapidated, poverty was everywhere. It was like the town had gone back three decades.

My heart sank, and I could feel the kids' disappointment. There was no bread, pet chickens, sheep, or life.

We had been greeted by ghosts parading the streets.

Like most of my in-laws, the town was dead – just like another city, 6000 miles away, nestled between the Welsh mountains.

11 September 2021 – A British Ghost

I was on a business trip to Wrexham, Wales, to meet the CEO of one of Britain's biggest pharmaceutical manufacturers.

Suffering from epilepsy, I could not drive, so I took the train from Plymouth (my adopted home city), taking me the best part of the day to get there.

When I arrived at the train station, I took a taxi.

During the trip, all I could hear was the complaining of the taxi driver:

'This town is dead. It used to be a bustling town just a decade ago till all these Eastern Europeans came and stole our jobs,' he said, pointing angrily to a car washing bay being operated, ostensibly by Romanians.

'The government does nothing to help us, and all the shops are closing.'

I looked at Eagles Meadow, the town's central shopping centre, and I could not help but empathise with his sentiment and despair.

These experiences made me ask:

What is it that makes some High Streets tick, and some die? What makes some SMEs thrive even in dire circumstances, and some die? Why do entire towns live through turbulent times, and some die?

All along, I thought it was just due to the changing environment – the internet, the rise of easy home deliveries. But as I looked deeper, I realised that all I had assumed, though partly true, was just lazy thinking.

My mind wandered back to the resurrection of the Welsh phoenix.

22 April 2023

Just a few months prior, in February 2021, two A-list screen stars, Rob McElhenney and Ryan Reynolds, were looking for a Hollywood story[1].

They had just three criteria: a team with a story, a community, and a potential to blossom.

The answer they found? Wrexham AFC.

Founded in 1864, it is the third-oldest football team in the world, playing at the oldest football stadium in the world – the Racecourse. The team has a cult-like following and has been owned by the fans since 2011. It is also the same town I had visited five months earlier.

Two years later and Wrexham AFC had been the subject of an award-winning Hollywood documentary, had won its first football title in 45 years, and had seen a record 921% increase in following on all platforms, with close to half a million followers on Instagram.

In addition, the Wrexham women's team won a trophy and secured promotion for the first time in their history.

Not only that, but Wrexham AFC has grown 300 per cent since being taken over two years ago, signing deals with worldwide companies such as Vistaprint, TikTok, and Aviation American Gin and the club has also featured on ESPN and Disney Plus.

A miraculous revolution – a phoenix rising from the ashes.

Through its football team, Wrexham town was brought back from the dead using the power of collaboration, community, and agility – themes we will explore later in the book.

We live in unpredictable times. The things we value, the people we care about, and the lives we lead all feel uncertain and unstable.

We all long for predictability and, indeed, stability.

The paradox is that though we are all intrigued by the shiny object syndrome (think of AI and fast home delivery), we love and desire for our institutions to last.

And companies know this. You only have to look at their logos to see how they tug at our heartstrings.

Selfridges: Since 1909
Boots: Since 1849
Morrisons: Since 1899
Plymouth Gin: England's Oldest Working Distillery since 1793
Fortnum and Mason: Since 1707
House of Fraser: Since 1891.

But these slogans can be illusory, as illustrated by another British High Street icon, Debenhams, which abruptly ended its trading after 243 years.

In man, yet another quality appears, which we call reason, whereby he is enabled to force his pain, which henceforth is preceded with acute mental suffering, and to foresee his death, whilst keenly chasing permanence.
C.S. Lewis (*The Problem of Pain*, 1940)[2]

Permanence, in its most accurate form, does not exist. All products, services and businesses have a life span.

As Phil Rosenzweig says, success is hard to sustain over long periods, especially at the pinnacle.

As I mentioned earlier, William Magnussen forces us to confront our mortality through the business lens.[3]

I am fully aware of the dangers of predicting the future using lessons from the past. The pace of change, the increase in knowledge, and the acceleration of technology are too pronounced to enable even the most accurate social scientists to do that. Even many companies discussed in Jim Collins' classic book *Built to Last* (such as Fannie Mae and Circuit City) and its European equivalent, *Enduring Success* (think of Nokia), have faltered over time.

Start-ups rarely survive their second birthday – even established firms in the UK and the US average a life of only fifteen years.

However, the basics and the underlying success factors rarely change, but the ways do.

But this does not distract from the elephant in the room – the problem that needs addressing and is staring us right in the face:

Are our High Streets in crisis?

There is no doubt about it: the essence of our High Streets is disappearing before our very eyes.

According to the Lords Report on November 2024,[4] there were over 10,000 store closures across UK High Streets in 2023. People have seen the loss of local department stores, pharmacies, clothing stores, pubs and banks.

The dominance of retail on High Streets is rapidly becoming something of the past.

However, the same report surmises:

> *Thriving businesses are essential for a busy and successful local High Street and business owners should be actively involved in the management of their High Streets.*

According to the latest report compiled by the Federation of Small Businesses, 69% of local businesses say there are vacant units on their local High Street.

45% of High Street small businesses say the availability of affordable commercial space is essential for the future of the High Street.

One in seven locations on our High Streets is empty, further blighting its optics and discouraging investment.

As Tina Mckenzie, FSB Policy and Advocacy Chair, writes:[5]

> *Since the pandemic, there has been a 70% decrease in consumer spending and a corresponding 47% in local business.*

> *To add to this puzzle, retail store closures have increased by 72%, hospitality closures by 69%, and financial services closures by 58%.*
>
> *Add an increase of 47% rise in crime and anti-social behaviour, and the complex problems facing our High Streets become clearer.*

Analysis by the Centre for Retail Research also painted a similar gloomy picture: about 47 sites shut up shop for the last time every day in 2023. Part of the report continues[6]:

> *As shops shut, jobs went with them. More than 151,000 retail jobs were lost in the UK last year, including from online retailers – an increase of more than 45,000 from the year before.*

The group's survey found that a little over 5,500 shops went under, while more than 11,600 were closed as larger chains decided to cut costs.

The Centre for Retail Research's director, Professor Joshua Bamfield:

> *Rather than company failure, rationalisation now seems to be the main driver for closures as retailers continue to reduce their cost base at pace.*[7]

The professional service firm PwC also stated:[8]

> *Research suggests that almost 50 stores per day closed down across the UK during the first half of the year.*

Figures from the Local Data Company suggest that between January and June, some 8,739 outlets closed across High Streets, retail parks, and shopping centres.

> *[But] ... three thousand four hundred eighty-eight opened during the same period, resulting in a net decline of 5,251.*[9]

Yes, all companies have a lifespan.

However, the primary concern is that the decline of that lifespan is accelerating. To see this, you only need to walk on the High Street of any town or city in the UK (and many Western countries). A company in the S&P 500 lasted 33 years in 1965. Now, the typical tenure is half that.[10]

This lifespan is even worse for BAME SMEs. Research by Professor Monder Ram of Aston University shows that BAME SMEs are twice as likely to start up as their white counterparts but are twice as likely to go bust within 42 months.[11]

Tina Mckenzie continues,

> With empty units blighting many town centres across the country, the outlook can sometimes look bleak, with business rates, parking charges, the planning system and rent all impacting the business community.
>
> We are at a crucial juncture for the future of our High Streets. Forward-looking and robust policy interventions are needed to not only help small firms grow and be successful, but also anticipate what they need to sustain themselves and adapt to a rapidly changing world.[12]

A study from PwC, quoted in the BBC, shows that almost 40 shops disappear from the High Street every day, and a typical SME on the High Street only lasts 10 years.[13]

And COVID is only partly responsible; this trend started before the epidemic.

In 2018, 22,000 jobs were lost in the UK alone.

City centres have suffered the most, and between 2016 and 2021, the UK lost 83% of its leading department stores.

Why? The BBC report surmises:

1. Squeezed incomes due to the shift to online shopping
2. Changing tastes of customers
3. Rising overheads: the British Retail Consortium estimates that the National Living Wage costs the industry between £1.5 and £3 billion a year, plus the increase in business rates, which costs another £2 billion, which rises yearly. A spokesman for the consortium put it this way: *'Business rates are deterring investment in local communities, causing shop closures and job losses in hard-pressed communities and preventing retailers from delivering what their customers want efficiently and cost-effectively.'*
4. Too many shops by retailers: some retailers over-expanded during the good years, leaving them dangerously exposed
5. Finally, many retailers are shouldering an unsustainable high debt burden – the now-defunct toy retailer Toys R Us, for instance, faced a VAT debt of £15m just before its collapse.

And yes, these are all true. The latter part of this book touches on what local and central governments can do to improve our High Streets and the characteristics of some towns across the country that have made their roads a resounding success.

There is an epidemic of failing SMEs in the UK and Western countries.

17,145 High Street businesses closed their doors for the final time in 2022. There is a decimation of the High Street.

Bill Grimsey, the former head of Wickes, who has led three reports on the future of town centres and High Streets, recently talked with the BBC:

You can't rely on retail any more for town centres and High Streets as the main attraction due to technology and the internet ... these spaces need to be reinvented for something else because we are social animals and we need somewhere to assemble, and it won't just be shops.[14, 15]

Is Bill Grimsey right?

Well, partly so.

However, most reports and literature look at this problem from the outside. There is no shortage of speeches, articles, and even books that call on government and policymakers to enact changes to preserve, maintain, and even improve our High Streets and make them more accessible, attractive, and enjoyable for local customers and perhaps even more crucially, for the up-and-coming generation to invest in brick-and-mortar companies on our High Streets.

The trouble is that, apart from lobbying (covered in the last part of this book), the impression is that the businesses on the High Streets are helpless and that customers are ambivalent.

The truth is, the actual situation is far more complex.

For example, the High Street pastries retailer Greggs has become an enormous success story, opening over 150 stores in 2023 alone.

Also, a recent YouGov survey has placed defunct High Street retailer Woolworths (which opened in 1909 and at one point had 800 stores in the UK but closed 15 years ago this year) at the top of the list of nostalgic High Street shops customers want to return to, with Debenhams second.

Nevertheless, High Street businesses also face mountainous challenges from within:

1. **The steady demise of Command and Control style of leadership**: In *For Profit,* Magnussen details the beginning of the corporation from the days of the Medici Bank to the monopolies of Google, Meta, Amazon and Apple and the rise of the start-ups (more of this later) Of particular interest was the rise of Ford Motor Company and how the Command and Control (the power of centralised leadership) began from those days which resulted in incredible efficiency and quality maintenance. However, the trail of bodies left in the wake in the name of efficiency was a cause for concern. The spread, proliferation and wide availability of knowledge, combined with increased distrust of leadership, has meant that there has been a gradual but steady power shift **away** from centralised leadership, where a few people had all the information and

held all the cards. Increasingly, as we will see later on in this book, success in the current setting involves leadership as coaching, collaboration and mentoring of the many, rather than a few people in the C-suite barking down instructions to everyone else.

2. **The explosion of choice**: Advances in technology, information availability and entrepreneurship, as well as changing tastes of consumers, have offered an exponential amount of choice available in every area of our lives – from TV shows, consumables, social media and many others. Everyone now has a voice, and getting heard amongst all the noise can be difficult. Advances in technology, the rise in AI, and lowered barriers to entry for many businesses imply challenges for businesses, particularly on the High Street. Competition for space and choice amongst High Street shops and with online start-ups – not only established ones like Amazon and eBay, but also relatively new ones like Etsy, Shein and Temu – have intensified competition to new levels. All these have also had a knock-on effect.

3. **The corresponding rise of the employee**: The recent upheaval of the last 10–15 years has shaken faith in institutions, and power is gradually shifting from management to employees, from government to people, from leaders to followers. The rise of the MeToo movement in France and the UK, and protests worldwide, have become a natural consequence of the demise of command and control. The phenomenon of 'Quiet Quitting,' 'The Great Resignation' and the rise in entrepreneurship is symbolic of this trend, which, even though it was already happening, has been accelerated by COVID. Pressure on pensions, the minimum hourly rate, and sustainability (whilst good for our planet and workers) also puts pressure on businesses.

Just as with the uprising of the serfs in the bubonic plague of 1348 (which killed upwards of 60% of Europe) the rise of COVID has shifted power to the employee, making them better placed to leave and find gainful employment elsewhere if they are not treated as individuals.

Companies that do not give employees more say, rewards, challenges, and route fulfilment will likely lose out. The year when most job hunters become freelancers, entrepreneurs, and solopreneurs rather than traditional employees may soon be upon us.

4. **The changing nature of work**: In her brilliant book, *Your Resource is Human,* Melissa Romo talks about the complexities of hybrid working, which has dramatically increased after the pandemic.[16] However, hybrid working is not the only change that has been noticed. In a recent article written in *Harvard Business Review*, bestselling author and professor Dorie Clark lists five ways to 'future-proof' the

working world in light of the rapid change we are seeing, such as the rise of AI and the noise of social media. She lists them as:

1. Avoiding predictability
2. Honing the skills machines strive to emulate
3. Doubling down on the real world
4. Developing a personal brand
5. Cultivating expertise.

We are increasingly being asked to use our minds, intellect, and creative instincts more.

Work that will thrive in the future is work that machines cannot replicate, which will involve much more collaboration, creativity – the rise of emotional intelligence and soft skills – and innovation at an increasingly rapid race, which brings us to the following phenomenon:

5. **The rapid acceleration of change and uncertainty:** Ray Kurzweil, an American technologist and futurist, has an uncanny ability to predict the future. In 1988, for instance, he spookily predicted that handheld devices would enable blind people to read sometime in the early 21st century. Twenty years later, the same thing happened.

Mark Buchanan formulated the theory called

The law of Accelerating Returns – the tendency for advances to feed themselves, increasing the rate of further advance, and pushing well past what 'one might sensibly project by linear extrapolation of current progress' (Nature Physics VOL 4, July 2008).[17]

In his brilliant book *Think Again*, Wharton Professor Adam Grant describes this pace of change beautifully:

With advances in access to information and technology, knowledge is not just increasing. It's increasing at an exponential rate. In 2011, information was consumed five times more than just a quarter of a century earlier. As of 1950, it took about fifty years for knowledge in medicine to double. By 1980, medical knowledge was doubling every seven years, and by 2010, it was doubling in half that time. The accelerating pace of change means we must question our tightly held beliefs more often than ever.[18]

This rapid acceleration of change means that companies, especially SMEs and organisations, must be ready to adapt and be flexible as quickly as the changing landscape. The well-known professor of change, John Kotter in his 2021 book, *Change: How Organizations Achieve Hard-to-Imagine Results in Uncertain and Volatile Times*, agrees:

> *The trend of change has accelerated as we've moved from an Industrial Age to an Information Age – examples of this increased pace and complexity are easily found: whilst it took the telephone 75 years to reach 10 million users, mobiles took only 12 years, and the iPhone took just three. A 2018 IBM study found that 90% of all data on the internet was produced in the immediately preceding two years.*[19]

We now live in the beginning of the age of AI, which has dramatically increased our sense of uncertainty. Depending on which side of the fence you are on, AI either threatens many jobs and the apocalypse is upon us, or it gives us the potential to create many jobs and usher in a new wave of technological brilliance. This has only added to the sense of uncertainty that we all face.

There is also the rise of the start-up (which I discuss in detail in Part III of this book) with companies such as Pharmacy2U, Uber, Amazon, JustEat, Ebay, notonthehighstreet and Etsy which have consistently and steadily eaten away market share from our High Streets.

80% of music is listened to online, half of books are bought online and there is the rise of internet fashion, such as Debenhams online, Boohoo, and Temu.

Netflix, Amazon Prime, and other streaming services have made it possible to watch movies and quality series from the comfort of your sofa. The rise of Just Eat means that families can now enjoy parties from their living rooms rather than the pub.

The rise in out-of-town retail centres which offer free parking, fewer security concerns and easy accessibility, have compounded the issues of High Street businesses.

These are seismic shifts and it is no wonder the list of High Street companies that folded just a few years ago is mounting: Debenhams, Hawkins Bazaar, PaperChase, Lloyds Pharmacies, SK: N, Ted Baker, Victoria's Secret, and the Arcadia Group. Some, like Jessops, are barely hanging on. The modern organisation, as we will delve into later, is struggling to create the agility, adaptability, speed, and learning needed to continue to compete and win.

But we all like to see our High Street companies thrive and chase Permanence.

How do I define Permanence?

In four contrasting, paradoxical ways:

1. **Permanence is not always about scaling**: This reminds me of a story I heard as a teenager in Ghana in the nineties.

A man used to do brisk business selling popcorn and drinks on the street. He set up shop early at nine o'clock and sold popcorn and beverages by the truckload and was done by 3 pm. He then shut up shop, locked his stall, went home, sat on the balcony with his wife, watched the world go by, and sipped his cold beer. This went on for years. One day, a consultant came to town.

He wanted to learn more about business and find work for his consultancy, so he booked an appointment with the popcorn seller.

He began to talk to him about scaling. 'You know,' he said, 'you could invest the money from the profits you made by selling this much popcorn into new machines, employing more people and building a bigger business. You could earn much more money this way,' he said.

The popcorn seller answered: 'What would I do with the extra money?'

The consultant said, 'You can have much more fun and money by just going supervising all these new popcorn sellers you have recruited, shut up shop at 3 pm and come and sip wine with your wife.'

The popcorn seller retorted, 'What's the point? I can do that now anyway!!'

There is now a new buzzword in business: Scale. Books on scaling are now selling by the truckload: *Masters of Scale* by Reid Hoffman; *The Voltage Effect* by John A-List; *Beyond Entrepreneurship* by Jim Collins. We now have 'scale-up coaches.' We discuss whether an idea is 'scalable.'

Success is not always about scaling – at least not in the way scaling is traditionally defined.

Later in the book, under Strategy, I'll introduce the Stand Your Ground concept.

2. **Permanence is about scaling:** In Part III of this book, I introduce the concept of Personal and Personnel Scaling.

Permanence is about establishing your core values, your why, your raison d'être, and growing into them (personal scalability); and your employees and colleagues (personnel scalability). This concept reminds me of how the Japanese built buildings to survive earthquakes: the foundations (values in business) are strong, rigid, deep and immovable, but the buildings (the visible part of the structure) were built to sway during the earthquake. Founders, entrepreneurs, and CEOs need to learn to balance developing and scaling their values while learning to foster the power of individualism and diversity in their companies.

3. **Permanence is about thriving:** Yes, Permanence is about thriving. It is appropriate for a company to spew out profits month after month, year after year, despite the outward (or inward) circumstances. It's good for a company to scale, expand, and succeed by whichever definition you use. It is appropriate for companies to give back to the environment.

Yet, we admire Permanence: Queen Elizabeth. Nelson Mandela. Bill Marriott. Olusegun Obasanjo. Jimmy Carter. Bob Marley. Richard Branson.

And more to the point of this book, some artists churn out album after album that regularly top the mainstream charts for decades and become multigenerational – Coldplay, Lionel Richie, Elton John, Sir Paul McCartney, U2, Queen. These individuals, even those who have passed, are still thriving.

4. Permanence is also about surviving: No company (or individual) can consistently produce positive productivity year after year. Permanence is also about weathering the storms, both internal and external.

I call this Standing Your Ground, and I talk about a few companies that have done that.

Harry Stebbings, founder of the *Twenty Minute VC* podcast remarks on X,
People can say what they want about what makes the best founders and leaders. The defining trait is resilience.

Can you go through the most challenging days, day after day and wake up every morning with a fire in your belly, saying to yourself: Today, today is going to be different. Yes, I can do this, I have what it takes?[20]

It's good to thrive, but Permanence sometimes means plain old grit and survival. We talk more about this later in the book.

One of the greatest fears, I must admit, whilst writing this book was the sucker punch I felt when I read Phil Rosenwieig's The Halo Effect and the Eight Other Business Delusions that Deceive Managers:

There will always be books, some good, some not so good, that try to discover elements that separate the best companies from the rest of the pack – that's not just inevitable; that's healthy.

He continues:[21]

Our thinking about business is shaped by several delusions. I hope managers will read business books more critically, free from delusion…. tempered by realism.

In *The Halo Effect*, he mentions eight delusions managers face, three of which I felt were particularly relevant to this book:

1. **The Halo effect delusion:** looking at a company's overall performance and making attributions about its culture, leadership and values.
2. **The delusion of correlation and causality:** just because two things are correlated does not mean one causes the other or vice versa. For instance, does employee satisfaction lead to high performance or vice versa?

3. **The delusion of lasting success:** almost all high-performing companies regress over time, so the promise of a blueprint for lasting success is attractive but unrealistic.

He's even more blunt:

Anyone who claims to have found laws of business either understands little about business (or physics) or both.

Bearing this in mind, I have tried in this book to avoid halos, measure variables independently, and realise that company performance is relative, not absolute. Chance, intelligent strategy and superb execution play a more significant role than we'd care to admit.

How did I try to do this?

Riding the waves and succeeding when your operating sector is in vogue is easy. This is exemplified by the rise of companies like Zoom and Peloton, which made outstanding profits during the COVID era but fell away when life returned to normal, or companies like Primark and Shein which profit in the age of cheap, throwaway fashion and the cost of living crisis.

For this book, I have selected the five most challenging sectors on the High Streets – not only by market share but by **changing habits** of customers:

- **Community pharmacy:** these are one of the most beleaguered sectors on our High Streets. Between January and June 2024 alone, 18 pharmacies closed every week. Big chains such as Boots and Lloyds have drastically reduced their pharmacy-only stores on the High Street or exited the sector altogether. The sector is described as having an uncertain future and is on life support, and pharmacies have threatened to reduce hours to cope. In addition to this, there have been massive disruptions to the sector. Start-ups such as Pharmacy2U, Pharmazon Direct, and Lloyds online now dispense up to 2 million prescriptions annually, stealing market share away from the traditional High Street community pharmacy.
- **Books:** Amazon alone accounts for 50% of books bought in the UK and between 70–80% of all online books. In addition, it owns Audible, the audiobook platform, and has about 90% share of all ebooks. Physical book sales have slowed down in 2023, according to Publishers Weekly.
- **Planned obsolescence:** the era of throwaway fashion is now at an unprecedented high. According to the Netflix show *Buy Now*, many companies encourage and intentionally create products that don't last so customers can discard them and buy new ones. Repairing and finding ways to extend what we have is actively discouraged. I have seen first

hand the results of this, in my native country, Ghana, which has the biggest site in the world for second-hand clothing. The pollution it causes is indescribable.
- **Physical music:** over the last decade, the rise of music streaming apps such as Spotify, Apple, Amazon, and YouTube have decimated the purchase of physical music products such as CDs, cassette tapes, and vinyl. According to data from the CMA, as of 2021, more than 80% of all music is listened to online.
- **Audio equipment and TV:** online sources such as AO.com and Amazon, out-of-town retailers such as Curry's, and the industry's fragmentation have threatened to reduce the market share of High Street sales severely.

> **Real success occurs when companies continue to beat the odds over a reasonably long period in chronically worsening sectors prone to rapid disruption in a challenging environment.**

This survival battle is old because it is a familiar one that academics and practitioners have wrestled with since the early 1960s.

Are the failures of companies due to business-related effects (the environment) as the majority of the literature suggests, or are they related to resource-based impacts (the firm's operations)?

The answer is a complex interplay, but I focus more on the latter in this book.

Too often, articles, the media, think tanks and books are too quick to blame the former (the changing environment), underestimating the ability of some firms to adapt and thrive despite these seismic shifts.

But as Peter Senge in his 1990 book, *The Fifth Discipline*, and Tracy Lane's book *The Living Organization*,[22] explain, like living organisms throughout evolution, some organisations have an uncanny ability to navigate these headwinds and emerge more robust and resilient.

This book is my contribution to this paradox. I mainly wrote it to explore this phenomenon, using examples from music, sport (which reduces the halo effect) and a few companies from different spheres that thrive amid this accelerating pace.

I have tried to balance this halo effect by observing companies at work in the most natural way possible and balancing interviews by led by real-time observation.

But now for the big question:

So why me, I hear you ask? What makes me qualified to write on such a controversial topic?

Over the last decade, I have developed a queer fascination and admiration in which some High Street SMEs and chains can grow and even thrive during these turbulent times.

But this is also personal.

I've witnessed the tears, pain, and cynicism of employees and staff – some of them close friends – who feel cheated. In this book, I detail many of their painful stories.

The effects of bad leadership. Waste. Mismanagement. Greed.

And I've also seen the opposite.

I am privileged to have two decades of experience working in and with scores of businesses on High Streets, not only up and down the UK, but in two other continents from an interplay of six different angles:

1. **As an employee,** I have had the privilege of working on the shop floor of many High Street healthcare chains and seeing what it's like in the trenches.
2. **As a manager,** I have managed dozens of High Street chains across the UK and Africa and have worked in middle management for decades.
3. **As a consultant and freelancer,** I have worked with and in many High Street chains in London and the South West of England and have been able to observe up close and help many small and medium chains achieve long-term growth.
4. **As a senior judge** for some of the top business awards in the UK, including the celebrated Signature Awards, I have had access to data from hundreds of companies, many of whom are located on our High Streets.
5. **As an entrepreneur,** my company, BlueCloud, fell victim to this all too common problem of failure, and we had to merge the business with my current company, Strategy Boutique, which caused a lot of pain and regret.
6. **As a researcher,** this book has its roots in an intensive two-year research project across over a hundred companies for my MBA thesis – and I attempt to answer some of the questions that build on from *Pay The Price*. Oddly, parts of this book were written before my first book. Since 2009, these burning questions have continually consumed my thinking and that year, incidentally, marked the highest number of firms going bust in the history of the UK when records began. Additionally, I have long admired enduring successful musicians who have remained relevant for decades, from which businesses can learn.

These experiences have shaped the structure of this book. Spider Webb, the principal protagonist in the novel *Slow Horses* says:

> *It distorts the data to provoke the target into a course of action he might not otherwise adopt.*[23]

In my opinion, interviews and questionnaires sometimes provoke inaccurate answers – they may encourage respondents to give answers they would not typically adopt.

And yes, I expect readers to study this with a healthy, critical realism. I hope that this book will start a vigorous debate on the future of our High Streets by placing a heavier emphasis on where it should, in my opinion, rightly belong – at the feet of the businesses.

So, bearing in mind all this, plus the short life cycle of High Street SMEs, I set the bar lower than classics of the same theme: Jim Collins' *Built to Last*, Alex Hill's *Centennials*, and Christian Stadler's *Enduring Success*, and rather than use comparison companies, I carefully selected High Street companies that are thriving amid chronically struggling sectors using five criteria:

1. The company must be at least 40 years old (almost four times the lasting average for a High Street SME and business).
2. It should have had at least one successor or be in the active phases of succession.
3. It should be an independent business enterprise on the High Street.
4. It should thrive in a declining or stagnating business sector and consistently perform better than its market since 2007. (Thrived through 2 downturns, the financial meltdown of 2008 and the COVID crisis of 2019).
5. Should be making a constant profit even through recession and other shocks.

Thus, I have chosen five main High Street Chains as my main focus (as well as a smattering of well-performing smaller chains, which I refer to throughout this volume)

Having explained the basis for this book, let us begin the next section by welcoming them to the stage….

Notes

1. ITV. The inside story of why Hollywood picked Wrexham Football Club: www.itv.com/news/2021-02-11/the-inside-story-of-why-hollywood-picked-wrexham-football-club, accessed January 2023.
2. Lewis, C.S. *The Problem of Pain*, Collins, 1940.
3. Magnuson, William. *For Profit: A History of Corporations*, Basic Books, 2022.
4. UK Parliament. Look beyond retail to reverse high street decline, says new Lords report, 28 November 2024: www.parliament.uk/business/lords/media-centre/house-of-lords-media-notices/2024/november-2024/look-bey

ond-retail-to-reverse-high-street-decline-says-new-lords-report/#:~:text=In%202023%20there%20were%20over,is%20something%20of%20the%20past
5 FSB. The Future of the High Street, Pgs 8–9: www.fsb.org.uk/resources-page/new-report-sets-out-future-vision-to-support-and-transform-our-high-streets.html
6 Centre of Retail Research. The Crisis in Retailing: Closures and Job Losses: www.retailresearch.org/retail-crisis.html
7 Centre of Retail Research. The Crisis in Retailing: Closures and Job Losses: www.retailresearch.org/retail-crisis.html
8 Simpson, Emma. Almost 50 shops a day disappear from High Streets, BBC: www.bbc.co.uk/news/business-58433461, September 5, 2021.
9 PwC and The Local Data Company. 2023. Store openings and closures in H1 2023, London, PwC UK, August: https://www.pwc.co.uk/industries/retail-consumer/insights/store-openings-and-closures.html, accessed December 15, 2024.
10 Kotter, John P., Vanessa Akhtar and Gaurav Gupta. *How Organizations Achieve Hard-to-Imagine Results in Uncertain and Volatile Times*, John Wiley, 2021.
11 Aston University. Time to change: A blueprint for advancing the UK'S ethnic minority businesses: https://publications.aston.ac.uk/id/eprint/43782/1/CREME_NWG_Time_to_change_report_FINAL_published.pdf.
12 Aston University. Time to change: A blueprint for advancing the UK'S ethnic minority businesses: https://publications.aston.ac.uk/id/eprint/43782/1/CREME_NWG_Time_to_change_report_FINAL_published.pdf.
13 PwC UK. High-streets suffer as 38 stores close across Great Britain each day in 2024 – but there's hope with convenience stores, coffee shops and value retailers showing net growth: www.pwc.co.uk/press-room/press-releases/research-commentary/2024/high-streets-suffer-as-38-stores-close-across-great-britain-each.html
14 Grimsey, Bill, et al. 2013. The Grimsey Review: An alternative future for the high street. London, *Bill Grimsey Review*: https://edemocracy.coventry.gov.uk/documents/s13961/Grimsey%20Review.pdf, accessed December 15, 2024.
15 Grimsey, Bill, et al. 2018. The Grimsey Review 2: It's time to reshape our town centres. London, *Bill Grimsey Review*: https://evapascoe.com/wordpress/wp-content/uploads/2018/07/GrimseyReview2018.pdf, accessed December 15, 2024.
16 Romo, Melissa. *Your Resource Is Human: How Empathetic Leadership Can Help Remote Teams Rise Above*, London, Practical Inspiration Publishing, 2023.
17 Buchanan, Mark. The law of accelerating returns, *Nature Physics*, vol. 4, p. 507, July 2008.
18 Grant, Adam. *Think Again: The Power of Knowing What You Don't Know*, Viking, an imprint of Penguin Random House, 2021.
19 Kotter, John P., Vanessa Akhtar and Gaurav Gupta. *How Organizations Achieve Hard-to-Imagine Results in Uncertain and Volatile Times*, John Wiley, 2021.
20 Stebbings, Harry (@HarryStebbings). People can say what they want about what makes the best founders. At the end of the day, the defining trait is resilience. X (formerly Twitter), May 2, 2022: https://x.com/HarryStebbings/status/1521562320908046337.
21 Rosenzweig, Phil. *The Halo Effect: … and the Eight Other Business Delusions That Deceive Managers*, New York, Free Press, 4, 2007.
22 Tracy, Lane. *The Living Organization: Systems of Behavior*, Praeger, 1989.
23 Herron, Mick. *Slow Horses*, Soho Crime, 2010.

Leaders

The main companies I refer to extensively are:

1. **Day Lewis Pharmacy**: Founded in 1976 by the late entrepreneur pharmacist Kirit Patel, High Street community pharmacy chain Day Lewis has consistently retained a profitable business amid challenging circumstances. According to the BBC, they now have over 260 branches across the UK in an era where pharmacies, pubs and banks made up half of the closures on Britain's High Streets in the first six months of this year. Eighteen pharmacies are closing weekly, with the largest chain, Lloyds Pharmacies, exiting the sector altogether. As of October 2024, one of the leading pharmacy chains, Boots the Chemists, has closed over 300 branches, calling them 'loss makers.' Boots could afford to do this, as only 35% of their revenue came from community pharmacies.[1]

   Day Lewis continued to outperform the market: gross profit increased by £4.7m to £115.9m (2021: £111.2m). The gross margin percentage increased by 0.5% to 26.6% (2021: 26.1%) driven by increased professional services performed in pharmacies.[2] Its founder, Kirit Patel, won an MBE for his contribution to community pharmacy and charity.

2. **HMV**: In an era of falling CD and DVD purchases, decreasing footfall to High Streets, and falling customer demand complicated by the rise of music streaming by Apple, Spotify, Amazon, YouTube and Deezer,[3] the High Street music retailer HMV should be dead by now. Indeed, it nearly kissed the dust until it was rescued by Canadian entrepreneur, Doug Putman, in 2019. Even though 20 stores had to close and 455 staff lost their jobs in 2013[4], a decade later, the retailer chain is enjoying something of a revival. Music Week states:

   The HMV revival continues. Since its rescue by Doug Putman five years ago, the entertainment retail chain has got to a point where it's now expanding once again, having survived the impact of Covid on High Street retail.[5]

Following its return to the London flagship store in November 2023 and a rare CD sales increase (as reported in Music Week), the company recently issued positive financial results. For the 12 months ending May 30, 2023, HMV's parent company reported that revenue increased by 18% year-on-year to £177.9 million. Pre-tax profits were £5.28m compared to £1.97m in the prior year"[6].

3. **Timpson:** Eyebrows were raised as James Timpson, son of Timpson's founder Sir John Timpson, was made prisons minister by UK prime minister Keir Starmer. High Street retailer Timpson is known for its key cutting, shoe and phone repair, and engravement services. In a throwaway culture where most of us would rather throw things out than get them fixed; in an era of the rise of fast fashion such as Shein, Temu, Primark and Boohoo, Timpsons stands tall and different – repair rather than rot; give old gadgets and shoes a new lease of life rather than encourage wastefulness; and implement what they call 'upside-down management' rather than command and control. As a testament to the prowess of Sir John Timpson, the founder, he was nominated to head a panel by the Conservative government in 2018 to head a panel to identify some of the most pressing challenges faced by England's High Streets and propose practical solutions for the government to take. I talk more about this in the last part of this book.

   It employs nearly 3,500 staff and has 1,325 stores and 110 franchises nationwide. According to the Retail Gazette, *'Timpson is celebrating record results after its profits soared "way beyond" its expectations. The cobbler and key cutters' pre-tax profits surged 66% to £40.6m in the 53 weeks to 1 October 2022 as sales soared 40% to £297.4m.'*[7]

4. **Watersones:** The advent of retail online giant Amazon, where books could be purchased cheaper than in bookstores, and the rise of Kindle e-books and others such as Audible.com, as well as the streaming of podcasts and books from Apple, Spotify and books summary website Blinkist spelt near doom for book High Street retailer Waterstones. And like HMV, this almost seemed to be the case until James Daunt was called in to 'rescue' the beleaguered company. And even though a warehouse glitch caused a significant dent in its financial performance this year, it still managed to close at a profit of over £11 million, and sales grew 13% to over £452 million last year.[8] Waterstones has spurred a butterfly-effect renaissance in independent bookstores nationwide, with many independent booksellers recording record profits.

5. **Richer Sounds:** Despite fierce competition from online sellers such as ao.com and Amazon, as well as High Street retailers such as Comet, Euronics, Argos and Dixons, High Street retailer Richer Sounds shows

no signs of stopping. Even though it has opened no new stores for the past 2 years, it has expanded its online offering and strengthened its stores. Companies House and Pomada.com said it made a pre-tax profit of just under £4.5 million as of April 2023 (£9.7 million before profit sharing and charitable donations).[9]

Apart from profits, these companies regularly show up on tables for good employee treatment and sustainability and have been relatively scandal-free.

There are lots of great companies on the High Street – Greggs, John Lewis, Lush, and Superdrug are all thriving companies – but the ones I chose were thriving despite a massive negative shift in their respective sectors.

This is not to say that these companies are blameless or the epitome of perfection. I've heard managers from some of these shops complain about how they're treated and that they experience a lack of support in some cases. However, the key is that most of the staff and middle management appreciate the trajectory and intentions of the CEOs/founders, all of whom remain alive (except Day Lewis' Kiri Patel, whose children have now taken over, with son Jay Patel as CEO).

Indeed, Jay Patel's mentorship as CEO has yielded a 94% approval rating from his employees: both pharmacists and other healthcare staff.[10] At the same time, Timpson, Waterstones, and Richer Sounds continue to be rated among the best companies to work for in the UK.

I have travelled across the country to many of their stores, interviewed staff, read their history and values and, in some cases, had exclusive interviews with the owners or worked as an employee or freelancer in some of their stores!

Based on this and other research, I've segmented this book into three parts to reflect the three-legged model of Permanence, which includes: the mindset, the operation, and the systems of Permanence.

1. **The Mindset of Permanence:** The entrepreneur who is building a small business and is thinking of achieving long-term success. The central imperative of this book is that long-term success starts from within and that there are characteristic principles of enduring staying power that remain the same. I draw on iconic musicians from different genres, such as Coldplay, Sir Paul McCartney, U2, Stevie Wonder and many others who have achieved enduring success, and bring their mindset for achieving success into the mainstream business world.
2. **The Operation of Permanence:** This is an examination of the business operational aspects of Permanence.

According to the decade of research we have conducted, there are five determinants for enduring success, which I have labelled as:

i. **Tangibility**: the ability to connect with customers over a long period).
ii. **Risk**: the balance of exploration, resilience and exploitation.
iii. **Intellectual capacity**: the crucial element of human resource.
vi. **Affordability**: the right product at the right time and the right price for the right customer.
v. **Strategy**: the right way to get to where you want and how to get there.

The dynamic balance of these five factors can ensure some measure of permanence.

3. **The Systems of Permanence:** This section of the book combines the mindset of operational aspects of Permanence to form a system of Permanence, much like Stephen Covey talks about sharpening the saw in his iconic book, *The 7 Habits of Highly Effective People*. It delves into two significant aspects: the scalability imperative and the **systems** imperative.

In this book, you'll find first hand information, interviews, stories, and observations from CEOs of these companies (and others) who've done just that. They have managed to merge the flexibility and agility of typical SMEs with the stability, uniformity, and economies of scale of larger companies.

I will start looking at the mindset of Permanence with the stories of some unlikely heroes: Snoop Dogg, Elton John, Celine Dion, and the 'evergreen' Coldplay.

Notes

1 Cunningham, Ed, and Henrietta Taylor. 2024. Boots announces more store closures: Full list of boots store closures so far (300 to shut by end of October 2024), *Time Out UK*, September 27: https://www.timeout.com/uk/news/boots-announces-more-store-closures-062823, accessed December 15, 2024.
2 Day Lewis Plc. Day Lewis Financial Statement 2023: https://daylewis.co.uk/wp-content/uploads/2023/01/Day-Lewis-Plc-Annual-Report-Financial-Statements-2022-23.pdf
3 Research and Analysis. Executive Summary. Published 26 July 2022, Digitisation had a significant impact on the music industry: www.gov.uk/government/publications/music-and-streaming-market-study-update-paper/executive-summary
4 Neville, Simon. HMV administrators axe another 464 staff and 37 stores, *The Guardian*: www.theguardian.com/business/2013/feb/20/hmv-administrators-cut-jobs-close-stores, February 20, 2013

5 Music Week. As HMV eyes expansion, owner Doug Putman talks new opportunities, vinyl, CD and the first five years: www.musicweek.com/labels/read/as-hmv-eyes-expansion-owner-doug-putman-talks-new-opportunities-vinyl-cd-and-the-first-five-years/089256, February 14, 2024.
6 Music Week. As HMV eyes expansion, owner Doug Putman talks new opportunities, vinyl, CD and the first five years: www.musicweek.com/labels/read/as-hmv-eyes-expansion-owner-doug-putman-talks-new-opportunities-vinyl-cd-and-the-first-five-years/089256, February 14, 2024.
7 Retail Gazette. Timpson pulls in profits 'way beyond' expectations: www.retailgazette.co.uk/blog/2023/06/timpson-record-results/#:~:text=Timpson%20is%20celebrating%20record%20results,40%25%20to%20£297.4m
8 Denny, Neill. Profits Boom at a Resurgent Waterstones, *Publishers Weekly*: www.publishersweekly.com/pw/by-topic/international/international-book-news/article/96896-profits-boom-at-a-resurgent-waterstones.html, January 22, 2025.
9 Butler, Ben. Profits Boom at a Resurgent Waterstones, *The Guardian*, August 17, 2025.
10 Chemist+Druggist. Pharmacy Manager of the Year 2012: www.chemistanddruggist.co.uk/CD003545/Pharmacy-Manager-of-the-Year-2012

Part I

The Seven Mindsets of Permanence

Introduction: The Seven Mindsets

The first foundational pillar of Permanence is the mindset:

> *'Everything begins and ends in the mind.'*
> Leon Brown, Grammy award winning singer

And to distil this, it may be worth looking outside business for the answer to an unlikely source of rich answers:

Music.

Artists who have lasted over four decades and are still making mainstream music with loyal multi-generational fans share the attributes of the seven Mindsets of Permanence.

They are:

1. **Resilience:** Weathering the knocks
2. **Identity:** Who am I?
3. **Transcendence**: Life of service beyond me
4. **Openness and agility:** Knowledge beyond me
5. **Diligence:** Plain old hard work
6. **Principle of the pie:** Enough to share
7. **Principle of the trail:** Competence versus compassion

Let's examine them one by one, starting with two well-known celebrities who have chased permanence for over two decades: Celine Dion and Snoop Dogg.

Chapter 1

Resilience
Weathering the Knocks

She lay there, as good as dead.

Then, her fingers began to twitch.

Then followed the spasms, the screaming in pain, and the involuntary twitching, which lasted a full 10 minutes. It was painful to watch.

It was so painful that the film director, Irene Taylor, thought she was dying and seriously considered cutting that scene out from the documentary when it was finished.

Even more astonishingly, just moments after this life-threatening episode, she was back in the studio, continuing her 2024 soundtrack album, I | AM.

She had been previously diagnosed with a rare immunological condition known as Stiff Person Syndrome, which causes the body to go into sudden spasms, similar to a severe epileptic fit. As someone who suffers from severe epilepsy myself, I could not help but marvel at this astonishing show of resilience.

At the end of the cut, with a grimaced but stubbornly focused look, she uttered a profound four-word statement, aptly summarising her astonishing music career, which lasted over fifty years.

I will not stop.[1]

The celebrity and legend that is **Celine Dion.**

Then there is the American rapper **Snoop Dogg** whose resilience is undeniable. He faced bans from Norway, the UK, and Australia for marijuana possession, violent disorder, and character concerns.

While creating his album *The Doggfather*, his friend Tupac was killed, he had legal troubles with Death Row Records, and he faced a murder indictment.

Snoop Dogg stated:

It shattered my spirit – I didn't cry, complain, or beg; I just stood strong.[2]

In 2024, over three decades since he was first discovered, he stood 6 feet 4 inches tall as the flag bearer at the Paris Olympics, literally (and metaphorically) showcasing his persistence and tenacity.

Resilience

It is possibly an overused word in today's terminology, but it's a universal trait of all leaders chasing Permanence.

The most enduring leaders possess optimism but balance it with tenacity and persistence in extreme difficulties.

But resilience goes beyond grit, determination, and weathering the knocks. It means going a step further to continually scan the horizons in one's life to detect potential hazards that will undermine one's ability to live a whole and productive life.

From this, we can learn as much from failure as we can from success.

Most companies and organisations rarely suffer from one big fatal blow – just like the collapse of the Roman Empire, it is a culmination of many little bites, 'little foxes' that get them in the end.

> *He that lets the small things bind him*
> *leaves the great undone behind him.*[3]
>
> Piet Hein

As he writes in his bestseller *The Power of Resilience: How the Best Companies Manage the Unexpected*, the undisputed expert on the issue of resilience, Yossi Sheffi, provides three simple principles for ensuring resilience:

> *Resilience involves developing prevention measures, response alternatives and detection systems that cost money and time, which seems to imply a choice between fragile efficiency and expensive robustness.*[4]

Although he writes primarily for companies, as is often the case, this principle can also be applied in our personal lives.

We will read more about Sheffi's ideas and findings later on in the book, but for now, let's look at his three top findings for maintaining resilience:

Detect, Prevent, Respond.

Detect indicates the principle of self-awareness and humility – knowing where we are weak and where we tend to fall at hurdles and entangle ourselves. A strong sense of personal identity gives a strong awareness of our strengths, positives, internal power, weaknesses, and where we are most likely to fall.

Prevent goes a step further. It is not enough to detect the potential hazard. Once we are aware of this, then we can put in measures to ensure we don't fall – that we develop resilience from all four pains: Red (self-sabotage), Amber (waiting), Green (voices) and White (unexpected problems).

Prevention affects our health, habits, happenings, and hazard signs. It also realises that we need help, even when we think we are lions, and it creates structures to help us.

Respond implies developing resilience, which also involves knowing when we need help – our tight circle of friends, our coach, our trainer, our doctor – and being openly vulnerable and asking for help when we know the little bites are beginning to take hold.

Even when death strikes and they don't make it, successful CEOs have implemented robust succession plans, enabling the company to survive without them. Later, I feature excerpts from an exclusive interview with two companies: Day Lewis Pharmacy and Timpson and I show how their leaders have implemented succession plans to ensure a smooth-running company after their demise.

In most cases, leaders and CEOs who run great, enduring companies have an underlying baseline, a strong underbelly that enables them to clench their teeth and withstand incredible shocks. More often than not, they rise from the ashes more muscular, more determined and, yes, more resilient.

Where does this come from? This is precisely what we discuss in the next chapter.

Notes

1 See Celine Dion Suffer Intense Seizure in New Documentary: https://youtu.be/VXoCHpWozNY?si=z7JQ6xTaxtfPQl9s
2 Hip Hop World. www.tiktok.com/@hiphopwrld24/video/7380517833756740871
3 Hein, Piet. Grooks. *Small Things and Great*, Hodder & Stoughton, 1969.
4 Sheffi, Yosef. *The Power of Resilience, How the Best Companies Manage the Unexpected*, The MIT Press, 2015, Pgs 202–214.

Chapter 2

Identity
Who Am I?

A leader who is striving for Permanence knows precisely who they are. They have delved deep into the recesses of their hearts and drawn from a rich reservoir in their inner world. Understanding who you are is the first step towards establishing your identity.

Leaders with mixed identities and a disorganised inner world often struggle to distinguish between their roles and authentic selves – they conflate what they do with who they are.

As Coldplay frontman Chris Martin expresses:

> *I'd love to be a surfer, but I'm just rubbish. If I weren't such a brilliant frontman of a brilliant band, I'd probably do this.*[1]

Years of success can lead to what I term a 'messianic fantasy,' which can infect a leader's personality and create self-aggrandising delusions about their identity. This phenomenon is especially prevalent in SMEs and family-owned businesses, where the company can feel like the founder's 'baby.' However, just as good parenting involves allowing your child to grow into an independent adult, successful leadership requires recognising that a business needs to thrive separate to its founder.

Nature provides prudent examples: the eagle pushes its offspring out of the nest, the lioness nudges her cubs to hunt, and female mammals wean their young off milk.

At the core of identity are two essential factors: **character** and **purpose.** Character is simply the ability to meet the demands of reality (as defined by author Henry Cloud[2]), while purpose – when discovered and embraced – is enduring, even if its expression changes over time.

My father exemplifies this: his purpose was to help people become better than when he found them, a mission he embodied through his work in law, through friendship, leadership as a chief, or his role as a father to me and my brother. Even at 85, when he stepped away from active legal practice,

DOI: 10.4324/9781003569527-3

his identity – his character and purpose – continued to shine. He could meet the demands of reality by retiring, yet he still found ways to fulfil his purpose of encouraging others. For me, as his first son living 6,000 miles away, his support was always just a phone call away, especially when I felt low or down.

Great companies emerge from this deep sense of identity and core values. Later, we will explore how a company's values often reflect the founder's.

Three company founders – Julian Richer, Sam Patel (son of Kirit Patel) and Sir John Timpson – are so clear about their identities and values that they have published books detailing their philosophies. Richer authored the bestseller *The Ethical Capitalist*, while Patel's *Nothing is Impossible* honours their father. Sir John Timpson has written extensively on topics from mental health to entrepreneurship and established Timpson University for top-down management training. More recently, his son and current CEO, James Timpson, has authored the Sunday Times bestseller, *The Happy Index*.

However, the pursuit of Permanence within a company can be significantly jeopardised when the founder/CEO's identity shifts into that of a self-serving idol, 'Messiah' – an issue we will address in greater detail in the next chapter.

Notes

1 Chris Martin, quoted in "Chris Martin Quotes," Coldplaying Forums, https://coldplaying.com/forums/topic/5619-chris-martin-quotes/, accessed October 7, 2025.
2 Cloud, Henry. *Integrity: The Courage to Meet the Demands of Reality*, New York: HarperCollins, 2006.

Chapter 3

Transcendence
Life Beyond Me

We all have an expiry date on the bottom of our 'tins.' As a practising High Street pharmacist, there are two types of expiry dates I deal with regarding medicines:

- **BBE:** Best Before End: after nearly going bankrupt with my first business, BlueCloud Health, my family struggled for basics. Plymouth has a shop called Rogers, whose tag line is: 'The UK's biggest gone past best before warehouse.' This shop specialises in products past their sell-by date – sometimes even months past – and which aren't suitable for traditional supermarkets like Tesco or Sainsbury's. However, these items remain edible and safe for consumers despite minor issues like discoloured labels, incorrect batches, or beginning of deterioration.

One day, I had just £20 available to spend. Everything was maxed out.

The bargains were incredible – almost 80% off a 16-pack of fizzy drinks, nearly 90% off snack bars, tinned tomatoes, and ready-to-prepare meals. That supermarket was a lifesaver for us during hard times.

We survived that week with enough food to last us through the next week before we got paid.

But the fact remained - everything in that store was past its best.

In business and leadership, there comes a time when you're still fit enough to govern, lead, and stay in charge, but you know deep down that your best days are behind you. As Africans, we are familiar with leaders who had gone past their best but continued to rule. Robert Mugabe. Paul Biya. Yoweri Museveni. Abdelaziz Bouteflika. Contrast those with leaders who knew their time had come before the world knew: Nelson Mandela. Sir Alex Ferguson. Jacinda Ardern.

As John C Maxwell says:

> *If you run well but are unable to pass the baton to another runner, you lose the race.*[1]

Sir Elton John, one of the world's most celebrated artists, can teach us a lot about Transcendence.

To say he is a celebrated artist is a wild understatement.

The Royal Academy of Music summarises his achievements:

> *Elton is the most successful solo male in the history of the American charts and the third most successful artist, behind only Madonna and the Beatles. Between 1970 and 2000, he logged 67 Hot 100 entries, including nine No. 1s and 27 top 10s. He achieved seven No. 1 albums in the three-and-a-half-year period from 1972 to 1975 – a period of concentrated success surpassed only by the Beatles.*[2]

He holds the record for the biggest-selling single of all time, *Candle In The Wind* (1997), which sold over 33 million copies[3].

On June 25, 2023, he headlined the famous Glastonbury Festival, where he gave a masterclass on succession that every business leader could learn from: he introduced new talent on stage, sang some of his collaborative music with the audience, seemed genuinely humbled to be there, and gracefully left the stage when his time was up.

All the things that Bob Iger, CEO of Disney, failed to do.

Just before the performance in Los Angeles started, there was breaking news that Bob Iger, aged 71, was retiring to retake control of the firm he had left just under a year ago, elbowing out his handpicked successor, Bob Chapek. Having retired from his position as Disney's Executive Chairman in 2021, Bob Iger, aged 71, returned to the company only a year later, taking up his previous role and elbowing out his handpicked successor, Bob Chapek. The irony was that this happened just before Elton John was about to perform the Los Angeles leg of his farewell tour. Strangely, Bob Iger had written a memoir, *The Ride of a Lifetime*, in which he exemplifies the messianic fantasy I alluded to earlier.

The Economist newspaper, which broke the story, says that far from this situation being unique to Disney, there is an 'American 40 year' succession problem. This problem is exacerbated significantly when the departing CEOs have achieved near-mythical status (Jack Welch, former GE boss, and Howard Schultz, CEO of Starbucks, come to mind). This is one of the reasons I chose the 40 year window timeline for SMEs earlier. The self-fulfilling prophecy is 'confirmed' because once these CEOs have departed, the companies' influence begins to wane and competitors start to grab market share – as happened with FedEx (Fred Smith was in charge for 49 years) and Rupert Murdoch's News Corp (70 years in charge), both of whom are named in the article.

And this is not limited to America.

In Japan, famed anime director Hayao Miyazaki, Director of Studio Ghibli, came out of retirement on November 25, 2021 once again to make a feature-length animated film. He had done this several times before, the first being in the 1990s. He then returned in 2020 to direct *Spirited Away* (which earned an Oscar) and, before that in 2013, *The Wind Rises*, a fictional biographical film.

However, not all cases involve a best-before date. Sometimes, they involve a hard stop.

- **Use-by date**: the hard stop. One day, I nearly lost my job as a pharmacist. I didn't correctly check that I dispensed a dangerous medicine that was out of date, causing panic. My 20-year career could have ended as the anti-inflammatory could have severely harmed the patient, but luckily, he checked the date. Unlike best before end, it's illegal to sell medicines past their use-by date; they must be destroyed. This applies to some businesses where a CEO's sudden death or incapacity can halt operations. I've seen this when a small company I freelance for lost its founder to COVID-19.

Day Lewis Pharmacy lost Kirit Patel to a heart attack, but fortunately, he had the forethought to already have trained his successors, Jay, Rupa and Sam Patel. In an interview, Jay noted how Kirit ensured his children were well-acquainted with the business and consequently, Day Lewis now thrives under new management while remaining a family business. As a CEO or founder, you have a BBE or use-by date. Every CEO, founder, leader, or entrepreneur must grasp the principle of Transcendence.

In both instances, the solution is the same: you begin training and implementing systems within as broad a pool of leaders as possible who will then be ready to step in. A company that falls to pieces after its leader goes through a best before or use-by phase most likely did not have a transcendent culture to begin with.

However, this is easier said than done – accepting transcendence is mentally challenging. In his book, *The Ride of a Lifetime*, Bob Iger acknowledges:

> *It's one of those moments, I imagine, when it's hard to know exactly who you are without this attachment, title and role that has defined you for so long.*[4]

He adds that all CEOs like to think they are irreplaceable. Yet good leadership demands the opposite. This raises the question: what kind of legacy will I leave behind? And yes, apart from legacy, CEOs also have to confront their inevitable mortality. It's a shame that Iger couldn't follow his own advice, even though his BBE was written on his tin. His best days were behind him.

There is a true story of an English headmaster appointed when he was around forty-five. The first thing he did was write himself a letter to be opened twenty years later:

Today, you are sixty-five. It has been twenty years since you took this appointment, and it is time to hand over the reins to a younger person. You will tell yourself that no one can replace you, that the school cannot do without you. But don't believe this for a second – it is self-aggrandising propaganda.[5]

When he reached sixty-five years old and opened the letter, he found that, indeed, he had those exact feelings. However, unlike the Disney boss, he took his own advice and released the leadership to someone younger.

Gordon MacDonald, in his classic book, *Ordering Your Private World*, identifies this kind of leader as a 'called':

A sense of stewardship, his perspective about his role, and his commitment to the principle of release mark a called person. These are the characteristics of a person who first builds his interior and private world, which flows out of his fountains of life.[6]

Author Henry Cloud agrees:

A transcendent leader realises that there are things much more significant than her, and her existence is not just about her and her interests but, ultimately, about the more substantial stuff she is. Her life is about fitting into those things, joining them, serving them, obeying them and finding her role in the big picture. Then, as a result, she ultimately becomes a part of them and finds meaning much more significant than life just about her. Life is about things that transcend her.[7]

But you don't have to wait until your Best Before Date before you master the principle of Transcendence. A Transcendent leader is so secure in his identity that he is intentional about being generous with his time, passing on everything he knows, and not being afraid to model his behaviour.

That's why Richer Sounds' boss was happy to let his employees own the company. That's why Kirit Patel visited most of his branches to deliver flowers and personally celebrate weddings and other milestones.

The founder of British High Street chain LUSH, Mark Constantine, has given 10% of the company to his employees and states:

I think having an element of employee ownership is one of the best things we've ever done.[8]

However, the issue may sometimes lie with an insecure successor, not the outgoing leader.

In his debut book, *Centennials, the 12 Habits of Great, Enduring Organisations,* Alex Hill recounts the unfortunate succession of David

Moyes to Alex Ferguson, former coach of Manchester United.[9] Alex Ferguson was Manchester United's most successful manager, winning the league trophy a record thirteen times after six years in charge and in the top three every other year. David Moyes sacked three of United's assistant coaches and half the existing squad and brought in some of the former team from Everton. Probably as a consequence, Manchester United ended up having their worst ever position in over twenty years, ending up seventh in the league.

It's a credit to Alex Ferguson that he didn't try to come in to rescue United – a sure sign of a Transcendent leader with a strong identity.

However, there is another crucial reason SME leaders may destroy the company if they stay too long.

It is called the difference between Fluid Intelligence and Crystallised Intelligence.

Arthur C. Brooks, in his bestselling book *From Strength to Strength, Finding Happiness and Deep Purpose in the Second Half of Life,* distinguishes between the two types of intelligence leaders have, which is directly proportional to their ages.[10]

In the first half of life, up to around 40 years old, entrepreneurs and most leaders have the most innovative times of their careers. This explains why iconic companies such as Facebook, Google, Twitter, and Third Web were all founded by leaders in their late twenties or early thirties. They were working in **fluid intelligence** – the kind of intelligence in the brain that fuels quick thinking, innovation, experimentation, and discoveries. This kind of intelligence typically peaks around the forties (though individual results sometimes may vary). This also explains why bands and artists such as Coldplay, The Rolling Stones, UB40, Abba, Oasis, Elton John, and poets such as T.S. Eliot, rely on fluid intelligence to produce new work, typically having produced their best original work in their late twenties and early thirties. Even the iconic Rolling Stones' newest 2023 album, *Hackney Diamonds*, has hardly made a ripple in the charts by their own standards.

It explains why sports pundits and judges are primarily in their 40s upwards (think of British TV sport pundits Gary Lineker, Alan Shearer and Ian Wright)

That intelligence wanes as they age, particularly past their mid-forties, and a metamorphosis begins. It is replaced by another type of intelligence called **crystallised intelligence.** This intelligence is based on a synthesis of already done work, pattern recognition, experience and time. This is why many bands, poets and others do not hit the bestseller charts in those ages or disappear unless they figure out a way to stay relevant by maximising their crystallised intelligence or collaborating with younger people who have fluid intelligence. This may imply freshening their bands by introducing new and young talent, such as Queen using Adam Lambert as their new vocal frontline or Coldplay collaborating with newcomers BTS, or Elton John with Dua Lipa. We will talk more about this in the next section, which is about Tangibility.

So, leaders beyond their forties who try to focus on innovation and new products (fluid intelligence) will have a hard time because their brain intelligence type has changed.

This is especially true for businesses that constantly rely on innovation to survive. This means that older leaders have to move to a more coaching, supervisory and teaching role, as well as a role that involves strategic pattern recognition, synthesising already-done innovative work and applying it to their company. Older leaders should be spotting new talent who can carry on the innovation and progress of the company with new ideas, interpreting what's out there, identifying and developing talent, ready to hand over the reins before hitting the hard stop.

Crystallised intelligence involves synthesis, not innovation, interpreting or trying to incrementally improve the original breakthrough. And you must be secure enough to have an eye on the bigger picture, the Transcendent picture.

Reggae icon Bob Marley puts it well,

Live for yourself, and you will live in vain. Live for others, and you will live again.

And that's why he had the confidence to say:

My music will go on forever. Maybe it's a fool to say that, but when I know facts, I can say facts. My music will go on forever.[11]

And yes, over forty years after he died in 1981, his music is still topping charts worldwide.

Such leaders have a keen sense of openness – the characteristic to which we now turn.

Notes

1. Maxwell, John C. Teams that don't bond can't build: www.instagram.com/johncmaxwell/p/Cwycm91ONY2, accessed November 7, 2024.
2. Royal Academy of Music. Sir Elton Hercules John, CBE, is one of the most highly acclaimed and successful solo artists of all time: www.ram.ac.uk/people/sir-elton-john, accessed February 10, 2024.
3. Wikipedia. List of best-selling singles in the United Kingdom: https://en.wikipedia.org/wiki/List_of_best-selling_singles_in_the_United_Kingdom, accessed November 14, 2024.
4. Iger, Robert. *The Ride of a Lifetime: Lessons Learned from 15 Years as CEO of the Walt Disney Company*, Random House, 2019.

5. MacDonald, Gordon. *Ordering Your Private World – Key Steps to Greater Resourcefulness, Effectiveness and Balance*, Moody Books, 1984.
6. MacDonald, Gordon. *Ordering Your Private World – Key Steps to Greater Resourcefulness, Effectiveness and Balance*, Moody Books, 1984.
7. Cloud, Henry. *Integrity: The Courage to Meet the Demands of Reality*, HarperCollins, 2009.
8. Cartlidge, Sarah. Lush boss says employee ownership is 'best thing its done.' *Daily Echo*: www.bournemouthecho.co.uk/news/23628419.lush-boss-says-employee-ownership-best-thing-done, July 4, 2023.
9. Hill, Alex. *Centennials: The 12 Habits of Great, Enduring Organisations*, Cornerstone Press, 2023, Pgs 54–56.
10. Brooks, Arthur C. *From Strength to Strength: Finding Success, Happiness and Deep Purpose in the Second Half of Life*, Green Tree Books, 2023.
11. Goodreads. Quotable quotes by Bob Marley: www.goodreads.com/quotes/23755-my-music-will-go-on-forever-maybe-it-s-a-fool, accessed November 15, 2024.

Chapter 4

Openness
Knowledge Beyond Me

An open leader is a secure leader. A secure leader understands their place in the world, is comfortable with their identity, and recognises that their purpose extends beyond their organisation. They know that isolating themselves, lacking the humility to learn, and failing to remain curious will lead to failure.

So, what does it mean to be open?

A significant insight comes from an interview with CEO James Timpson, published in Marketing Week:

> *The Timpson CEO picks up ideas all the time, spending 20%–30% of his time examining other companies.*[1]

Timpson is part of a business group that meets once a month and regularly seeks advice from friends and his father on issues like the impending inflation crisis. This group also includes Richer Sounds CEO Julian Richer and Day Lewis CEO Jay Patel.

This essence of openness is captured in one key trait: collaboration.

This trait is emphasised after identity because only a leader with a strong sense of identity can recognise that living in isolation and fearing the admission of ignorance are signs of stagnation.

In his bestselling book *The Tipping Point: How Little Things Can Make a Big Difference*[2], renowned author Malcolm Gladwell introduced the term 'connector' to describe individuals who bridge different social worlds. The essence of a true leader isn't measured by the number of social media followers or by being the loudest voice in the room. Instead, the 'law of the few' defines an open leader's character – those who can forge connections beyond their immediate sphere or specialisation.

Many books have been written about the value of being an open leader. For instance, Christian Stadler's book *Open Strategy* discusses the importance of involving front-line staff in a company's strategic planning beyond just the boardroom.

In their paper published in *Harvard Business Review* in January 2010, INSEAD professors Ibarra and Hansen outlined what it takes to be a collaborative leader:[3]

- Connecting people and ideas from outside the organisation to those within it
- Modelling collaborative behaviour at the top
- Leveraging diverse talent
- Providing strong guidance to prevent teams from getting caught in endless debates

I have witnessed first-hand how modelling collaborative behaviour, leveraging diverse talent, and creating connections have significantly contributed to Day Lewis' success, even as many pharmacies nationwide have closed down. Kirit Patel forged strong ties with companies outside his industry such as Timpson, the High Street key-cutting company, to learn from their success.

Mark Higgins, CEO of Devon High Street retailer Beacon Electrical, attributes the company's 45 years of success to collaboration. Beacon was the first Hotpoint-sponsored company in the country and has leveraged its connections with Euronics, an international association of over 11,000 independent electrical retailers in 37 countries. Euronics functions as a leading global electrical retail group on behalf of its members based in Amsterdam and it has built strong relationships with customers, of whom I am one. Beacon has consistently outperformed much larger and more established competitors, such as John Lewis, AO.com, and Currys.

Timpson has also established strong partnerships with prisons nationwide, effectively leveraging its diverse talent by engaging directly with inmates. The CEO exemplifies this collaborative behaviour by leading from the top.

Part two of this book, The Operation of Permanence, will delve into the spirit of openness and collaboration that characterises almost all successful small businesses. We will also explore a common thread among musicians who have remained prominent in the industry for decades, with examples including Coldplay, Elton John, Madonna, Beyoncé, Snoop Dogg, and Switchfoot.

Collaboration signifies a more profound understanding – the realisation that you face formidable challenges as a business leader on the High Street and cannot succeed alone. However, if your identity is strong, you will understand this truth deeply, making you open to learning, especially in a fragile business environment where decline is prevalent.

I appreciate how rapper Snoop Dogg articulates this:

When I collaborate, it's about bringing out the best in someone else, and it's also about ensuring they bring out the best in me – collaboration is about blending different flavours to create something delicious.[4]

Another fundamental aspect of openness is humility – a word that is easy to spell but challenging to embody. The saying '*pride comes before a fall*' is especially relevant here. True humility involves accepting ourselves fully, including our imperfections. This should not be confused with false humility, where individuals who deserve recognition downplay their achievements; such behaviour benefits neither themselves nor their communities.

Notes

1 Rogers, Charlotte. Timpson CEO: Our business shouldn't exist anymore, *Marketing Week*: www.marketingweek.com/timpson-ceo-business/, accessed December 5, 2024.
2 Gladwell, Malcolm. *The Tipping Point: How Little Things Can Make a Big Difference*, Abacus Press, 2002.
3 Ibarra, Herminia and Morten T. Hansen. Are you a collaborative leader? *Harvard Business Review*, July–August 2011: https://hbr.org/2011/07/are-you-a-collaborative-leader.
4 Buring for Success. Snoop Dogg quotes on collaboration: https://burningforsuccess.com/snoop-dogg-quotes/, accessed August 21, 2024.

Chapter 5

Diligence
Doing the Work

How does a superstar like Madonna keep herself in the limelight for over four decades?

What is one of the open secrets of the seeming immortality of Elton John?

Madonna scheduled an 81-date tour that began on 14 October 2023, at the O2 in London and ended on 4 May 2024, with a free concert in Rio de Janeiro, attended by over 1.6 million fans – the biggest in her career and the largest crowd ever for a standalone concert.[1]

She is 64, with a career spanning nearly four decades, and still keeps up gruelling schedules like this – delivering performance after performance. It's one of the reasons she remains so successful, with nearly 41 million listeners on Spotify.

Elton John's Farewell Yellow Brick Road tour is even more impressive: a whopping 330 shows across five continents, beginning in Allentown, Pennsylvania, on read 8 September 2018, and concluding in Stockholm, Sweden, on July 8, 2023, including headlining the world-famous Glastonbury festival along the way, despite being in his seventies, having had multiple joint replacements and bouts of ill health.[2]

The time for just working hard, putting out a record and hoping it sails to the top of the Billboard Charts and changes the face of music is over.

This is why successful bands and musicians tour, post, and interview so much – to get their music out there to old, ever-adoring fans and to attract new ones.

The founders of the companies on the High Street I have looked at have also had to put in the hard yards.

But their goals were different. Unlike their successors and modern companies, which now have the task of keeping their companies at the forefront of customers' minds, nobody knew initially who they were or what they stood for. They had to plough the ground, sow the seed, work the ground, and pioneer their companies amidst formidable changes.

DOI: 10.4324/9781003569527-6

They had to work hard to let people know they existed. There was no Facebook, no Instagram, no podcasts for them to go on, no Google rankings for them to use SEO, no AI to complement their tasks – there was barely any internet.

It's probably the reason Kirit Patel had a heart attack.

And probably the reason why Eddie Stobbart, founder of the logistics company Eddie Stobbart, worked so hard; why he was frequently found asleep on his desk the following day.

And even though we have different challenges, there is intense competition. Quiet Quitting. The Great Resignation. The Internet. There are way too many voices, too much noise, and too many choices; the solutions haven't changed and the principle of hard work hasn't changed either.

Connections need to be made. High Street companies must work hard to ensure that employees demanding better treatment are seen, heard, and understood. They must also work hard to keep customers, execute strategy, and keep the doors open.

However, not all hard work is good work.

In a groundbreaking study, Professor Nancy Rothbard surveyed a representative sample of workaholics with mental health struggles, loneliness, and even early deaths. She found no health issues with what she called 'engaged workaholism,' where people brought meaning into their work and had an overarching purpose that tapped into their deeply-held values.[3]

This is made more accessible by one word: PASSION.

Retail expert Graham Soult emphasised this recently in his interview with the magazine Retail Gazette:

> *If you look at some of the success stories of struggling retailers that have come back from the brink, it's often because you've got somebody involved who is passionate about the product.*[4]

The CEOs of all five High Street companies are distinguished by their passion for their work.

Doug Putman, the boss of HMV, Jay Patel of Day Lewis, and John Timpson (and later on his son James) have all been passionately involved in their sectors since they were young.

James Daunt, CEO of Waterstones has sold books since he was 19 years old and opened Daunt Books decades ago (which is still a going concern).

Julian Richer started selling hi-fi equipment when he was 14 and opened his first store at 19.

That is what renowned author and coach Marshall Goldsmith calls *The Earned Life* in his book with the same name:[5]

We live an earned life when the choices, risks and efforts we make in each moment align with an overarching purpose, regardless of the eventual outcome.

He continues:

A truly earned life makes three simple requirements of us:

- *We make our best choice supported by the facts and the clarity of our goals. In other words, we know what we want and how far we must go.*
- *We accept the risk involved.*
- *We put out maximum effort.* (**Hard work and diligence – emphasis mine**)

Engaged workaholics are typified by living an earned life.

One of Kirit Patel's aims in life was to have fun. He scaled Mount Kilimanjaro, went skiing, and had regular family skiing trips with his family. As a result, having fun was one of the enduring tenets he left with his company. This is the concept of personnel scalability (which I touch on in the third part of this book). Even though he paid the ultimate price for his hard work, he lived an earned life.

Sir John Timpson is another entrepreneur who has lived an earned life. He has written several books and fostered over 90 children. This personal trait of his extends to his company which regularly employs ex-convicts as well as people serving time in prison to work in its stores (an example of personnel scalability discussed in part 3 of this book). Over 12% of Timpson employees have some sort of criminal record.

There is now a common slogan that many high-profile celebrities have passed around:

Work smarter, not harder

As if those two were mutually exclusive.

The fashion now is 'cheat sheets' and 'done for you' programmes. Most people want to take shortcuts and find 'cool and quick methods' of completing the work.

Yes, working smart has its place, but nothing can replace diligence, hard graft, and putting in the work.

Simply put, most competitive advantages eventually diminish and die over time. As Morgan Housel said in his 2023 bestseller, *Same as Ever*, a key determinant of sustained success is to '*keep running*':

Few products, musicians, etc., ever remain relevant for decades. No competitive advantage is so decisive that it can enable you to rest on your laurels – and the ones that do tend to seed their decline.[6]

A proper mindset of permanence is just plain practical hard work. But that's not all. Like Coldplay and Elton John, you need to keep running, and one way to 'work smart' is to find a good team that will cheer you on and lessen the load.

Umuntu ngumuntu ngabantu: I am because we are.

This is the famous Zulu proverb that we will examine next.

Notes

1 Wikipedia. Farewell Yellow Brick Road: https://en.wikipedia.org/wiki/Farewell_Yellow_Brick_Road, accessed February 15, 2025.
2 *The Economist*. What Disney can learn from Elton John: www.economist.com/business/2022/11/23/what-disney-can-learn-from-elton-john, 23 November 2022.
3 *Knowledge at Wharton*. The Truth About Being a Workaholic: Why It Isn't Always Bad for You, November 29, 2017: https://knowledge.wharton.upenn.edu/article/truth-workaholics-isnt-always-bad/, accessed July 18, 2024.
4 Retail Gazette. Does HMV have a future on the UK's High Street?: www.retailgazette.co.uk/blog/2019/10/does-hmv-have-a-future-on-the-uks-high-street, accessed October 15, 2019.
5 Goldsmith, Marshall and Mark Reiter. *The Earned Life: Lose Regret, Choose Fulfilment*, Penguin Business, 2022.
6 Housel, Morgan. *Same As Ever: Timeless Lessons on Risk, Opportunity and Living a Good Life*, Harriman House, 2023, Pg 131.

Chapter 6

Principle of the Pie
Enough to Share

Richer Sounds should be dead by now.

Instead, they have won the Retailer of the Year eight times (so far), with their first win in 2010 and their latest in 2024. Despite all the online competition, they are still the UK's largest High Street hi-fi retailer after 40 years.[1]

As an audiophile, a lover of all things sound, and an irresistible lover of SMEs, I know that every company and retail space gives off a je ne sais quoi, an energy, a vibe, that either draws you in or repels you as you enter. In the next section of this book, I explore this phenomenon, which I have called Tangibility.

The vibe, culture, and energy in every Richer Sound retail space is palpable. Still, the positive vibration is difficult to pin down, which we will cover in the next part of the book.

But a lot of it is down to the staff.

Julian Richer, CEO of Richer Sounds, recently devolved company ownership to his employees. They own the company – it is their business and as a result, they have a real stake in how it is run. The staff are very knowledgeable and friendly, taking time to get to know their customers and going to great lengths to make that sale, develop a community, and participate in it. Their superior training is evident.

Yet this mindset doesn't just happen.

The employees are self-made experts – they share a passion for music and movies. But the most significant thing that struck me is their almost unanimously held, optimistic view of the company, which is mirrored by customers and external viewers.

This does not apply just to Richer Sounds. The other companies featured also have a particular mindset about sharing their successes: from Julian Richer emailing each employee to congratulate them on personal and business successes; to Jay Patel giving £50 to each employee to celebrate their wedding and offering generous bonuses for targets; or even down to 'little' things like free ice cream on a hot day. John Timpson makes available free holiday homes for his managers; the High Street department store John Lewis, and cosmetics chain Lush, also practise the same principle in their stores – perhaps a significant reason why John Lewis is still standing after 83% of department stores have disappeared from the High Street in the last decade.[2]

They share the tenet of the Principle of the Pie.

This pie extends beyond the company. These staff members have taken the initiative to build strong communities around their companies locally and nationally. They are loved and respected in their communities.

Why? Because they enjoy a share of the Pie.

Even though I believe in an open strategy, I firmly believe that what leaders, CEOs, and entrepreneurs believe deep down feeds into the organisation's culture. Good leaders powerfully lead themselves with their values, and this leadership, almost like a positive virus, infects their companies.

I call this the principle of *Personal Scalability*, which we will discuss in Part III of this book.

Later on in Part II of this book, I discuss how the CEO's mindset toward employees significantly impacts success and morale. Do founders view hiring as a favour or just see their staff as essential stakeholders? Are they genuine in their commitments?

For over twenty years on the High Street, I've observed the consequences of these attitudes, from mass resignations and 'quiet quitting' to sabotage. This leads us to the final chapter, which explores the balance between genuine care for employees and a strong commitment to high standards.

Notes

1 Wikipedia. Richer Sounds: https://en.wikipedia.org/wiki/Richer_Sounds, accessed February 15, 2025.
2 Simpson, Emma. UK loses 83% of department stores since BHS collapsed: www.bbc.co.uk/news/business-58331168, accessed August 27, 2021.

Chapter 7

Principle of the Trail
Balancing Competence and Compassion

As a leader, what trail do you leave behind as you walk the path called Life?

Dr Henry Cloud, in his book *Integrity*, talks about the balance of tasks (competence) and relationships (compassion).[1]

Leadership expert John Adair talks about the balance of the 'work' and the 'people.'[2]

We all intuitively know this.

Staff and employees will frequently talk about a boss who 'knew his stuff' but was 'difficult to get along with' or a boss who was 'nice' but made frequent wrong professional calls and judgements.

They are talking about the balance between competence and compassion.

That is what I call the Principle of the Trail.

I touched on this principle in my debut book, *Pay The Price*.

A High Street healthcare business that made frequent losses and was sold had a middle manager who exemplified competence: he knew his figures, was highly adept at the nuts and bolts of the business and knew how to keep employees in line. He was my manager in my younger days and I used to dread his visits. He came in all guns blazing, bullied me and my staff and left us feeling frustrated and demotivated. His recommendations were usually correct, he was excellent at his job, but his lack of empathy, people skills, and low emotional quotient took its toll.

Complaints mounted about him and even though his results were good, the trail of broken relationships he left behind was too pronounced to ignore. He was eventually fired after staff members started leaving in droves.

He sacrificed compassion for competence.

On the other hand, I worked for a small business owner who was dignified, professional, honest, a fantastic father, and had a distinctive smile. But there was a paradox: people were also leaving the organisation in droves, all bitter, twisted, and hurt. After a while, I joined that exodus.

It was a paradox because he was *too caring*. He lacked the courage to fire or discipline persistently incompetent employees, refused to act when tough calls had to be made personally, and made mistakes in his leadership and

DOI: 10.4324/9781003569527-8

professional capacity. His compassion was off the scale, but his competence was lacking. As a result, the company is stuck in Formative Mode, neither growing nor thriving.
He sacrificed competence for compassion.
Both extremes by a leader do not bode well for the long-term health of any business.

One thing that struck me about the thriving High Street chains I examined was how disciplined they ran their companies **and** how deeply they cared for their employees. Jay Patel of Day Lewis could mention most of his pharmacists by name, their birthdays, and events. He shared his family celebrations with his employees. But he also insisted on and expected high standards and ensured the bottom line was looked after.

Richer Sounds boss Julian Richer manages all 52 branches, personally emailing the managers to congratulate them on success and ensures they are well looked after. He also monitors the numbers and ensures that tasks and sales in all 52 branches conform to his high standards.

Charlotte Rogers, writing in Marketing Week, after interviewing James Timpson, summarises his words beautifully:

> *'Kindness is integral to us,' he explained. Regarding hiring leaders, kindness is one of the key attributes we look for. We do not see any conflict in being a kind employer with high standards. We only want 'amazing colleagues' to work with equally amazing people; if they don't, we consider ourselves to have failed.*
>
> *The way we look at it is that we want people with an amazing personality, and how we describe them is an eight, nine, or ten out of ten. Ideally, we want the nines and tens out of ten, but eight is good enough, and we can help them improve.*
>
> *If you're a nine out of ten colleague and you've got to work with someone who's six out of ten, you won't enjoy your job. It'll cost you a commission, and things will start to go wrong.* **We are ruthless in ensuring that people who aren't amazing find themselves in a business elsewhere.**[3]

Róisín Currie, CEO of the popular UK High Street bakery chain Greggs since 2022 and recently appointed a CBE, exemplifies what this chapter is about: clarity of purpose (competence) combined with genuine care for people (compassion). In terms of the former, she has pushed for bold expansion, partnering with Primark on branded lines, growing the estate beyond 2,600 shops to over 3,000, as well as modernising logistics to stay competitive in a challenging economy. Yet her achievements are rooted in something deeper. Rising from Group People Director to the top role, Currie makes every decision through a people lens.

She invests in colleagues via wide-ranging inclusion programmes, has ensured Greggs has met the UK's leading Diversity, Equity and Inclusion standard, the National Equality Standard (NES), and keeps customers at the heart of every product adjustment. Beyond the business, she chairs the Employers Forum for Reducing Reoffending and launched Greggs' Fresh Start scheme, which offers paid roles to those leaving prison (similar to Timpson above). Under her leadership, Greggs has become increasingly profitable; their financial results show a pre-tax profit of over £203 million, an 8.3% rise from 2023. Currie's track record proves that when a leader combines sharp strategy (competence) with genuine care – for employees, customers, and the wider community (compassion) – you don't just grow a business. You build something that lasts.

And Chrissie Rucker, founder of The White Company, built her High Street and online empire with a deep belief in calm, purpose-driven culture – not just for customers, but for her people. What began as a mail-order catalogue in her spare room has grown into a national brand known for quality, trust, and timeless design. But behind the scenes, she credits the company's lasting success to its values and its people-first culture:

For me, great business is about values and people. If you get the culture right, performance follows.

Her leadership is a reminder that clarity of purpose (competence) and consistency of care (compassion) – even in fast-paced retail – can build both loyalty and longevity.

This is the principle of the trail – the dynamic balance between competence and compassion.

So, these are the seven mindsets that enable Permanence.

But more is needed to just have a mindset. It is not enough to just put them into practice consistently.

These mindsets should evolve the company to practice the operation of Permanence – a dynamic loop of five different practices (determinants) that, combined with the mindsets, form a robust framework that helps companies and their leaders anticipate, weather, and even thrive beyond the inevitable storms.

We now turn to these five determinants, starting with the story of an unlikely hero in my backyard and what we can learn from Britain's corner shops.

Notes

1 Cloud, Henry. *Integrity: The Courage to Meet the Demands of Reality*, HarperCollins, 2009.
2 Adair, John. *How to Grow Leaders: The Seven Key Principles of Effective Leadership Development*, Kogan Page, 2009.
3 Rogers, Charlotte. Timpson CEO: Our business shouldn't exist anymore, *Marketing Week*: www.marketingweek.com/timpson-ceo-business

Part II

The Operation of Permanence

Introduction to the Five Determinants

Louise Parker, the CEO of Bread and Roses Pub in Plymouth, is a trailblazer and one of the first black women to run a pub in the South West of England. Despite facing challenges like racism and personal loss, she persevered, fuelled by her roots in the Windrush generation.

Louise transformed her pub into a vibrant community hub by introducing live bands and focusing intensely on making a positive local impact. This innovative and collaborative approach has set her apart in the region, positioning her pub as Plymouth's only Social Enterprise Pub.

According to the Guardian, over 2,600 pubs closed in the UK in the past five years, but Louise has thrived, recently celebrating her pub's 10th anniversary.

During a lunch together, Louise shared her journey of resilience, which illustrated the Five Determinants Model:

- Tangibility
- Affordability
- Human Capital
- Risk and Resilience
- Strategy

These dynamic determinants emerged from over a decade of research involving more than 50 companies and extensive interviews with successful business leaders. They should be viewed as a dynamic loop rather than static factors, varying by organisation, location, and stage of development.

We will discuss this dynamism further in Part III of the book. For now, let's explore the first determinant, beginning with a favourite quote from one of my favourite authors.

Chapter 8
The First Determinant
Tangibility

During her illustrious, award-winning career, Dr. Mandeep Rai, a former BBC and Reuters journalist and global expert on company values has visited over 150 countries. She has distilled a specific value that embodies each nation's essence.

She quotes:

> Whenever I visited a new country to report, I was struck by the same realisation. Wherever you go, there is something evident yet unspoken, a cultural language that influences many aspects of everyday life. You notice it on the streets, in the cafes, in business meetings, around the kitchen.[1]

If we pay close attention, this 'something evident' exists in diverse countries and various businesses. These emit an implicit yet unspoken vibe, energy, and resonance – an attribute that makes something almost magical perceivable through all five senses. (Dr. Rai hinted at this in her 2019 TED Talk, delivered in Hungary[2], regarding how values can serve as a distinguishing tangible factor for businesses, just as they do for countries.) We explore this further in chapter 10 of this book. A customer told me after visiting a community pharmacy that had just changed hands:

> The shop felt cold as I entered and appeared to have lost its warm and welcoming feeling – it had now become very quiet – I did not enjoy my experience there.

Writer and Researcher Kerry Lee states:

> In an era when digital convenience often reigns supreme, physical stores face the challenge of declining foot traffic. Despite the undeniable appeal of online shopping, which offers unparalleled speed and convenience, brick-and-mortar stores still hold significant customer value, providing tangible,

Figure 8.1 The Five Determinants Model: Determinant 1: Tangibility.

sensory experiences and serving as community hubs that foster human connection.[3]

These physical locations are strategic assets for retailers that reduce transportation costs and enhance profit margins. However, to counteract the trend of diminishing footfall, physical stores must evolve, offering unique advantages that online platforms cannot replicate.

Kerry Lee perfectly summarised this first determinant of permanence on the High Street.

I call this phenomenon **Tangibility.**

One day, while walking to get a haircut, I walked on Mutley Plain, a busy High Street in Plymouth. It is known for its many barber shops and salons catering to the city's diverse population. Some shops were empty, with barbers idle, but I found one store, Headline Barbers, bustling with customers.

Which one did I go to for my haircut?

On that same street, there are dozens of bakeries, confectioneries, and cafes, all of which are doing well. However, one particular cafe, Early Bird, had a long queue of customers waiting to go in even before the shop opened at 9 a.m.

I noticed the same phenomenon in Seville, Spain, when one restaurant had queues and queues of hungry customers waiting patiently. In contrast, others stood empty with bewildered-looking staff.

Again, I have seen the same in an ice cream parlour and pasta restaurant in Rome, a local restaurant in Accra, Ghana, a famous meat restaurant in Nairobi, and a small coffee shop on the High Street in St Budeax, Plymouth.

It was like an energy that drew customers and clients to a particular business.

After walking into many SMEs, especially those that have physical spaces and sell services and goods, I concluded:

- It wasn't the price because, in most cases, the price differential between the shops was almost negligible.
- Yes, factors like cleanliness, a good process, quality of service and location on the street played a considerable part, but I couldn't fully explain what I saw.

The story I gave at the beginning of this book about my mother's long-standing connection to Selfridges is an example of tangibility. There is a familiarity to the business, a stable core, a warm fuzzy feeling that endures – yet has a disruptive edge. This edge keeps innovation, changing, adapting, and moving, sometimes fast, sometimes slow, but all to the beat of the customer and its environment.

We will discuss this more later in the book when talking about strategy.

This explains why such businesses with tangibility still attract crowds, feel relevant and fresh, and can maintain their bases, even over decades and sometimes centuries.

Speaking of maintaining their bases:

On 8 September 2023, an earthquake on the Richter scale of magnitude 6.8 hit the North African Country of Morocco, killing nearly 3,000 people. A couple of days later, torrential rains hit Derna, a city in north-eastern Libya, which killed 11,000 people. In both tragedies, outdated infrastructure was a massive factor, which meant that the buildings were incapable of handling the impact, resulting in unnecessarily high death tolls, as recounted by Professor Shideh Dashti of the University of Colorado Boulder.[4]

Contrast this to the buildings in Japan.

Japan is in one of the most earthquake-prone zones in the world. It is also home to some of the most resilient buildings on Earth, such as the Skytree building in Tokyo, the second-tallest building in the world when it was inaugurated in 2012. The resilience is achieved by a reinforced foundation, which in some cases sits on rubber pads to absorb the seismic shocks, and the construction of the actual building using mesh and other materials designed in a particular way to enable the buildings to 'dance' as the earthquake strikes.

And the lessons the design of these buildings teaches us can also be applied in the business world.

32 Chasing Permanence

To succeed over the long term, SMEs need to recognise their base, establishing the firm's foundation and anchoring it in values that rarely, if ever, change but allow the actual business to 'dance' across the years to withstand shocks.

Surprisingly, so have the long-lasting musical artists we have looked at: Coldplay, Elton John, Madonna, U2, and bands that have lasted two to three decades and are still household names today.

They have a stable core and style, but like the buildings in Japan, they work hard to maintain a long-term connection with multigenerational fans.

Pauline Brown, former North American chairman of the group LVMH and author of the bestseller *Aesthetic Intelligence: How to Boost it and Use it in Business and Beyond*, talks about the concept of 'aesthetic intelligence':

> *How executives, entrepreneurs, and other professionals harness the power of the senses to create products, services, and experiences that stand out, resonate with their customers, and create long-term value for their businesses.*[5]

Again, Pauline is talking about the phenomenon of Tangibility.

Selfridges in Central London beautifully encapsulates this, as do all the High Street Companies and SMEs we have studied: Day Lewis Chemists, Richer Sounds, Beacon Electrical, Timpsons, Waterstones, HMV, and even the little High Street pub Bread and Roses.

How does tangibility play out? I explain using the three Cs: Customer Agility, Collaboration, and Community.

The Essence of Tangibility

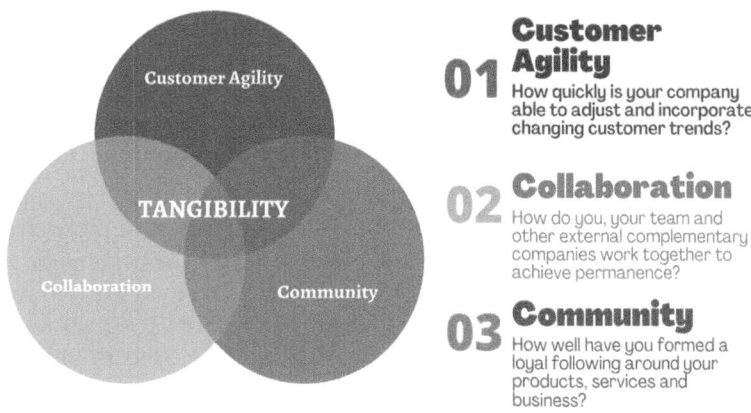

01 Customer Agility
How quickly is your company able to adjust and incorporate changing customer trends?

02 Collaboration
How do you, your team and other external complementary companies work together to achieve permanence?

03 Community
How well have you formed a loyal following around your products, services and business?

Figure 8.2 The Essence of Tangibility: Customer Agility, Collaboration and Community.

Starting with Customer Agility, I'll illustrate with a review I was sent by a customer of a High Street Business:

1. **Customer Agility:**
An example which happened in a healthcare store I was involved in recently:

> *Help, please!*
> *I have been struggling to get this item, which is crucial to my health.*
> *The staff said they could order it. This was in the city centre with limited and expensive parking so they promised it would be in stock by the following week. I went there the following week only to find it had not been looked at. I found this unacceptable as I had limited mobility. As I was sitting there in the queue, I realised that 90% of the customers were complaining about the same issue.*

But here's the strange bit:
I had worked with the owners in the past to try to improve their customer service, just recently. The manager of that branch had sent me this message just a day before this review (coincidentally).

> *Hello, Steven! We are now running like clockwork.*

This difference in perception between employees and customers at any given time is a lack of customer agility.

Customers' needs (and wants) remain the same, but the mode of delivery needs to change continually to meet those needs better.

This is where our High Street Business can learn from what the Economist calls '*the Eternal Bossman*' – *Britain's corner shops*:

> *Corner shops have adapted to British society. Supermarkets emerged in the 1950s, squeezing out small shops. They survived thanks to arrivals from Punjab and Gujarat who seized the chance to work for themselves. Corner shops produced politicians like Margaret Thatcher and Priti Patel.*
>
> *Corner shops thrive on convenience and vice. Previously, they sold cigarettes, alcohol, newspapers, and adult magazines, but now they are the last resort on the High Street. With the retreat of post offices and banks, essential services like cash payments and parcel collections are underserved.*
>
> *The corner shop has evolved, filling the gap.*[6]

I start with customer agility because, in this book, it is the foundation of business permanence.

For High Street SMEs and businesses, exceptional customer service is essential. It forms the bedrock of tangibility and, indeed, of success as a whole. That's why it cannot be overemphasised how important it is to look after staff and motivate them to maintain customer agility.

In an interview with the Talk Retail blog, private equity specialist Neil Debenham talks about the High Street retailer HMV:[7]

> *The reality is that any business – of any size and in any sector – needs to be agile and respond to changing market conditions.*

This is particularly important regarding digital platforms and the increasing trend towards purchasing online.

> *Rather than becoming complacent with an existing product or service, businesses need to listen to their customers and look at the state of the current market to understand how to keep pace with changing demands.*

Get this wrong, and the whole business falls apart.

Again, Steve Hewitt, Executive Chair at Britain's leading sportswear brand GymShark, when being interviewed for the website blog, Retail Gazette:

> *Driving our growth is innovation or – as I prefer to say – **agility** and disruption. This means we can respond swiftly to trends and changes in the market in a way that our competitors cannot.*[8]

Leading pharmacy retailer Boots the Chemist has closed over 300 stores in the past two years as a measure to 'consolidate its business,' but the real reason was revealed in an interview with the BBC by managing director Sebastian James, who was parachuted in to try to turn around the loss-making flagging High Street behemoth.

> *There's no doubt that trading conditions are tough on the High Street, and healthcare and retail face a challenging reality. Boots is not immune to these pressures.*[9]

The retailer's focus was now on making stores more '**differentiated and personalised**, with the best brands at the best value.'

Ronseal, a UK DIY company, was founded in 1956.

In 1994, it was beginning to face an existential crisis and turned to the advertising company HHCL for help. After brainstorming, they devised a powerful slogan that has become the third most-used slogan ever.

After that slogan, sales shot up, and the company has become a brand leader in its field.

Do you know what your customers need? Sometimes we think we do, but there is mostly a deeper meaning.

And sometimes, the need is more fundamental than we think. The most famous entrepreneurs we all talk about, Henry Ford, Steve Jobs, and

Richard Branson, are renowned because they could anticipate the 'need behind the need.' Henry Ford allegedly said that if you asked customers what they wanted, they'd say they wanted faster horses. Customers did not wish to hire faster horses, they just wanted a better, more reliable mode of transportation to get them from A to B quicker and more reliably. So, the fundamental problem to solve was better transportation. Most customers at that time had never seen a car, but Henry Ford was able to anticipate this.

You think you may be in the car business, but really, you are in the transportation business.

Researchers Govindarajan, Kopalle, and Danneels have researched this kind of customer agility. They published an influential paper arguing that there is a difference between mainstream and emerging customer orientation. Most SMEs are oriented toward mainstream customers, and the researchers found that mainstream customer orientation is negatively related to disruptive innovation.[10]

In other words, as author and Professor Christian Stadler said to me recently: 'If a small business is wondering whether opening one more hour on a Saturday is worth it, asking its (mainstream/existing) customers makes sense.'

Mainstream customer orientation is found to have a near-zero correlation with emerging customer orientation, indicating that the two can coexist and be pursued simultaneously.

We will discuss this further in Part III of this book, The Systems of Permanence.

The best employees, apart from top management, who can identify those trends are the customer-facing ones.

This is where the advantage of the open strategy for High Street businesses reigns supreme.

When I work within, or for, many SMEs, I am continually amazed at how many founders, leaders, and CEOs have forgotten this basic principle.

The basic needs must be met before building on better service delivery methods.

Let's take for example, the field of my speciality, community pharmacy.

I mentioned earlier the astonishing rate at which High Street pharmacies were closing. While this is undoubtedly due to many factors, some outside the control of pharmacists (covered in Part III of this book), I am sometimes amazed at how patients' basic needs are not being met.

Patients attending pharmacies want their medicines in stock and dispensed safely, quickly, and efficiently, and their health needs met with minimum fuss by knowledgeable, highly trained professional staff in a friendly, clean, safe, and enabling environment.

That's it. That is the foundation.

But it's surprising how so many High Street pharmacies lack this: long waiting times, lack of stock, poor customer service, and a lack of qualified staff and pharmacists.

Failure to provide this foundational need has made the sector vulnerable to disruption with the rise of internet pharmacies such as Pharmazon Direct, Pharmacy2u, and others entering the market with phenomenal success.

In my work with High Street community pharmacies nationwide, I have seen customers offered free medication delivery, elaborate apps to manage repeat prescriptions, health checks, vaccinations, treatment of minor symptoms, and online access to the pharmacist or healthcare professional. But these appear to have not yet stemmed the tide.

In other words, if the foundational aspects are missing, all other add-on services are irrelevant.

That is why typical pure top-down approaches are so devastating for SMEs and possibly why traditional hierarchical companies such as pharmacies, pubs and restaurants are shutting down at an accelerating pace.

In the same breath whilst Boots the Chemists is shutting down over 300 pharmacies due to *'challenging market conditions'* whilst Day Lewis is buying up pharmacies and expanding its presence on the High Street.

Same market. Same sector. Different outcomes.

Day Lewis' systems are built around customer agility – even down to its bags, which have QR codes to facilitate customer feedback, which is fed to management to facilitate agile change.

Because the management structure between front-facing staff and upper management is optimised, High Street chains and SMEs that involve their frontline staff in strategy and employ quick, trusted communication and autonomy can swiftly adapt to changing delivery needs. Those who do this consistently and effectively are more likely to achieve permanence.

However, to allow this to happen, there is one big caveat:

TRUST.

James Timpson, says,

> *We trust branch colleagues to do whatever they believe will give an amazing service: They can change prices, invent new displays, and they can pay up to £500 to settle a complaint.*[11]

and James Daunt of Waterstones agrees:

> *We have achieved success by trusting our local managers to lead their stores the way they see fit, and we allow them to just get on with it.*[12]

Julian Richer of Richer Sounds adds:

> *Ultimately, I do believe that companies that fail to serve their customers well do not last.*[13]

Harvard scholar and bestselling author Ranjay Gulati, in his paper *Silo Busting: How to Execute on the Promise of Customer Focus*[14] writes about four sets of activities crucial for customer-centric companies that are actively trying to build customer agility:

Co-ordination: Ranjay surmises that to deliver customer-focused solutions, division of labour, information sharing and decision making should move as effortlessly as possible between boundaries (or departments or silos as he calls them).
Cooperation: Metrics and incentives should be developed to reward customer-focused collaboration. All too often, staff and employees closest to customers are incentivised the least, have the least authority to act on behalf of customers, and are overlooked for promotion and benefits.
Capabilities: Customer-facing employees sometimes need training and experience to be more generalist, have deep knowledge of customer needs, and be able to make quick, autonomous decisions to achieve the best outcome within a pre-agreed framework.
Connections: By combining offerings with various partners to create high-value solutions. We talk more about this in the sub-topic of collaboration below.

This principle even extends to NGOs and charities flourishing on the High Street.

I recently met with social researchers and bumped into a woman I'll call Kate. Kate works for one of the largest charities in the UK. We met for coffee, and she told me how a High Street charity had changed its whole approach to allowing families to visit their dying loved ones with just months (or even weeks to live) based on feedback she had given from the 'shop floor.'

She had just met a woman with just months to live.

This charity's policy was to list the people allowed to sit with a patient as they were dying and in most cases, just one person was allowed.

So this woman, who had a massive family who loved her, had to choose just one person who could be with her as she was dying and she was upset that multiple people were not allowed on the list.

That meeting touched Kate, and she decided to act. Fortunately, this NGO has always had a relatively easy pathway to contact senior management, so she arranged a meeting with the 'big guns' up the ladder, as she called them.

That meeting had a dramatic effect – the charity changed its entire system to accommodate multiple family members on the list.

Customer agility at its best, even for a High Street NGO.

To consistently maintain customer agility, ensure the main reason for your business, identify the need behind the need for which you established the company, and continuously and rigorously find ways to do exactly what it says on the tin.

This book repeatedly returns to the essence of personalisation, which distinguishes successful High Street companies and SMEs from their less successful competitors.

As Katie Tucker says in her brilliant book, *Do Penguins Eat Peaches?*[15]

> *The single biggest mistake businesses make is that they think they are their customers – 'I know my customers; they are just like me'... Your customers are real people. They are real people in the real world, living their messy, imperfect lives. If you want people to buy your stuff, you need to find them and talk to them so you can understand them better. One of the biggest killers of dreams is assumptions without proof.*

As Katie says, there are three essential toolkits for maintaining customer agility.

Things we will be coming to in this book again and again:

Curiosity, Empathy and Courage.

I have seen this again and again. It's only a matter of time before a company that loses its curiosity loses its business because curiosity, courage and empathy involve a simple sentence:

Being present in the moment.

However, for a business to remain tangible, it needs more than customer agility. Two other factors which are just as important, also affect SMEs – collaboration and community.

Going it alone in these times of oligopoly, with only a few companies dominating the market in many sectors, is becoming increasingly complex.

To remain competitive and relevant, SMEs must learn to work together internally and externally.

They must learn what all the musical artists who have stayed relevant over decades instinctively know: they need to learn the simple art of collaboration and I begin to illustrate this concept with the little-known story of a well-known band.

2. Collaboration

On June 28, 2019, a black musician made history.

Michael Ebenezer Kwadjo Omari Owuo Junior, the British-Ghanaian grime artist otherwise known as Stormzy, headlined the Pyramid Stage at the world-famous Glastonbury festival. He was the first British black male solo artist to do so in the festival's 55-year history.[16]

It was a monumental performance hailed by politicians, musicians, and fans due to the collaboration with several musicians, rappers, drama performances and poetry.

But one person stood out for me during the performance.

He came in without fuss, sat by the piano, and began playing. The crowds went crazy. Stormzy joined him, and they sang for just over two minutes. After a big bear hug, he got up quietly and left.

Coldplay frontman, Chris Martin.

Those two minutes at Glastonbury partly signified why Coldplay has over 73 million followers on Spotify and is consistently in the top ten of the most famous musical artists in the world when, in the words of the Guardian newspaper, *'bands are dying.'* [17]

They continue to top charts and remain multigenerational, mainstream, famous, and relevant even after 27 years.

It is no secret.

It is condensed into one word.
Collaboration.
Coldplay is the king of collaboration.

They were formed 27 years ago in 1997 after four friends, Guy, Johnny, Will, and Chris, met at University College London. They are one of the world's most popular bands, with over 100 million albums sold, seven number one albums, seven Grammys, nine Brit Awards and are named the 6th most popular artist on Spotify (at the time of writing) with nearly 93 million followers.

For the past two decades, Coldplay has collaborated with musicians as far-flung as BTS in Korea, Kanye West, The Chainsmokers, Beyonce, Jay-Z, Billie Eilish, Selena Gomez, Rihanna and Dua Lipa.

This trend continues even in their latest 2024 album, Moon Music, with collaborations with various music stars of varying popularity: British Grime rapper Little Simz, Afrobeat superstar Burna Boy, Pop star Ayra Starr, and classical and electronic superstar Jon Hopkins.

Beyond music, they have also collaborated on a massive nationwide TV advert with the world's leading logistics company DHL.

However, this is not limited only to other parties. They have learned the art of what I call intra-collaboration.

As the world's #1 leadership expert and author, John C Maxwell puts it:

Teams that cannot bond cannot build. [18]

In an interview with leading podcaster Conan O'Brien, Coldplay frontman Chris Martin said:

The surest way that Coldplay has stayed together has been the sharing of two things – credit and money – and how we have all utilised our different strengths as a band, and how we've remained friends after 27 years

A band's unique thing is their chemistry, especially if none of you are prodigious players or particularly handsome – the one thing you have is your uniqueness – so we hold on to that. [19]

What makes Coldplay all the more remarkable is that traditional mainstream bands are disappearing off the grid at an astonishing rate.

As the Guardian correspondent Dorian Lynskey said in 2021:

Popular music's centre of gravity has undeniably moved towards solo artists, at least regarding commercial success. This paradigm shift has been evident for a while now.[20]

The similarities between staying as a band and continuing to be successful on the High Street are uncanny because they face the same challenges:

- The advent of technology
- Expensive set-up and sunk costs
- The advent of social media
- The difficulty of intra-collaboration among team members, particularly with the sustained rise of individualism

Elton John has had the presence of mind, openness and humility to collaborate with numerous other artists (I mentioned Dua Lipa earlier), such as Eminem – another multigenerational, ground-breaking hip-hop artist and the 10th most famous artist worldwide, according to Spotify.

Many other long-standing artists, such as Bob Marley and 2Pac, still going strong decades after their deaths, have one big thing in common: they have all tapped into the incredible power of collaboration.

And all the small businesses that I studied have had the same principle (see page 16) and even internet-based firms such as AO.com.

In an interview with Jay Patel, he talked about the power of collaboration – Day Lewis has collaborated with companies in entirely different sectors, such as Timpson and Skills4Pharmacy, in order to introduce apprenticeships and other skill-building schemes.

But this kind of intra-collaboration doesn't just happen. It takes time and effort to build.

In their paper "Social Intelligence and the Biology of Leadership"[21] written for *Harvard Business Review*, Daniel Coleman and Richard Boyatzis write about the responsibility of leaders to foster intra-collaboration.

They discovered that certain behaviours of leaders, *'especially by exhibiting empathy and becoming attuned to others' moods, affect the brain chemistry of their followers'* and perhaps even more crucially, their own brain chemistry, in a sense, resulting in the brains being metaphorically almost *'fused as one.'*

They go on to say:

We believe that great leaders are those whose behaviour powerfully leverages the system of brain interconnectedness, placing them on the opposite end of the neural continuum with people with serious social disorders such as autism and Aspergers' syndrome, which are characterised by the underdevelopment in the areas of the brain associated with social interactions.

We will talk more about the way followers mirror their leaders in the part of the book about scalability. Still, Boyatzis and Coleman list seven attributes of a leader that foster collaboration:

- **Empathy:** Understanding what motivates your team, no matter how diverse they are
- **Attunement:** listening attentively and thinking about the feelings of others
- **Organisational Awareness:** Appreciating the culture and values of the business
- **Influence**: Getting support from key players and persuading others by engaging in discussion and appealing to their self-interest
- **Developing Others**: Investing personal time in coaching, mentoring and providing feedback with compassion
- **Inspiration:** Building pride, articulating a compelling vision and fostering a positive emotional tone
- **Teamwork facilitation:** soliciting universal support and encouraging cooperation

In other words, the leader's behaviour can energise or completely deflate your business through mood contagion.

That 'off feeling' one gets when entering a retail outfit or business environment is not ethereal. It is the literal mood contagion at work. When customers say "I could almost cut the atmosphere in the store with a knife", thats what they mean.

> **I'll even further argue that mood contagion can quickly spread from followers to clients and customers, contributing massively to the 'negative energy and vibe' customers feel when interacting with the business. This will inadvertently negatively affect tangibility – customers' connection with your brand.**

Build in first, then out.
Inter-collaboration:
One cold morning, my wife Dela and I were browsing one of our local High Streets when we came across a little shop called Bud Houseplants. This shop sold freshly cut flowers, plants, and memorabilia. Curious, we went in and were greeted by with a cheery smile from Julie, the owner.

Just a few months prior, a shop just three doors down the road from Bud had closed its doors for the last time, hit by both the recession and COVID.

Dela bought a colossal plant, much to my chagrin – our house was already full of plants of various sizes and shapes.

But even before we bought the plant, Julie asked us if we had checked out the other new shops opening next to her on the same High Street – a shop selling zero-waste foods and a new coffee shop around the corner. She enthusiastically persuaded us to visit those shops, which led us to make even more purchases.

This was High Street collaboration at its best, resulting in a win-win situation.

In my present long-term consultancy role, I try to lead by Julie's example and:

- I get my hair cut at the barbers across the road
- I buy my groceries from the grocery shop down the street
- I have business meetings in the restaurant down the street.
- I buy gifts for loved ones from the art shop down the road from me
- As an African, I buy my African produce from the continental shop three doors down from me
- I order my pizza from the handmade pizzeria around the corner
- I frequent the pub directly opposite the pharmacy and have met the owner at a business lunch
- I actively advertise my fellow High Street neighbours' products and services in my pharmacy
- I sometimes take my family for dinner at the delicious nachos restaurant down the road
- Dela uses the nail bar that was recently opened down the street

The pharmacy has now become one of Plymouth's top community pharmacies within a year, partly due to this intercollaboration.

Why?

Because the other High Street shops responded:

1 **They reciprocate the support** – all staff utilise the pharmacy for their health benefits and suggest our services to their customers, which enhances sales and revenue.
2 **They offer valuable insights** – from both their customers and themselves that have helped us improve our responsiveness to customer needs.
3 **They share positive experiences** – word of mouth remains the most effective method for attracting new customers.

Collaboration goes beyond just other shops; it includes security agencies, Business Improvement Districts, and local governments, which are discussed in more detail in the latter section of this book.

Sometimes, I can envision all High Street stores, especially in smaller towns and boroughs, uniting to provide a 10% discount card to all fellow High Street employees. This initiative would encourage intra-shopping, further promoting collaboration while connecting smoothly to the third aspect of tangibility:

3. **Community**

   "Community is the discipline of belonging, where customers become members through shared spaces and rituals that keep them returning and draw others in."

   She sat there, almost lifeless, on the toilet seat.
   We thought we had lost her.
   She had battled COVID for over a week and we thought her body had finally given in.
   An emotional call to 999 saw an ambulance arrive in 10 minutes to cart her off to the hospital, and we watched on helplessly. We were not allowed to visit – we just had to wait.
   Luckily, after being put on oxygen, she was discharged the next day, still really ill.
   What struck me was how our friends and family rallied together for support. It didn't matter who they were then: middle or working class, rich or poor, black or white, old or young, English or African – they did our shopping, bought our necessities, got us takeaway, medicines, whatever we needed.
   And every evening, clapping for our heroic NHS workers filled the streets.
   The whole of the UK – indeed, the whole world – was united against this deadly disease which nearly claimed my wife, Dela.
   The paradox of COVID was that even though we were isolated, we were united. Even though we could not meet, and pubs and restaurants were closed, we were all fighting a common cause. Even though we had fundamental differences, there was equal anger against a common enemy, The virus did not discriminate.
   Even though now the cost of living crisis is biting hard, I suspect we are generally more unhappy because the old divisions that used to tear us apart have resurfaced.
   The progressive death and destruction of one of the greatest needs of humanity seems to have made a comeback.
   It is the death of the community.
   Building a community around your products and services takes collaboration to the next level: using customer agility and collaboration to create a dedicated following around your brand. To do this, it is crucial to monitor changes in consumer behaviour, which continue to evolve and change over time.

I have noticed that thriving SMEs are doing just that: using customer agility and collaboration to cater to today's consumers.

The progressive death of the community has given rise to two contrasting and paradoxical developments after the pandemic.

The rise of the hermit customer is balanced with the need for connection in a post-COVID world.

I illustrate this paradox from a member of my household.

Dela typically exemplifies the paradoxical dichotomy that exists today as we move past the immediate aftermath of the COVID pandemic.

She doesn't like to go to the shops to buy clothes, jewellery, or books; instead, she prefers to have them delivered to her home. She loves to be home with the family and share experiences, such as watching movies on Netflix and the occasional takeaway from the local chippies or Chinese. Instead, she'll order lots of sizes from her favourite online shop and return the ones that don't fit and then go to the shops to try them on physically.

She is the typical hermit customer.

However, she regularly sets aside time to meet her close friends at the popular local cafe. She loves to go there because the cafe has built a thriving online community that sends her deals and new recipes, acknowledges her visits with rewards, and greets her by name. The prices are reasonable, the food is unique and extraordinary, and she can connect and maintain a physical connection with her friends.

She is the typical community customer.

These two seemingly contrasting behaviours provide a unique opportunity for High Street businesses and SMEs: if they can offer a sense of community while catering to the same dichotomy of people being hermits, then we are practising proper customer agility. The best High Street stores can beautifully tap into both seemingly paradoxical trends, and this is a crucial strategic advantage that online competitors cannot match.

This is why 'old-fashioned' High Street shops such as HMV and Waterstones paradoxically attract more younger customers.

It is due to the desire for convenience, coupled with the human need for touch, taste and smell, as well as the need for community: where people of similar tastes – music, books, and health – assemble. In short, there is a tenuous tension between a backlash of digitalisation (community) and the need for convenience (hermit)

Doug Putman, head of HMV, puts it well:

> *The true intersection of something being great is online with some physical component. Everyone's still trying to figure out exactly how to do it and what that special sauce is. I think HMV is getting there.*[22]

This increased digitalisation of the world Doug Putman talks about has also given rise to a darker side of humanity:

The Rise of Loneliness.
Steven Bartlett, entrepreneur, author and leading podcaster writes:

As our internet connections get stronger, meaningful conversations get weaker.

He thus hosted a physical dinner party for listeners of his podcast to try to begin to tackle this crisis:

The main thing we care about is for people not to feel so alone.[23]

It is a strange paradox that loneliness is on the rise despite the multiple ways we connect through social media, video conferencing, and mobile phone technology.

And this loneliness has devastating consequences for communities in the Western world:

The BBC estimates that the leading cause of unemployment in the UK for those under 44 is the issue of mental health problems, which undoubtedly is a consequence of the lack of community.[24]

Researchers at the Office for National Statistics in the UK have been tracking this epidemic since 2018[25] and estimate that 25% of adults felt lonely, which resulted in 2.5 million experiencing chronic loneliness.

This figure jumped to 3.3 million in 2021.

The British Red Cross supports this, reporting that 9 million people in the UK felt lonely. Almost a third said they had gone nearly a month without a meaningful conversation, leading the UK to be labelled the loneliest country in Europe.[26]

Neither is this phenomenon limited to older people, as is commonly believed.

Gen Zs are also significantly less sexually active (and interested) than Millennials or their Gen X parents, with only 30% saying they've had sex, down significantly from previous generations.

Even youngsters were not exempt from this epidemic, with 1 million youngsters between the ages of 16 and 29 feeling chronically lonely – and loneliness is more likely to affect the youth, another BBC report finds.[27]

Author and podcaster Carey Nieuwholf says the heart of it isn't a revival of purity culture but rather a deep loneliness plaguing the next generation. Gen Zers are twice as likely to report feeling lonely as people over 65.[28]

Vivek Murthy, the 19th and 21st Surgeon General of the United States, who served under three presidents – Obama, Trump, and Biden – wrote a book on loneliness, titled *Together: Loneliness, Health, and What Happens When We Find Connection.*[29] He wrote it just after COVID which he believed to be the most significant healthcare crisis in the Western world. The evidence is clear: people have fewer friends who truly know them, a substantial contributing factor to this epidemic.

In a report he authored titled, *Our Epidemic of Loneliness and Isolation*,[30] he emphasised four points:

1. Humans are wired for social connection, but we've become more isolated over time
2. Social connection significantly improves the health and well-being of all individuals
3. Social connection is vital for strengthening relationships and improving public health
4. We can advance social connections and improve our nation's public health

He also writes:
[Businesses should] ... create opportunities and spaces for inclusive social connection and establish programs that foster positive and safe relationships, including among individuals of different ages, backgrounds, viewpoints, and life experiences.

I hear you ask, how does this relate to the subject of the High Street?

Companies that capitalise on this epidemic to form a community around their offerings while catering to the hermit consumer are more likely to succeed over the long term.

In today's fast-moving and changing environment, the new leadership model is centred around the human being. The leaders of the best-performing High Street companies work to connect the business to the larger world – the community, society, and the local economy.

As far back as 1989, the anthropologist and emeritus professor Ray Oldenburg published a book called *The Great Good Places* and publicised the theme of the '3rd space.'

In the older days, members of communities lived their lives in 3 spaces:

- The first space was the home: this was family. This was the physical space that people bought – the home – Oldenburg postulates that the home represents environments that are *'informal and isolating.'*
- The second space was work, where people physically met to perform a particular task or work organisation – the office, which he says is *'formal, structured and mission-driven.'*
- The third space was for recreation for like-minded individuals; the pub, the football stadium, the cafe, main streets, and beer gardens – regular, voluntary, informal and happily anticipated gatherings beyond the first two spaces; a neutral space which is regular, voluntary, informal and happily anticipated.

He goes on to say that they:

promote social equality by levelling the status of guests – providing for grassroots politics, creating habits of public association, and offering psychological support to individuals and communities – beyond the realm of home and work.[31]

Even as far back as in 1989, Oldenburg was primarily concerned about the disappearances of third spaces, which were congruent with the suburbanisation of modern societies. The pandemic and the disappearance of businesses from the High Street have accelerated this trend.

The current epic of loneliness has been magnified by the blurring of lines between the first and second spaces and the near disappearance of the third space. It is this third space which encapsulates the meaning of the community.

SMEs in the services and goods industries that are doing well and have emerged stronger after the epidemic have noticed this growing trend of hermit customers (the rising numbers of people who prefer to stay at home), combined with the increasing epidemic of loneliness.

High Street businesses can help combat loneliness and build a community around their offerings and those that are able to do this optimally will have a sustained competitive advantage.

Back to Louise Parker – the pub owner I mentioned earlier, who encompasses this principle.

She had opened the pub with a business partner who had been secretly squandering the money from the pub. One day, the police turned up at her doorstep. Unbeknownst to her, the business was on its knees with debt. A complex litigation followed, nearly leading to the pub being forced into bankruptcy, but Louise refused to give up.

She won the battle and renamed the pub 'Bread and Roses,' transforming it into the city's first and only social pub, operating as a community-focused hub and arts. There is space with a café for everyone to use, various clubs and free activities during the day, and progressive live musicians and events in the evening.

The bar's values:

Visit us at the bar, and we will serve you with passion in our heart, ethics from our mind, live music for your ears, and creativity to inspire.

Based on this strategic change, Louise transformed the pub into one of the city's most profitable and popular venues.

Engaging with a community will mean different things to different businesses – some businesses can build a community around their offering (such as Waterstones and HMV), or some companies will have to open up their staff, services or products to positively affect their communities (such as Day Lewis, Richer Sounds or Timpsons).

A few High Street examples:

Day Lewis Pharmacies are championing FREE medicine delivery services, fostering community programmes and building a community-based model focused on emphasising repeat prescription services. They are hiring local staff and, unlike other pharmacy chains, actually leaving the comfort of their spaces and going out into their community – whether it is to give immunisation in schools, give talks in community settings, or hold health outreaches in supermarkets. Individual stores are free to develop innovative ideas to drive engagement in the community within a pre-arranged framework with minimal interference from top management.

Richer Sounds also has a robust home delivery service for its hermit customers. It is actively building an online community of people who share its passion for audiovisual equipment, doing community-based programmes, and having staff who are passionate about what they do and their customers. They also support undiscovered musicians through their charity, Richer Unsigned, give donations through their charity, Acts 435, and get involved in many community projects. Many of their employees, for instance, are budding musicians and DJs.

They also have VIP Club members who receive a six-year free warranty, personalised care, and front-of-the-queue service.

As we will see later, Richer Sounds donates the highest percentage of their profits (15%) to charitable causes.

Waterstones, the UK's number-one bookstore, finally returned to profit this year using the same principle: building an online email community, fostering quick home delivery, creating a sense of community by providing cafes in their bookstores where strangers could meet, and facilitating book signings by authors either for sale (which I was encouraged to do when they stocked my first book) or in person, where connections around fans of an author could meet and facilitate friendships.

During Christmas, for instance, they invite readers into each of their stores, where the staff offers complimentary mince pies and mulled wine. Authors then sign copies of their books, hang around, answer questions, and interact with readers and staff.

Morris S. Evans, biographer of James Daunt, Waterstones CEO, states:

> *Daunt Books was also inspired by Daunt's ambition to open a bookshop that focused on community. He envisioned Daunt Books as more than simply a bookstore; he saw it as a cultural hub where people could come together, talk, and share their love of reading. The store frequently organised author events, book signings, and reading clubs to that aim. These activities*

promoted a sense of community and involvement, which increased the store's attractiveness.[32]

Warhammer, a proprietary fantasy game miniatures maker and High Street retailer based in Nottingham, had its best year in 2024 since its conception in 1983. It has 134 stores throughout the UK, including a massive store on Tottenham Court Road, London. It reported sales of £495 million, up from £445 million the year before. Its strength is built firmly around its devoted community, which meets in its stores to play, have meetings, purchase games, and pick up online orders.

HMV, which recently marked its 100th anniversary, has twice faced administration. However, it has found renewed success by transforming its business model and diversifying its offerings:

In April this year (2024), HMV saw a 150 per cent increase in footfall compared to previous occasions when lockdown restrictions were lifted, and there is a real sense that people don't want to lose their local High Streets.

HMV's revenue increased by 18% to £117.9 million, with pre-tax profits of £5.28 million last year. In the July 2021 edition of the Retail Gazette, a spokesperson said,

Nothing can replace speaking to someone face-to-face who is as passionate about what you're buying as you are, and our stores offer a real sense of community for music, film and TV fans.

HMV's head of music, John Hirst:

'We're opening up our stores to lot more local artists as well; it's about creating events in stores, particularly at the weekends,' he said. 'So we've opened for local artists to perform in our stores, and we've relaxed our rules on stocking local artists' products so local acts can drop into their nearest HMV and get their stock on the shelf there.'[33]

For instance, one of UK's biggest hiphop stars, Aitch, performed live in many HMV stores across the country in 2025, where he met fans and signed records for his new album, 4. Their new flagship Birmingham store, Europe's most prominent (called the Vault), is a prime example – with a footprint of 25,000 sq ft, it stocks 100,000 LPs and CDs, 20,000 Blu-ray and over 40,000 DVD titles, and also offers a significant performance area at its centre, thus creating a sense of community around music. Doug Putman has just undertaken a bold move to relocate to a five-storey facility right in the heart of Oxford Circus, London's premier shopping centre, using the same principle.

Sports Direct and Game recently collaborated, allowing Game to stave off hot competition from online retailers and simultaneously reduce high sunk costs by renting space within Sports Direct stores. In this space, they hosted video game parties where groups of youngsters could hold parties, meeting in a shared space where they could play video games together using high-resolution pictures and explore new games while accessing Sports Direct's massive sports equipment. Partly as a result, Game is flourishing even as other similar companies in the same sector are going under.

VUE, a High Street cinema chain, recently partnered with Sky TV, Vitality Health Insurance, and Go-Compare.com to offer its customers free tickets and build a community around these offerings. VUE also rents its halls for conferences, live football matches, and opera and music performances.

This has helped keep the company afloat even as the popularity of Netflix, Amazon Prime, and other home offerings rose. The company has tried to build its strategy around caring for the hermit customer by incorporating community into its retail offering.

The British Red Cross: One of the popular High Street charities, the British Red Cross, has recently been organising fashion shows in their stores. They offer a fashion show, live DJ, music and complimentary drinks – all for free.

Booths, a high-end supermarket in Northern England, recently eliminated self-checkouts and encouraged its checkout assistants to interact with customers. This move was designed to promote human interaction between staff and customers, reduce loneliness, and foster community in its stores. Thus, Booths enhanced the overall customer experience.

This community initiative can even reach towns with bustling High Streets centred around a single attraction: **Hay-on-Wye** in Wales, renowned for its bookstores and book festival; **Totnes** in Devon celebrated for its independent artistry; **St. Ives** in Cornwall, which boasts quirky fine art shops; and **Folkestone** in Kent, home to the UK's most extensive outdoor art collection. Visiting these towns lets you fully experience their essence, immersed in the city's character and tangibility.

A prime example was my time working at a High Street pharmacy and being involved in a collaborative project in Padstow, Cornwall. All the High Street shops united to extend their hours, provide free mulled wine and mince pies, and welcome the community into their stores. The atmosphere was fantastic, with streets filled with shoppers and High Street employees mingling, sharing laughter, and shopping at each store. It painted a vivid picture of what a High Street could evolve into.

The key to community is uniting people around a common cause, and SMEs need to use ingenious means, depending on the sector and field in which they operate as I have illustrated above. This is a strategic advantage that online stores would find difficult to compete with. Amazon, for instance, tried this and flopped, as we see later in this book when we discuss strategy.

The primary goal of communities for businesses is to enhance tangibility – to promote a visceral bond between the consumer and the High Street Business.

To quote again from HMV boss Doug Putman:[34]

> *When HMV went into administration, there was an outpouring of people who were genuinely upset.*
>
> *It was pretty clear that the customer didn't want to go and buy from somewhere else. They wanted HMV to be around.*
>
> *What you want to believe is that the customer is rooting for you to be successful. If enough people give you the benefit of the doubt, you can turn something around quickly.*

And this aspect of permanence is not limited only to businesses or towns.

Chris Martin of Coldplay:

> *A lot of the things we are good at as a band are not conventional – the main thing we care about is the interaction and communication – partly for own sake as humans not feel alone, but also to feel like you're a community ... and [we want to] share our positivity and as we get older, that has become more and more of our focus.*[35]

The band Wolf Alice's frontman, Joff Eddie, agrees:

> *We're fanatical about bands and being in a band. A good band creates a community. They have an ecosystem that, as a fan, you feel like you want to be part of. Despite all that's been said about individualism, there is still a hunger for that collective feeling.*[36]

The Power of Community

Mary Portas, author of *Work Like a Woman* and architect of the Kindness Economy, has long argued that the future of the High Street depends not on volume, but on **community, connection, and human-scale experiences**. Her work reframes retail as a civic space – a place where relationships, not just transactions, determine value.

The key to community is not just building one or getting people to join but getting those already in the community to stay– and not just to stay but to enjoy their time while visiting.

Keeping the community is more critical than evangelising for more followers.

This is not to say that marketing and prospecting for new customers are unimportant. Of course, they are. However, the issue is that businesses spend far more time looking for and marketing new customers than keeping the ones they already have satisfied and happy.

It's like a leaky container: no matter how much you pour in, the container will stay empty if the base is full of holes.

As I have experienced more and more, HMV, Day Lewis, and Waterstones have proved that if you look after your primary community, they'll do most of the evangelising for you.

You can only build a lasting, strong community with customer agility and collaboration, forming the other two legs of customer agility and using them as a springboard to facilitate community. It is then that community acts as an evangelist for your service or product because, despite the evolving scene, one thing will never change (despite the rise of Trustpilot, Google Reviews, and others): the power of word of mouth to facilitate expansion. Driving new customers to your product or service is crucial to the survival and thriving of your High Street Business or SME.

As a small business expert in the health retail space, I have found that nothing drives engagement and tangibility more than this.

One of the main ways to ward off the internet and online competition is to keep the community as the third leg of tangibility.

In this age of AI, where what it means to be human is constantly under pressure, more and more of what we do is being handed over to machines – and that's only going to accelerate. But what won't change – in fact, what may grow even more vital – are the relational parts of our existence. Our connections, our relationships, are not just a part of who we are – they define us. As I've said before, we're living through a global relational crisis. And the businesses that understand this – that choose to lead with care, connection, and community – will be the ones that last. The ones that matter. The ones that endure.

Therefore, the pursuit of tangibility is ultimately the pursuit of the resurrection of community, and the companies that do it well will ultimately survive and even thrive.

That explains why, on many local High Streets, banks, shops, and chemists are being replaced by barbering shops, cafes, meeting areas, and play areas for children.

However, not just the use of community sets these businesses apart.

The facts and evidence are irrefutable: footfall is decreasing on the High Street.

But this phenomenon does not have to spell doom for High Street businesses.

That is why the secret of using the community to your advantage, especially for SMEs with limited resources, is spending the most on your primary customers – those returning for repeated services. For most High Street SMEs and businesses, all customers could be segmented into three,

Primary customers: those who keep coming repeatedly and rely on your services.

An example from my field as a High Street pharmacy SME specialist:

My primary customers are those with chronic health issues who visit monthly for medications to manage conditions like diabetes, high blood pressure, and respiratory diseases. They also include vulnerable individuals needing home deliveries, nursing home care, or specific products.

These core customers often make up 60–80% of a pharmacy's revenue. Losing them to a competitor isn't just inconvenient – it's financially damaging. That's why we prioritise them. We go beyond transactional service: we listen, we personalise, we deliver on time, and we keep the essentials in stock. The bond we build with these individuals is deep and enduring. Yes, some of the benefits we offer – like free delivery or bespoke products – may not always be profitable in the short term. But they are strategic sacrifices that help secure long-term loyalty and consistent income. Primary customers should be the backbone of any community business. Think of them like season ticket holders at a football club – they're invested, they keep showing up, and their belief in you gives your business staying power. This isn't about chasing volume for its own sake. It's about depth over breadth. Too often, small businesses waste energy chasing new leads or serving customers who aren't a good fit. That's exhausting – and expensive. Instead, focus on doing your best work with the people who already trust you. Serve them with excellence, innovate for them, and let them become your evangelists. Get that right, and they'll bring others through the door. And that, in the end, is the golden word every High Street Business dreams of: footfall.

The rationale behind this approach may seem unconventional; however, it is essential to recognise that the dissatisfaction of specific customers can be pivotal in achieving a higher level of satisfaction among others:

- Identifying the primary target audience – we will discuss this further in the next section under affordability.
- Defining the unique value proposition to be presented to them and communicating this clearly to employees.
- Streamlining all strategic and operational activities to align with these objectives.

Then there are your secondary customers: those who utilise services occasionally, while tertiary customers engage with the services seasonally or as a one-time occurrence.

My **secondary customers** are those who occasionally return for services. Being situated near a large university, my secondary customers primarily use our services during term time, for convenience, or when they need help having had difficulty somewhere else. Even though they may form many customers, their net value to the company will create around 20–30% of business over the long term, depending on the season. They are the ones who have not formed a special bond with the organisation but use their services predominantly for convenience or experience. These will be the customers who occasionally buy tickets for a football team because they are celebrating an occasion, or there is a big match in town, or the tickets have been given as a gift.

My **tertiary customer**s use the pharmacy's services on rare occasions, such as when their regular outlet does not have the goods they require in stock or for annual services their local providers do not provide, such as vaccination services. Their net spend may be considerable but not reliable. When their need has been met, they may never be seen again. Unless there is a high possibility of turning tertiary into primary customers, resources spent here must be kept to a minimum. This may be equivalent to the away fans of a football team or a fan that happens to be in the area and fancies a good day of football.

In the pharmacy retail business, my tertiary customers may be highly profitable. They may spend incredibly heavily per customer, which may boost the bottom line considerably. However, resources should not be spent on them at the expense of the primary return customers, as their patronage may be a one-off.

It is possible to convert tertiary customers into secondary customers, but any community by the SME or business should primarily be to primary customers. They will be your evangelists, your primary source of income, the ones you can cultivate a strong, enduring bond with and provide most of your steady income.

Of course, this does not eliminate the need for marketing and spreading the word about your services and products. Your marketing must be in tandem with your commitment to your primary customer base. Otherwise, what I call *customer haemorrhaging* will take place – you will gain customers as quickly as you lose them, particularly now that it's so easy to switch.

The most successful artists build their brands on the principle of segmenting. Elton John, Coldplay, and Taylor Swift have all built their empires by obsessing over their season-ticket holders first.

Coldplay follows the same playbook. Before every arena show, the band's team studies fan-forum requests, then sprinkles surprise songs and interactive LED wristbands into the set so the faithful feel seen. Add the band's sustainability pledge – planting trees for every ticket sold – and you have a values-driven bond that keeps core supporters bragging about their 'Coldplay experience' long after the confetti has settled. Word of mouth from these evangelists fills the cheaper seats with casual listeners.

Taylor Swift is the masterclass. She names 'Swifties' in her speeches, hides Easter eggs in videos for them to decode, and re-records old albums so her base can own the new masters alongside her. At concerts she reserves the best floor spots for verified fans, not scalpers, and drops surprise songs so every show feels exclusive. That level of personalised care turns primary fans into marketers: they tweet, post, and podcast the experience, dragging in secondary and even tertiary listeners who want a slice of the magic.

The common thread? Each artist pours their best creativity and resources into the inner circle first. Those core fans then do the heavy lifting – spreading the music, filling venues, and sustaining revenue – exactly what High Street businesses need if they're to keep footfall strong and profits steady.

To conclude, let me tell you a personal story of how tapping into community values literally saved the life of one of our clients.

Anthony Parker is an in-house delivery driver who works for the pharmacy chain Wellcare (where I was freelancing at the time) who have been in business for over 40 years. His role is to deliver medication and other supplies to primary and vulnerable patients and sometimes patients who cannot get to the pharmacies quickly.

He makes it a point to visit the patients to see how they are doing, sometimes even sitting down briefly for a cup of tea, a quick chat, or just to say hello.

This contrasts with other delivery services offered by big chains or internet services such as DHL, Amazon, or EVRI, whose priorities are speed and efficiency, not care and community building. I'm always fuming when supplies are left out in the rain, tossed at the back of my garden window, or placed in my bin that's just been emptied.

One day, he set out to deliver medication to a patient – I'll call him John. Usually, Tony knocks on the door and John yells to come up. Tony provides the medication, has a quick five-minute chat, and then goes to his next delivery. Over a couple of years of delivery, they created camaraderie and a routine.

On this occasion, he called up to John. The door was wide open, which was unusual. He shouted out, "John!!"

There was no answer but Tony heard a squeaky noise from the upstairs bedroom – an ordinary delivery driver would have dropped the parcel in the front bin, left a note, and vanished, but not Tony.

He crept gently up the creaky stairs.

The squeaking got louder.

As he knocked on the bedroom and opened the door, he saw that John had fallen off his bed, got wedged between the mattress and some furniture, and could not breathe. He had begun to turn blue – only God knew how long he'd been there.

Tony rushed in, dislodged him gently from the bed and called an ambulance.

John survived by the skin of his teeth.

As he came and told us the news, tears were streaming from his face.

Most importantly, John lived, and our High Street community pharmacy had a patient forever.

The power of connecting the hermit customer with the community.

Intra-community: As I mentioned in the five significant changes at the beginning of this book, the future of work is changing in favour of the employee.

As evidenced by the recent strike actions within the NHS and public companies in the UK, employees are defying, in their unique ways, this old approach of command-and-control top-down management.

The future of work now lies in the community: apart from a place where we go to work, type at our desks, grab a cup of tea, and then head home at a set time, it is dying.

Now, employees are demanding more. The use of work as a third space for employees is accelerating rapidly. Hybrid working, which accelerated after the pandemic, is a hot topic.

To summarise the principle of Tangibility, Morris Evans put it succinctly in his biography of James Daunt:

The reassuring, nostalgic smell of a bookstore was disappearing, and the allure of perusing actual shelves was being replaced with cold, impersonal clicks. This was the grim reality the bookselling industry faced until James Daunt stepped in. Daunt's bold choice to forgo a lucrative career in investment banking to launch his bookstore and turn Waterstones into vibrant centres of culture highlighted the priceless importance of a sense of community and individualised client care.[37]

Doug Putman of HMV agrees that vinyl is stepping into that (tangibility) gap because the digital backlash is growing among younger generations.

Everyone wants these tangible things. Having 10,000 pictures on my phone is nice, but it's not the same feeling as having them in a photo album. I think music is like that, too. Yes, you can listen to it on your iPhone, but there's something about putting on a record. I feel like an old soul because everything's gone too far digital. Everything is phone, phone, phone. But sometimes, it's nice to pause and enjoy things. I don't pretend HMV is the saviour of that, but having the ability to buy things that are 'touch and feel' – books, vinyl – I think these things will stick around.[38]

This explains my confusion when my 18-year-old daughter recently dragged me to HMV to buy vinyl records of her favourite artist, Tyler the Creator, and order a record player. The shop was full of young customers, mainly Gen Z and millennials, which surprised me.

Emma Bridgewater offers perhaps the clearest modern illustration of those 'three Cs' of Tangibility. A Cambridge graduate who founded her Stoke-on-Trent pottery in 1985 after failing to find a suitably charming mug for her mother, Bridgewater built a brand that is *felt* as much as bought. Customer Agility shows up in her fast pivot from a single mug design to hundreds of sponge-painted patterns and in the way the factory now personalises pieces on-demand for birthdays, weddings, even dogs' names. Collaboration is literal: visitors tour the working factory, paint their own plates alongside artisans, and share tea in the café, turning production into co-creation. Community is sustained by a fiercely loyal collector base – annual 'collectors' days' sell out in hours and by Bridgewater's decision to keep 200-plus skilled jobs in Stoke rather than outsource overseas. In short, the brand proves that when customers can *touch*, *create* and *belong*, Tangibility becomes an asset irreplaceable by algorithms or AI.

But Tangibility alone isn't enough. Even when your offering looks and feels right, success can still slip through your fingers if there's a deeper misalignment – one that's harder to spot but just as vital. It's to this quiet, often underestimated force that we now turn.

Notes

1. Rai, Mandeep. *The Values Compass: What 101 Countries Teach Us About Purpose, Life and Leadership*, John Murray Business Books, 2022.
2. TEDx Talks. Rai, Mandeep, *A Compass for Values*, TEDx John von Neumann University, Feb 2024: www.youtube.com/watch?v=mxi-iZMz8bQ, accessed January 15, 2025.
3. Lee, Kerry. Reimagining Retail: Where Online Meets the High Street, *Retail TouchPoints*, September 4, 2024: https://www.retailtouchpoints.com/features/design-perspectives/reimagining-retail-where-online-meets-the-high-street, accessed September 20, 2024.
4. Dashti, Shideh. What the devastating floods in Libya, earthquake in Morocco can teach us, 19 September 2023: www.colorado.edu/today/2023/09/19/what-devastating-floods-libya-earthquake-morocco-can-teach-us
5. Brown, Pauline. *Aesthetic Intelligence: How to Boost It and Use It in Business and Beyond*, HarperCollins, 2020.
6. The Economist, The Eternal Bossman, December 18, 2024: https://www.economist.com/britain/2024/12/18/the-eternal-bossman.
7. Talk Retail. Is HMV at risk of going into administration again?: https://talk-retail.co.uk/is-hmv-at-risk-of-going-into-administration-again/, accessed November 10, 2024.
8. Retail Gazette. It's not about innovation: it's about agility and disruption: www.retailgazette.co.uk/blog/2021/09/its-not-about-innovation-its-about-agility-and-disruption, accessed September 21, 2021.
9. BBC. Boots store closures 'right thing to do': www.bbc.co.uk/news/business-48797246, accessed November 10, 2024.

10 Govindarajan, Vijay, Praveen K. Kopalle and Erwin Danneels. The effects of mainstream and emerging customer orientations on radical and disruptive innovations, *Journal of Product Innovation Management*, 28(s1), November 2011, Pgs 121–132.
11 Timpson Group. Our Culture: www.timpson-group.co.uk/about/our-culture, accessed October 16, 2024.
12 Evans, Morris. *James Daunt Biography: How a Passion for Literature and Strategic Acumen Revitalized Iconic Bookstores Across the Globe*, Independently published, 2024.
13 Richer, Julian. *The Ethical Capitalist: How to Make Business Work Better for Society*, Penguin, 2019.
14 Gulati, Sanjay. Silo busting: How to execute on the promise of customer focus, *Harvard Business Review*, May 2007.
15 Tucker, Katie. *Do Penguins Eat Peaches?: And Other Unexpected Ways to Discover What Your Customers Want*, Practical Inspiration Publishing, 2023, Chapters 2 and 3 (Kindle Version).
16 The Guardian. All hail Stormzy for historic Glastonbury performance. Musicians, politicians and fans praise first headline show by black solo British artist: www.theguardian.com/music/2019/jun/29/stormzy-historic-glastonbury-performance
17 Lynskey, Dorian. Why bands are disappearing: 'Young people aren't excited by them': www.theguardian.com/music/2021/mar/18/why-bands-are-disappearing-young-people-arent-excited-by-them, *The Guardian*, March 18, 2021.
18 John C., Maxwell: Instagram Post 4 Sept 2023: www.instagram.com/johncmaxwell/p/Cwycm91ONY2, accessed 24 August 2025.
19 O'Brien, Conan. Host, Conan O'Brien Needs a Friend, featuring Chris Martin, Spotify podcast audio, March 20, 2023: https://www.youtube.com/watch?v=V61NWC0djbc.
20 Lynskey, Dorian. Why bands are disappearing: 'Young people aren't excited by them.' www.theguardian.com/music/2021/mar/18/why-bands-are-disappearing-young-people-arent-excited-by-them, *The Guardian*, March 18, 2021.
21 Lynskey, Dorian. Why bands are disappearing: 'Young people aren't excited by them.' www.theguardian.com/music/2021/mar/18/why-bands-are-disappearing-young-people-arent-excited-by-them, *The Guardian*, accessed August 29, 2025.
22 The Raconteur Daily. How HMV's boss has revived the beleaguered brand: www.raconteur.net/growth-strategies/hmv-oxford-street-sunrise-records, accessed November 15, 2024.
23 Linkedin. As our internet connections get stronger, meaningful connections get weaker: www.linkedin.com/posts/stevenbartlett-123_as-our-internet-connections-get-stronger-activity-7046737768265216000-QvKm, accessed November 11, 2024.
24 BBC News. More people in early 20s out of work from ill health than early 40s – study, *BBC News*, February 26, 2024: https://www.bbc.co.uk/news/education-43711606.
25 Office for National Statistics. Mapping loneliness during the coronavirus pandemic: www.ons.gov.uk/peoplepopulationandcommunity/wellbeing/articles/mappinglonelinessduringthecoronaviruspandemic/2021-04-07?utm_source=chatgpt.com
26 Co-op. New study reveals triggers for loneliness epidemic in the UK: www.co-operative.coop/media/news-releases/lonely-life-stages-new-study-reveals-triggers-for-loneliness-epidemic-in-the-UK?

27 Co-operative, Lonely life stages: New study reveals triggers for loneliness epidemic in the UK," Co-operative (media news release), December 8, 2016: https://www.co-operative.coop/media/news-releases/lonely-life-stages-new-study-reveals-triggers-for-loneliness-epidemic-in-the-UK, accessed July 25, 2025.
28 Nieuwhof, Carey. The Art of Leadership Podcast: Jean Twenge on Rising Anxiety, Depression, Isolation and Smartphones in Gen Z, and What That Means for Them and for Leaders: https://careynieuwhof.com/episode435
29 Murphy, Vivek. *Together: Loneliness, Health and What Happens When We Find Connection*, Wellcome Collective Books, 2020.
30 Murphy, Vivek. Our Epidemic of Loneliness and Isolation: www.hhs.gov/sites/default/files/surgeon-general-social-connection-advisory.pdf
31 Oldenburg, Ray. *The Great Good Place: Cafes, Coffee Shops, Bookstores, Bars, Hair Salons, and Other Hangouts at the Heart of a Community*, Paragon House Publishers, 1990.
32 Evans, Morris. *James Daunt Biography: How a Passion for Literature and Strategic Acumen Revitalized Iconic Bookstores Across the Globe*, Independently published, 2024.
33 Music Week. HMV opens up in-stores to unsigned bands: www.musicweek.com/live/read/local-news-hmv-opens-up-in-stores-to-unsigned-bands/077117#:~:text=HMV%20head%20of%20music%2C%20John,the%20weekends%2C%20"%20he%20said, accessed November 11, 2024.
34 Talk Retail. Is HMV at risk of going into administration again?: https://talk-retail.co.uk/is-hmv-at-risk-of-going-into-administration-again/, accessed November 10, 2024.
35 The New Yorker. Coldplay's self help pop: www.newyorker.com/magazine/2024/10/07/coldplays-self-help-pop?utm_source=chatgpt.com, accessed September 30, 2024.
36 Lynskey, Dorian. Why bands are disappearing: 'Young people aren't excited by them': www.theguardian.com/music/2021/mar/18/why-bands-are-disappearing-young-people-arent-excited-by-them, *The Guardian*, March 18, 2021.
37 Lynskey, Dorian. Why bands are disappearing: 'Young people aren't excited by them': www.theguardian.com/music/2021/mar/18/why-bands-are-disappearing-young-people-arent-excited-by-them, *The Guardian*, 18 March 2021; Evans, Morris: *James Daunt Biography: How a Passion for Literature and Strategic Acumen Revitalized Iconic Bookstores Across the Globe,* Independently published, 2024.
38 The Raconteur Daily. How HMV's boss has revived the beleaguered brand: www.raconteur.net/growth-strategies/hmv-oxford-street-sunrise-records, accessed November 15, 2024.

Chapter 9

The Second Determinant
Affordability

Sometimes, the difference between why two companies in the same sector, on the same street, serving the same clientele, thrive or go bust comes down to one factor:
Affordability.

Affordability is crucial to maintain productivity.
And that doesn't mean just cheap prices. I define affordability as:

> **The Right Product, at the Right Price, in the Right Place, at The Right Time, with the Right Customer.**

By this notion, Poundland, the British discount chain, is affordable. Most of their products cost a pound. They are rarely situated in expensive shopping centres, but in less costly venues to cater to the right clientele and they brand themselves to attract the right customers.

Poundland, Britain's discounted High Street chain, is affordable.
But so is the high-end retail outfit Selfridges.
They are affordable because they use the same affordability model: they have the right products at the right place and customers at the right price.

Running out of cash is a significant reason why SMEs and entrepreneurs fail, and this may happen for any of following five reasons:

The right product: stock type, availability, prices, quantity, and controlling costs are needed to ensure a healthy profit per sale. The right product also involves perceived value, as Kevin Holt says in his book *Differentiation Strategy*:[1]

> *Value is the customer's overall assessment of a product's utility based on what is received and what is given.*

Steven Bartlett puts it even better in his book *Diary of a CEO, the 33 Laws of Business and Life*:

> *Value does not exist. It's a perception we reach with expectations we meet.*

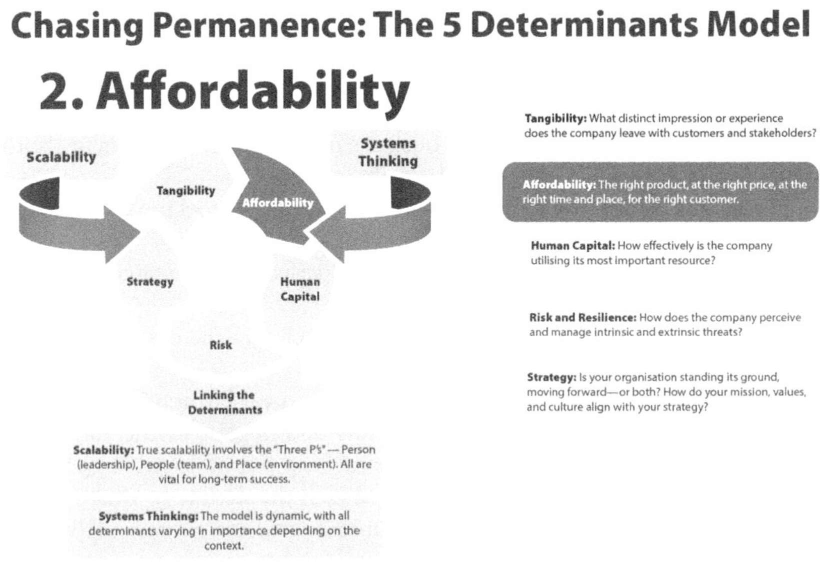

Chasing Permanence: The 5 Determinants Model
2. Affordability
Scalability
Systems Thinking
Tangibility
Affordability
Strategy
Human Capital
Risk
Linking the Determinants
Scalability: True scalability involves the "Three P's" — Person (leadership), People (team), and Place (environment). All are vital for long-term success.
Systems Thinking: The model is dynamic, with all determinants varying in importance depending on the context.
Tangibility: What distinct impression or experience does the company leave with customers and stakeholders?
Affordability: The right product, at the right price, at the right time and place, for the right customer.
Human Capital: How effectively is the company utilising its most important resource?
Risk and Resilience: How does the company perceive and manage intrinsic and extrinsic threats?
Strategy: Is your organisation standing its ground, moving forward—or both? How do your mission, values, and culture align with your strategy?

Figure 9.1 The Five Determinants Model: Determinant 2: Affordability.

THE FIVE 'RIGHTS' OF AFFORDABILITY:
AFFORDABILITY
Are your profit margins sufficient to sustain and grow your business?
1
THE RIGHT PRICE
Do your prices align with your target customers while giving you healthy margins?
2
THE RIGHT PRODUCT
Do your products or services match your target customers?
3
THE RIGHT TIME
Are you timing offers and using promotions or discounts effectively?
4
THE RIGHT PLACE
Does your location match your target customer both virtually and physically?
5
THE RIGHT CUSTOMER
Are you attracting and retaining the right customers to grow your business sustainably?

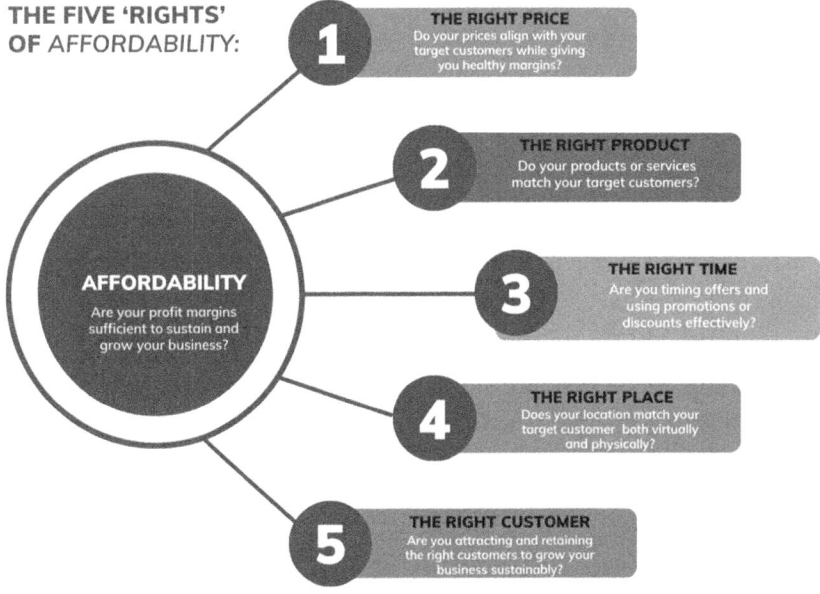

Figure 9.2 The Five 'Rights' of Affordability.

The Right Product: Matching the right service or product to the right environment.

The Right Price: Pricing products appropriately to reflect their target customers

The Right Place: Situating the business in the right environment, both virtually and physically, to attract the right audience

The Right Time: Seasonal adjustments in price – stocking products in different locations to reflect the right season

The Right Customer: Aligning your offering perfectly to your target audience.

Frank was an up-and-coming middle manager of a medium-sized chain of pharmacies on Britain's High Streets.

One of the shops he managed was in Devonport, near Plymouth's city centre.

Over the years, a decline in manufacturing and neglect by the authorities gave rise to a community with a complex melting pot of crime, drug addiction, violence, and homelessness, combined with the decline of what used to be a vital submarine hub that manufactured a large proportion of Britain's submarines.

The area had now become one of the most deprived in England, in the bottom 3% of the country, with widespread poverty.[2]

The head office of the major High Street pharmacy where he worked had rolled out a national strategy to standardise all 450 stores, sending the same planogram to every branch and expecting each one to stock exactly the same products.

Thus, the local pharmacy, located in one of the most deprived areas of the UK, sold high-end Gillette blades, expensive lotions and make-up, high-end multivitamins and supplements, and costly over-the-counter medicines.

Frank complained to top management. For one, the residents of Devonport could not afford these items, and two, the proliferation of drug addiction and poverty meant that shoplifting was rife.

He was ignored.

The pharmacy began to lose money by the truckload – not only through shoplifting but also through reduced staff productivity.

The staff spent most of their time preventing shoplifting rather than providing customer service.

This was partly why, eventually, the High Street chain had to sell up when its parent group amassed huge losses.

The stories above reflect the crucial importance of the concept of affordability. The second instance resulted in ultimate failure and loss due to the wrong strategy of uniformity of branches throughout the country, regardless of the dynamics at play.

Let's take this in turn.

1. The Right Product:

I gave an example of how the right product can dramatically affect your business' bottom line. I have lost count of how many SMEs and High Street independents stock products that are not in tandem with their environment. The trouble is that these products don't sell as well so they also create the most significant danger to the business – the build-up of unproductive stock.

The right product depends on many factors, but the community or area in which the business or service is situated is pivotal.

One day, a few months ago, when I was working in a High Street pharmacy, I noticed three totes full of over-the-counter medicines and vitamins in a corner.

I quietly asked why they weren't on the shelves.

'These medicines are out of date,' said Amelia (not her real name), the store manager.

A rough calculation revealed that £500.00 worth of stock had been wasted. The reason was apparent.

This community pharmacy was next door to a giant supermarket selling the same products at less than half the price.

But that wasn't the only ridiculous situation.

In the following weeks, professional stocktakers came to the branch to do a stocktake. They noticed all the empty shelves where the out-of-date products had been removed. Without questioning why, they ordered the same stock and filled the same shelves!

This is a cumulative loss of £1000 in just a week. This High Street chain had over 400 branches in various streets across the UK.

So, a quick conservative (if not scientific) estimation resulted in a loss of £400,000, enough to hire 200 staff for a year!

The right product is not limited to the wrong type of product, but also the quantity of the right product.

Generally, 80% of sales will come from the top 20% of products. However, the top 20% of products can only be identified through intensive research, knowing what competitors are stocking, and customer agility.

A double conundrum.

One of the most influential and productive ways to succeed is to focus on a particular product, service or market, devote resources, expertise and time to it, and become significantly better than the competition. I discuss this further in my first book, *Pay The Price*. The resources of the SME or even a High Street chain are not infinite. They are typically constrained – and the worst possible outcome is to spread these resources so thinly that you end up like a jack of all trades, or as Jim Collins calls in his book BE 2.0, an 'also-ran':

One of the most effective strategies of a small to mid-sized company is to focus on one particular market or product line and, within that area of focus, become significantly better than the competition.[3]

I speak of 'the signature dish' – where you are known for which slice of the pie you specialise in. Also-rans are in the worst possible scenario: they remain stuck in the formative phase, where they have progressed beyond a start-up but have not succeeded. They are trapped in the middle.

Only after laser-focusing on the right product does the second most crucial area, affordability, become relevant.

Prices.

2. The Right Price:

The right price is now closely related to the right product. It is almost impossible for High Street businesses to match internet companies' prices (and sometimes efficiencies). Competing on cost is a sure way to fail.

A close friend just ordered some reading glasses off the internet and the prices were almost 60% cheaper than a regular optician on the High Street – it will always be challenging for High Street stores to compete on the same level on just prices. There are only two ways SMEs could compete: symbiotic collaboration (symbol group model) and/or the value-add model:

- **Collaboration** (symbol group model): I have already touched on collaboration, when talking about tangibility. However, there is another form of collaboration, where many independents and SMEs come together to form one buying entity, which gives them extra buying power. This is known as the 'symbol group' or 'virtual chain model.' For instance, Euronics[4], an international association of over 11,000 independent collaborating electrical outlets, is based in Amsterdam, Netherlands.

Devon High Street retailer Beacon Electricals is a member of Euronics and as a result of this collaboration, it has access to many top brands from Europe that are not available anywhere else, allowing it to keep its prices lower than most of its big-chain competitors. Numark, part of the Phoenix group, is a similar buying group for 5,200 independent pharmacies across the UK. Each pharmacy is an independently owned outlet, but joining Numark enables individual independents to take advantage of symbiotic 'group purchasing' deals, which reduce their costs. Phoenix is known for its excellent service, prompt delivery, and extra services such as signage, template documents and advertising.

- **Value Add:** Noakes, Habermehl, and Kerr are a small chain of High Street opticians operating in South West England since 1979. They are a prime example of justifying higher prices using the value-add model.

They specialise in premium personalised treatment, emergency eye care, extended appointment times, high-quality frames, myopia control, and exceptional customer service – services which are not always available with the bigger chains. They also drive engagement by collaborating with local universities for student placements and focus on delivering top-tier clinical care.

Investor Warren Buffett says:

The single most important decision in evaluating a business is pricing power. If you've got the power to raise prices without losing business to a competitor, you've got an excellent business. And if you have to have a prayer session before raising the price by 10 per cent, then you've got a terrible business.

Of course, it is possible to run on a third strand: competitor based. However, a terrible strategy is to compete based on costs alone because this starts a price war which business experts term 'the race to the bottom.'

Reducing prices does, though, have a place in successful affordability. Lowering prices is possible, actually crucial.

Yet as we will see in the next section, it can work only with one other element.

The clock.

3. The Right Time:
Affordability also depends on seasonality, with virtual companies such as Amazon running Christmas deals, Black Friday deals, etc., SME discounts may sometimes seem enticing, but extensive discounting eats heavily into profit margins

As Catherine Erdly, author of *Tame Your Tiger: How to Stop Your Product Business Eating You Alive,* states:

Discounts (and promotions) are like spices. A little creates interest and excitement, but too much ruins the dish.[5]

Anderson Hirst in his book, *Sales Management for start-ups and SMEs,* reiterates:

If you don't have tight pricing control, a reasonable 10% discount to close a deal means you would need to double your sales volume based on a 20% gross profit! The attitude of death before the discount is useful, in part because it is closely linked to the idea that what is given free has no value.[6]

The goal is to attract as many customers as possible to buy products or services at a total price. Too many promotions and discounts can lead to customers being so used to getting discounts that they wait or delay buying altogether.

A way to enable customers to buy at full price most of the time with promotional or targeted discounts is the value-add system I touched on earlier such as a free wrapping service at Christmas, free delivery, product stacking, or even extended opening hours.

Another way to showcase timing is seasonality – weather, occasions such as World Kindness Day, Black History Month, etc., where products and services can be rotated and given prominence depending on the season. Most pharmacies, for instance, advertise antihistamines and sun lotion during the summer, and other SMEs feature a summer menu and so on.

This principle can be applied to timing. Overusing discounts and promotions leads to high customer expectations, meaning they will never buy items at full prices, leading to a never-ending cycle of discounting that eats deep into profit margins.

The key is generating interest and buzz at particular times without ruining the business' cash flow.

Timing is everything – but so is placing.

4. The Right Place:
Location, location, Location.

Fixed costs, in addition to stock, are among the biggest drains on SMEs. Over the years, some of the most successful SMEs I have researched have maximised their locations to reduce costs.

A typical example is HMV. A decade or two ago, HMV was a High Street favourite when streaming had not yet peaked, and CDs, DVDs, CD players, etc., were the most popular music-playing methods. However, with the advent of Spotify and streaming services, HMV risked going out of business as customers turned away from traditional ways of buying music and film to streaming services such as Netflix. Possibly learning from the famous bankruptcy of Blockbuster, the company had to restructure.

It concentrated mainly on developing a dedicated fan base of niche customers who were still fans of CDs and vinyl. This fan base meant that expensive locations on main shopping centres and High Streets were no longer necessary. In Plymouth, for instance, the local HMV has moved from Drakes Circus – the main shopping centre – to a cheaper location down the road, potentially saving thousands of pounds monthly and because it has carved a niche and a community for itself, a premium location is no longer a prerequisite for success. As the profits grew and the business became more resilient and cash-rich, they could afford to relocate to prime areas, such as Oxford Street in London and Dale Street in Birmingham.

Other successful SMEs, such as Beacon Electrical, have adopted the same tactic in the city's suburbs. Hybrid, remote, and the inevitable ascent of AI have made location switches easier.

Many companies struggling on the High Street have failed to consider this personalised approach to location. I talk about how thousands of pounds have been wasted because companies have not matched the right products to the correct location.

Practical examples: does the location have free parking? Is it easily accessible? What is the competition (both direct and indirect) in that area? If it doesn't have free parking, then speedy customer service is even more essential, as customers will watch their clock to ensure they don't incur heavy parking tickets. Resources should be prioritised in such areas to enable better service and again, the shop floor staff are best placed to give the best recommendations.

The story I told about Frank earlier in this chapter has as much to do with price as it has with location.

Although still on the High Street, Richer Sounds has moved locations to cheaper suburbs or negotiated terms to own its properties outright, endeavouring to provide free parking for its customers where possible.

In my research for writing this book, community and location go hand in hand. If you're a High Street SME with a strong buzz or a loyal niche following, your customers themselves become a tangible asset – especially for niche businesse – making your physical location less of a deciding factor.

However, the right place is not limited to physical locations. Virtual locations also play a huge role. A premium SME or High Street chain dealing with top-tier services or goods advertising on a site such as Facebook Marketplace may not send a good signal.

Location does not only apply to physical buildings.

As I write this, IBM and many businesses have pulled advertising on X (formerly Twitter). The reason? X located IBM's adverts next to anti-semitic content at a time when Israel and Palestine were receiving the world's full attention.

Many SMEs advertise their products and services through channels or videos on YouTube or TikTok that do not match their offerings which may ultimately devalue their brand.

Recently, I was shocked to see soft pornographic content advertised just before a devotional by a faith group. Following the devotional, I had to focus on the content, not the advert that kept popping up beside it.

Matching your online presence with your physical offering is vital to ensure maximum bang for your buck.

This is a nagging failure in too many High Street stores I have worked in, consulted for, or researched.

I once worked in a High Street health chain, where a customer chose to receive her goods from the store's online branch.

Unfortunately, there were some problems with the delivery so the customer came into the store and asked for help. None was given, as she was told 'you need to go back and contact the online team, as it has nothing to do with us.'

In an article for the blog *Retail Touchpoints*, consultant and researcher Kerry Lee writes:

> To revitalise High Streets, it is crucial for retailers to merge online and physical retail strategies effectively. Embracing experiential retail, integrating cutting-edge technology and ensuring a seamless and convenient shopping journey is pivotal in rejuvenating physical stores. As retailers innovate and adapt, this hybrid approach promises to enhance customer satisfaction, loyalty and overall profitability of the retailer.[7]

Your location must complement your offering, and your products or services need to align with the expectations of the customers you serve.

5. The Right Customer:

Just before the pandemic, I was recruited to turn around the fortunes of another struggling retail business near the High Street of a major UK city. The owners were distressed because they had been subject to an inspection by the regulatory authorities and were on the verge of being closed down. When I started the process, I could immediately spot multiple problems.

One of the first issues was the lack of products suitable for the community. The health and beauty retail outfit sold high-end make-up and had stands for L'Oréal, Max Factor, and L'Occitane (a luxury French retail cosmetics brand), as well as stocking high-end multivitamins.

The trouble was that the city had just built a world-class shopping centre across the road which housed many more better-known shops that also stocked these products. The shopping centre was near the University, so thousands of students used it.

Shoppers were deserting the small health and beauty shop in droves and it was nearing collapse – thousands of pounds worth of make-up was on shelves, and the medicines and cosmetics were nearing expiry.

No wonder.

We had to sell off and dismantle the make-up stands quickly, drastically reduce the prices of the high-end cosmetics, and fill the retail space with quality, but affordable, practical and functional lines: shaving cream, moderately priced deodorants, inexpensive cosmetics.

We just left a few high-end products to cater for the cash-rich retired patients and customers and the considerable number of middle-class families that lived in the area. However, we had to bear in mind that they could also get these same products just across the road in the massive shopping centre so and these products were just for convenience (and let's face it, for optics as well).

Within months, sales had skyrocketed.

Most business books also routinely overlook another crucial aspect of choosing the right customer: sustainability. There is a reason for the proliferation of charity shops on our High Streets. Many people dismiss them as unwelcome scavengers of empty buildings, but the truth is far more nuanced. My 18-year-old daughter once sat me down and gave me a lesson when I dared question her love for shopping at charity shops instead of traditional online or High Street shops:

- Her first reason was the fact that buying pre-loved clothes reduces the impact on the planet by reducing the massive problem of waste.
- Her second reason? Every item bought in a charity shop goes directly to make someone's life better, be it for cancer, pets, mental health, or poverty.
- Third: they offer volunteers such as the retired, an opportunity to contribute to society, have a community (for example, those with coffee shops), combat loneliness and share their stories.
- The fourth, most minor and slightest reason? Prices.

It's not that she suffers from poverty or lack. But at the forefront of her mind is the planet. And so it is for millions of customers her age who are increasingly becoming the dominant force with buying power, and increasingly becoming dissatisfied with big business.

The more High Street businesses factor sustainability into their everyday decisions, the more they do their bit for the planet. As a side effect, they also secure their future financial relevance and sustainability. It is the ethical, moral, and right thing to do.

TED speaker, author, friend and marketing Thought Leader, Nupur Gadkari, has done intensive research into this issue of sustainability and is pushing for it to be included in the 4Ps of marketing as the 5th P – the Planet.

She states:

In traditional marketing, you have the marketing mix – the famous 4Ps/ 7Ps: Product, Price, Place, and Promotion. Sustainability is becoming extremely important, and customers are increasingly conscious of this. How brands consider preserving the planet with the products/services they offer is now a key aspect of their purchasing decision. The Marketing mix has to have the 5th (or the 8th P) THE PLANET. Per the United Nations's 17 SDGs, today it is imperative to ask: was the product made in a sweatshop? Does the making of this product involve child labour? Have the raw materials been ethically sourced?[8]

Customers increasingly want to feel like they are making a difference in their community and the world. Again, this comes back to Tangibility: customers are likelier to associate themselves viscerally with shops that share these values.

Again, an example from Richer Sounds from the Guardian newspaper:

The bald fact remains that Richer Sounds, the slightly maverick hi-fi retailer, generally donates more of its profits than any other privately owned company. The business, founded by Julian Richer, gives away 5% of its annual earnings to a wide spread of good causes. Since setting up a charitable foundation in 1994, that has amounted to £1.1m, including £225,000 in the most recent financial year.[9]

Again, customers are noticing:

Of over 70,000 on Trustpilot, 98% are five stars, and as mentioned previously, they have won Retailer of the Year eight times (so far), with their first win in 2010 and their latest in 2024.

Many High Street businesses: Next, Nike, Primark, and Apple, as well as online brands, Amazon and SHEIN, for instance, have suffered irreparable damage from using questionable ethical practices in sourcing their products. This shift in consumer preference is particularly pronounced in younger generations – millennials and Gen Zs who rapidly become the majority of purchasing customers today.

This feeds into another feature and lesson of the right customer –

> **The lesson of personalisation.**

This is a point that we will visit repeatedly throughout this book.

The era of one-size-fits-all is rapidly dying. To succeed in this world of so many choices, High Street businesses and SMEs will increasingly have to balance a personalised approach with familiar uniformity across branches, sectors, and even departments of the same branch. But personalisation is nothing without people.

To illustrate this, the next section will begin with the inspirational story of how a US immigrant transformed a dilapidated, abandoned building and turned it into one of the world's largest health-based yoghurt factories.

Notes

1 Holt, Kevin. *Differentiation Strategy: Winning Customers by Being Different*, 1st Edition Routledge, 2022.

2   Plymouth City Council, Plymouth Report for HWB (PDF): https://democracy.plymouth.gov.uk/documents/s97566/8c.%20Plymouth%20Report%20for%20HWB.pdf, accessed September 20, 2024.
3   Collins, Jim and Bill Lazier. *BE 2.0 Turning Your Business into an Enduring, Great Company*, Random House Business, 2020.
4   Euronics. Euronics UK, https://www.euronics.co.uk, accessed October 7, 2025.
5   Erdly, Catherine. *Tame Your Tiger: How to Stop Your Product Business Eating You Alive*, Practical Inspiration Publishing, 2023.
6   Anderson, Hirst. *Sales Management for Start-ups and SMEs*, Routledge, 2024.
7   Retail Touchpoints. Reimagining Retail: Where Online Meets the High Street, September 4, 2024: www.retailtouchpoints.com/features/design-perspectives/reimagining-retail-where-online-meets-the-high-street#:~:text=To%20revitalise%20high%20streets%2C%20it,pivotal%20in%20rejuvenating%20physical%Kerry Lee, accessed November 19, 2024.
8   Sanjiv Speaks. E3: Forged in Adversity: Breaking Barriers & Embracing Challenges with Nupur Gadkari (quoted with permission): www.youtube.com/watch?v=pLJ-54bAwh8
9   Teather, David. "Rich Rewards." *The Guardian*, November 5, 2001: https://www.theguardian.com/society/2001/nov/05/11, accessed November 15, 2024.

Chapter 10

The Third Determinant
Human Capital

On a cold morning in January 2005, an immigrant from Turkey took a crucial drive – one of the most important of his life. He was driving in upstate New York, trying to find an 85-year-old yoghurt plant which was closing down.[1]

The prevous day, he had received a flyer in the mail advertising it for sale.

He had no money and hated business, but something about that flyer caught his attention. Like his life, he had no idea where this factory was.

But after driving round and round, he finally found it after a dead end (ironically).

It was rundown. The paint was peeling, the machines were rusting, and the factory was old and cheap.

All 55 employees had been laid off, and only five were left.

Rich, the production manager, was from a third-generation family of yoghurt makers.

All he could see were the people. They were huddled together. Stoic. Brave. Silent. The decision to close had been made by one of the world's leading food manufacturers from numbers based on a spreadsheet.

Five years later, that old factory had grown to become America's biggest manufacturer of organic Greek yoghurt. The whole town had revived. A vast community had sprung back up.

The immigrant entrepreneur was Hamdi Ulukaya, and the factory was Chobani.

Years later, he asked how he had turned it around.

He did not hesitate or mince his words in his 2019 TED talk,

> *The dumbest idea I have ever heard is what the business playbook says – business exists to maximise profit for its shareholders. In reality, companies should take care of their employees first.*[2]

He has since given shares in the company to all 2000 employees. The new anti-CEO playbook is about community.

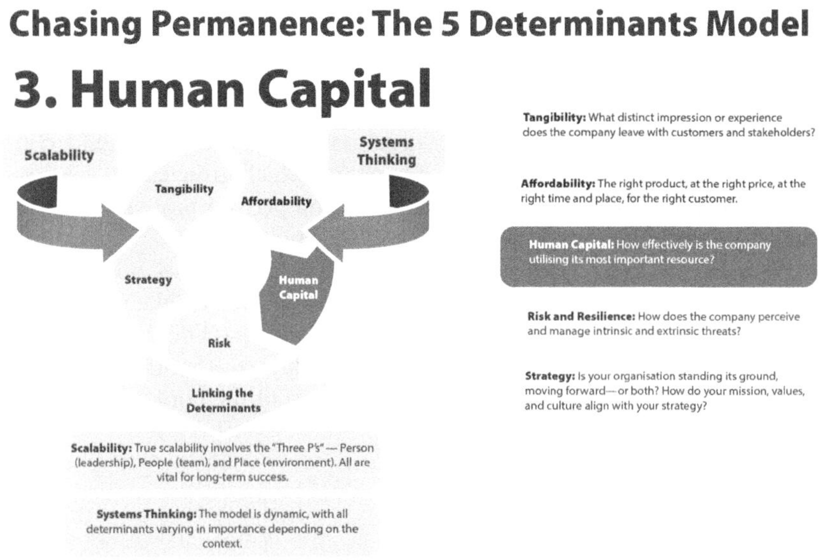
Chasing Permanence: The 5 Determinants Model
3. Human Capital
Scalability
Systems Thinking
Tangibility
Affordability
Strategy
Human Capital
Risk
Linking the Determinants
Scalability: True scalability involves the "Three P's"— Person (leadership), People (team), and Place (environment). All are vital for long-term success.
Systems Thinking: The model is dynamic, with all determinants varying in importance depending on the context.
Tangibility: What distinct impression or experience does the company leave with customers and stakeholders?
Affordability: The right product, at the right price, at the right time and place, for the right customer.
Human Capital: How effectively is the company utilising its most important resource?
Risk and Resilience: How does the company perceive and manage intrinsic and extrinsic threats?
Strategy: Is your organisation standing its ground, moving forward—or both? How do your mission, values, and culture align with your strategy?

Figure 10.1 The Five Determinants Model: Determinant 3: Human Capital.

This experience, shared on TED, has been one of its most popular talks, viewed over 4.5 million times.

Underlying his radical philosophy, he was chosen in 2024 as one of the top 50 leaders by the prestigious Thinkers50, the world's most reliable resource for identifying, ranking, and sharing the leading management ideas of our age.

Corey Hajim, the business curator of TED, summarised it perfectly:

> *Instead of looking for a community that would sacrifice to attract his business, he invested in people on the brink of despair and dreamed about what was possible. And together, they built something amazing.*[3]

The one thing that High Street businesses must do to build something unique and lasting is to put their employees first.

There is no shortage of nice-sounding slogans and fancy posters on walls, end-of-mission statements, excellent welcoming booklets, training programmes, conferences, and meetings, or books and pamphlets that sing this song in virtually every company.

In the past two decades, I have worked, consulted, and patronised hundreds of High Street businesses, and I have seen all the above in spades and buckets.

Sadly, the real shortage is often the need for leaders who walk the talk.

In his landmark award-winning book, *Irresistible: The Seven Secrets of the World's Most Enduring, Employee-Focused Organisations*,[4] author Josh Bersin, after he studied over 5,000 companies across the world, lists seven secrets which the world's best-run organisations focus on to build companies which he calls 'irresistible' – companies which grow faster, are more profitable, innovate and lead their markets – and perhaps more importantly, instil loyalty in employees, customers and stakeholders.

With all the High Street businesses I surveyed for this book – both large and small – this was the one thing they did right. Unlike most prominent companies, which say these things but present a different reality, the employees on the shop floor independently confirmed what the CEOs said.

This story forms the focus of what this section of the book is all about.

Josh Bersin lists the secrets:

1. Teams, not hierarchy
2. Work, not jobs
3. Coaches, not bosses
4. Culture, not rules
5. Growth, not promotion
6. Purpose, not profits
7. Employee experience(satisfaction), not output

I have repeatedly seen this phenomenon in my twenty years working in SMEs and large chains.

Fatima (not her real name) was a hard-working woman who had worked in healthcare retail, the care sector, and a food-producing company.

In her latter job, the premises had CCTV, which is customary in such organisations.

However, the situation in that company was different.

The proprietor had CCTV – not on potential shoplifters, but on the staff. Everything was controlled from the minute they walked in, to the minute they walked out. Fatima described the place as being like a prison. She was trying for a baby through IVF, and the company offered her absolutely no support.

She was hardworking, dedicated, and loyal, but when the opportunity to work again in the healthcare sector arose, she left for a lesser wage.

Bianca (not her real name) was a dedicated staff member who had worked for a large multinational for a quarter of a century. She was highly experienced and loyal and worked a massive daily shift during those years.

She was also neurodivergent, autistic and had hearing issues and as a woman in her fifties, she had never been properly diagnosed.

She finally mustered the courage to leave the organisation and ended up in a small High Street health retail shop chain.

She hoped that working for an SME would lead to better treatment and a more fulfilling role as a healthcare practitioner.

How wrong she was.

She was made to be a front-facing staff member and asked to work directly with customers, but they found her rude, unwelcoming, abrupt, and unhelpful. Partly because of this, they began to leave in droves, and this particular branch was at risk of closure and being sold off.

I was called in as a freelance healthcare consultant to work to turn around this struggling High Street branch.

When I interviewed the staff, the problem became clear – Bianca was unfairly blamed for everything. She was stressed and wanted to leave, but nearing retirement, her low self-esteem held her back. Additionally, her ironclad contract meant the company would face severe financial penalties if they terminated her. It was evident Bianca had been in the wrong role for too long. We promptly reassigned her to the back of the retail department, where she managed procurement, daily operations, and back-office processes. The change was immediate – Bianca flourished and became an invaluable member of the team. After 25 years, she had finally found her true place.

As leaders and managers of SMEs and High Street shops, we often hear about the importance of human capital.

We are told how important and precious our staff are and how they can be looked after.

The true story of Bianca highlights the massive issue of the Great Resignation and Quiet Quitting that we hear so much about today.

Speaking of values, Rajiv (not his real name) worked as a healthcare professional for one of the biggest healthcare providers in the UK. In the two decades he served, he made a name for himself and the company. His customers loved him, and his colleagues and staff adored him. He was passionate, kind, and caring.

But one day, he heard whispers on the grapevine that his branch on the High Street was closing. His fears were confirmed when the area manager turned up in his store and read him the riot act. The shop was closing. He was about to lose his job. He was offered a relocation dozens of miles from where he lived. He was caring for his elderly parents and had just endured a painful divorce. He had poured his heart and soul into the business, and it was now one of the chain's most successful stores in the city.

As we spoke, he was almost in tears. The pain was not from the fact that the store was closing because he understood that times were hard, but his problem was how badly he had been treated, tossed away like a rag doll despite his years of service.

And it was not just Rajiv. There was Mary, Dayo and the dozens of healthcare professionals I interviewed.

I quickly looked at the 'values' this particular company advertised on its website. Here it is, paraphrased:

Our team members are passionate about providing expert advice and services, and we pride ourselves in having great teams to deliver all our customers' healthcare needs.

Spot the gulf between the two?

All the above stories are real stories that have happened to people I know personally. I was there to see their tears, pain, and sorrow, not only because they had lost their jobs and means of livelihood but also because they felt betrayed by their faceless organisation.

They all thought (perhaps naively) that because they had stood up for the business, the company would do the same for them when it mattered most.

Nope.

The press statement this company released made the decision seem even more painful and difficult.

I compared this to employees I interviewed from the companies I examined: Timpson, Day Lewis, and Richer Sounds. The contrast couldn't have been starker.

These firms' employees regularly spoke about how recognised they felt, their ability to move higher up the hierarchy, or even to be partners in owning their stores. They also spoke of the bonuses, the words of affirmation, and the reaffirming visits from the top hierarchy of the organisation.

Day Lewis recently bought a new pharmacy near my house in early 2024. In a brief interview with the previous managing pharmacist, she said:

The best thing that could ever have happened to my pharmacy is when Day Lewis bought it out.

Or a comment made by an HMV employee when I asked him about why he worked for the company:

There's no other company I'd rather work for.

And they could recite the company's values. The passion I felt from the employees was palpable, no matter which branch I visited (and I visited a fair few), sometimes to Timpson to get my shoes fixed in different stores, or to visit a Richer Sounds store to speak to management.

The High Street cosmetics store LUSH displays its values on a large blackboard behind the checkout for all to see. This allows customers (and staff) to check the alignment between the written values and the shop floor, promoting 'happy faces.' Does the store's vibe match the values, setting it apart from competitors? Research for this book suggests 'yes.'

Staff understand, remember, and, most of all, believe and enact these values, enabling them to positively affect their daily work. These companies are, of course, not perfect but you can see and perceive their 'values compass.'

As Richer Sounds CEO Julian Richer recently wrote in the Sunday Times.

I have first-hand proof that looking at one's staff is good for business.[5]

How?

He explains:

- *Much-reduced labour turnover saves you three large piles of cash: less on recruitment, less on training, and sparing yourself the cost of losing an experienced employee. Any bookkeeper worth their salt can easily quantify these – and you will be surprised how much is involved.*
- *A happy workforce working sensible hours will take less time off for sickness. You don't want to think about the alternative: the additional costs for the business in having to arrange expensive, inexperienced cover; the lost sales because your customers are receiving a rushed service or aren't getting served at all; and the added stress for the remaining staff – which, if they become ill as a result, is a cycle of despair you don't want. But add up these costs anyway – you will be horrified.*
- *Less shrinkage – the euphemism we shopkeepers use for theft. This would primarily be internal from your workforce, but also external – mainly shoplifters and sometimes outsourced staff such as cleaners, who rarely get paid a real living wage (while not condoning the practice, if they earn too little to be able to 'live', it is little surprise they feel forced to steal).*

This saving can be huge. We have a turnover of about £200 million, and the retail norm for shrinkage is between one and two per cent of sales, so our bill should be between £2 million and £4 million, year in and year out. With us, though, it is a fraction of 1 per cent – less than 0.1 per cent – which saves us millions of pounds a year, and we are only a small business.

Our accountants will happily confirm that these savings cover the cost of our 12 company holiday homes several times over (and that ignores, incidentally, the rise in the properties' capital values over time).

- *Happy staff give better service. The members of the Which? Consumers' association have kindly voted us (Richer Sounds) the best retailer of any kind once again this year.*

I also visited other stores in the same sector and their competitors and realised the massive difference.

In today's world, millennials, Gen Z, Gen Xers, and others have abundant options: information is freely available and unemployment is low, yet employers often struggle to find the right skills.

As leaders, money and financial compensation are essential to all employees. However, in my two decades working with and in High Street businesses and SMEs, I have seen this not to be consistently accurate.

Author Josh Bersin agrees:

The cost of losing an employee can range from tens of thousands of dollars to 1.5–2.0 x the employee's annual salary. These costs include hiring, onboarding, lost productivity, training, and internal company impact.[6]

Bersin describes employees as 'appreciating assets' i.e. the longer they are with a company, the more knowledgeable they become of the company's systems, projects and culture, and the more value they provide.

Studies have shown that financial compensation is not the only reason employees leave or do not give their best when working.

Sadly, this could mean the difference between success and failure for many companies.

To ensure success and avoid Quiet Quitting you're better off keeping the staff you have and training them to align with your values.

But how do we do this?

Your leadership values will ultimately guide and form your company's culture.

So, as an SME or High Street founder or leader, you must begin with your values. These values are shaped by your natural bent as a human (your present), your life experiences and cultural grounding (your past), and your aspirations (your future).

This is one thing Doug Putman, Jay Patel, James Timpson, James Daunt and Julian Richer have in common.

Locating your values is crucial for the company's success and should not be taken lightly. As I mentioned earlier, your values should be personal, which sets you apart from other leaders and businesses.

I mentioned Dr Rai's TEDx Talk around values and her book, *The Values Compass.*[7]

After you have located and finalised these values, it is time to practise my Authenticity Framework®.

THE AUTHENTICITY AND VALUES FRAMEWORK

Figure 10.2 The Authenticity and Values Framework.

The Authenticity Framework starts with values and ends with vision and consists of four key steps:

1. Find it – identify the values that truly drive you. This means selling those values to yourself so they move from your head to your heart and become deeply ingrained.
2. Live it – commit to these values fully. Many businesses struggle here because leaders may know their values but haven't truly embodied them, causing a disconnect between words and actions.
3. Show it – begin communicating your values through your behaviour and company culture. This is often the most challenging foundational work.
4. Tell it – share your values clearly and consistently with your team and customers, extending your vision from the founder's core beliefs.

Executing these four steps is the toughest foundational work a company will face, yet it is what turns a founder's deeply held beliefs into a compelling, credible vision that the whole organisation can rally behind.

The purpose is set out in the foundational vision and beliefs – what, in *Pay the Price*, I call the honeymoon period.

Jay Patel talked to me about how the values his father and founder of Day Lewis held dear. Kirit always prioritised his family and he loved trying new things every year: he scaled Mount Kilimanjaro (the highest mountain in Africa), took his kids skiing, and gave them responsibilities at a very young age – and no matter how busy he was, he made sure his children were always a priority.

Table 10.1 Day Lewis Values

1	**To Look After Our Customers**
2	**To Be Disciplined and Professional**
3	**To Be Different Through Innovation**
4	**To Keep Our Caring Family Culture**
5	**To Have Fun**

So, when he founded the company, the values he set for the company were essentially the values he had lived by as an individual.[8]

I was amazed when I went to different branches of Day Lewis (without his knowledge) and saw how these values were lived out in the community. Generally, the staff showed their appreciation and confirmed the values that Kirit had instilled in the company 45 years ago.

Jim Collins called this 'finding the right people to board the bus.' Day Lewis concentrated on finding the right people, instilling values, and granting them autonomy within a pre-arranged framework.

They had successfully used the Authenticity Framework, so it was no wonder they were growing while other chains in the same sector were shrinking.

Kirit had found his values, lived, showed, and successfully communicated them.

Then, from this comes the purpose.

But that's not all.

It's straightforward to list values such as honesty, authenticity, and so on, but the values you espouse should be what you hold deep down in your gut; what sets you apart.

Once the company's values and mission are established, everything else falls into place, particularly the thorniest issue now: recruitment.

Recruiting and hiring workers for your organisation becomes more accessible (and paradoxically more difficult).

As Chip and Dan Heath say in their book *Made to Stick*[9], these values should not be displayed on a wall but ingrained in every organisation member and discussed in everyday language.

In my travels to Waterstones, Timpson, Day Lewis, and Richer Sounds stores across the country, I have been struck by how deeply the values of their founders have been ingrained into the company's psyche. Every store manager of Timpson or Richer Sounds knows the company's values and sees value in 'making those values stick.'

Again, to quote Josh Bersin, he calls this hiring process 'Select To Fit':

The best organisations have a strong sense of who they are. They understand what makes them successful and learn to hire people who fit those characteristics. Instead of relying on misleading traits such as previous experience, irresistible companies build unique elements into the hiring process to identify employees that fit.[10]

In the old system, employees were employed according to the job vacancy available. Whilst this will still hold for many companies – mainly highly regulated businesses: education, healthcare, law, etc. – an additional layer must be considered in the recruitment process.

The hiring bias has been toward experience rather than character. In addition to qualifications, the best companies hire employees according to values and culture.

In my two decades of experience, I have found that the best employees I have recruited have not always been those with no experience but those who are courageous and curious – ready to learn and teach the values and culture of the organisation into their daily lives and also have the character needed to fulfil their obligations.

Skills and experience can be taught, but it is almost impossible for the same to happen with values and character.[11]

In my first book Pay the Price, I argue that the honeymoon period consists of the 'holy trinity' of Person, Purpose, and Passion.

The most crucial factor is the person – not their skills or experience, but their character, internal compass, and build.

Julian Richer puts it like this:

Once candidates have been selected for an interview, it is essential to ensure they are qualified for the job and understand and accept the company's broader values. Overall, our policy is to hire for personality and train for skills.[12]

Hiring people who align with your value system and culture is far more valuable than hiring based on experience.

Once these have been sorted, half of the human capital work has been done. Jim Collins discusses this in his books *BE* and *Built to Last*.

Getting the Right People on the Bus in the Right Positions.

However, while this holds, I believe times have changed since Jim Collins' book. The changes in the last decade mean that getting the right people on the right bus is no longer enough.

Two significant positive and negative developments have occurred in the last decade, and paradoxically, they all stem from the same root.

Timpson have a typical example of this kind of hiring.

Mark Fallick, a senior Timpson manager, said they have a 'Mr Men' box where all boxes (or at least 90%) must be a *'heck yes'* before recruits are hired.

Hiring for Richer Sounds is a rigorous process: candidates have a fully paid 'trial day' where their ethics are judged, then they interview with HR and, ultimately, with the Operations Director. If approved, they undergo background and reference checks before being hired.

It's possibly no coincidence that **Which?** magazine customers rate these companies so highly. These companies, including John Lewis, Waterstones, Richer Sounds, and Timpson, are known for their excellent treatment of staff. This list is similar to companies rated highly by their employees on the employee research site Glassdoor.

Over the last century, there has been a gradual shift in power from corporations to employees. This is one of the five significant changes I enumerated in the introduction of this book.

It is worth considering how the reasons for working have changed over the last century in one irrevocable direction – towards the employee:

- **1930s to 1960s: The era of job security.** The essence was on a job for life; job security. After the financial crash of the 1930s, the Great Depression, and the devastating effects of World War II, poverty, joblessness and despair were widespread. Most employees were just happy to get a job where they could provide for their families, get job security, and have a pension. In the absence of laws that protected employees' rights, the power of companies was almost absolute. They could hire, fire and work employees as they desired. Taylorism – the effect of drawing as much productivity as possible from each employee was the accepted norm – the assembly line where each employee performed a specific task repeatedly for the whole of the day: entering figures, screwing on a bolt, turning on and off a switch for the whole day ... week ... month. It was not uncommon for workers to collapse or sustain wounds after a shift day with little compensation. But then came the strikes and revolts.
- **1960s to 1980s: The era of employee revolt.** Slowly, the wheels of employee power began to turn. Revolts right across the world started to take hold. African and Asian countries began to revolt against colonial enslavers and gained independence. Figures such as Martin Luther King and Malcolm X caused a mass revolt against racism and segregation.

The seventies and eighties marked massive strikes against Thatcherism in the 80s. This wind of change, which accompanied the boom of the late 60s to late 70s, also affected businesses. Pensions, better holidays, and better employee working conditions began to emerge. Employee agility – the ability of employees to move from one job to the other – began to take hold. However, all these benefits were still patchy and were not enshrined in law. Though in the US, the Reagan era was concurrent with the decline in labour effectiveness and the rise in deregulation, as opposed to the increase in labour strikes in the UK, there was an irreversible march towards better employee rights, culminating in the 1990s.

- **1930s–1960s: The era of employee benefits.** During this era there was a rise in the unions in the US, and even though the minimum wage was enshrined in law by President Roosevelt in 1938, it wasn't till 1996 and again in 2007, that significant amendments were made in the US. Similar changes were also being made in the UK: the national minimum wage, 1998; maternity pay, 1993; paternity pay, 2003 and a rise in union power with the Blair administration in the early 2000s.
- **2010s–present: The era of employee personalisation.** Strikes, the George Floyd and Me Too movements, the COVID pandemic, the rise of millennials to working age, and the rise of social media's power have all accelerated the pace of the inevitable march towards employee power.

I call this era the era of personalisation (Table 10.2). Increasingly, workers are no longer satisfied with being paid well, having holidays, and receiving benefits – they increasingly want to be treated as individual human beings, where their voices, personalised needs, rights, and ambitions are being heard and acted upon.

The resource provider company Gartner puts it this way:

The last three years were a catalyst to elevate personal purpose and values. Unfortunately, 82% of employees say it's essential for their organisation to see them as a person, not just an employee, and only 45% believe they are seen that way.

This translates into soul-searching about whether one feels valued in one's work or merely creates outcomes and value to benefit others. Dissatisfaction with the answers increases employees' intent to leave a job.[13]

Table 10.2 The March of Employee Power: Four Eras of Rights and Influence in the UK and US (1930s–Present)

Era	Headline Theme	Historical Backdrop	Workplace Reality	Representative Milestones
1930s–1960s The Job Security Era	"A job for life"	Great Depression → WWII devastation → post-war reconstruction	• Job security prized above all • Taylorism/assembly-line grind • Employers held near-absolute power	1943: Ford's 8-hour-day moved to other industries 1950s: early health-and-safety protests
1960s–1980s The Employee Revolt Era	"We demand a voice"	Civil-rights, anti-colonial, anti-apartheid, and anti-Thatcher strikes	• Wave of walk-outs & wildcat strikes • First real pushback on pay, hours, conditions • Job agility begins	1968: Memphis sanitation strike 1978–79: UK "Winter of Discontent"
1990s–2000s The Employee-Benefit Era	"Show me the package"	Global growth, tech boom, New Labour in UK, Clinton/Blair "Third Way"	• Minimum-wage laws bedded in • Rise of maternity/paternity rights • Health insurance & pensions upgraded	1993UK: Statutory maternity pay 1996US: FLSA wage hike 1998UK: National Minimum Wage Act
2010s – present The Personalisation Era	"See me, not just my role"	Social-media megaphone, #MeToo, George Floyd, pandemic reset	• Purpose-driven work & flexible models • DEI and mental-health demands • Talent holds negotiating power	2017: #MeToo movement 2020: mass remote-work shift
Looking ahead	Era of Employee Experience?	AI, ageing workforce, climate imperatives	• Hyper-personal contracts • Skills-based hiring • Continuous reskilling	TBD – but the trajectory is clear

Workers increasingly want to pursue their purposes within the organisation, see a direct route to growth, and be compensated fairly for their work. Thanks to remote working, hybrid working, the rise of AI, the shake-up of the traditional family, women no longer accepting sexual discrimination, people wanting fairer pricing, and environmental considerations, the psychic distance between the home and the workplace is blurring.

Companies that continually face redundancies, quiet quitting, and prominent resignations have largely failed to adapt to the changing working environment.

In short, many companies are stuck in the 1980s and 1990s, while the environment is now in the 2020s.

I'll discuss the cultural misfit between the environment and success when we discuss strategy later in the book.

This is the genesis of tension between them, which is the cause of many of the problems of High Street companies.

An article published on the BBC agrees:

People are also now looking at work and the role they want it to play in their lives differently and switching to jobs that better align with their new values.[14]

This change has negative and positive connotations that must be handled tactically.

The negative connotations are the hardening and calcification of different opinions due to the rise of 'noise,' where division across different lines is hardening, where people find it challenging to listen to each other, and where opinions are hardening.

In my two decades of working on the High Street, I have seen employees beginning to be drawn apart by this negative spin-off of personalisation:

1. The rise intensification and hardening of personal opinions.
2. The demise of the one-size-fits-all narrative.

How do we handle this negative spin-off of personalisation where everyone wants their opinions to count equally?

I offer my thoughts on these using two principles borne after personal experience, interviews and academic research:

1. Dealing with the rise of personalised divisions in the workplace: the 'Principle of the Bucket.'
2. Harnessing the rise of personalisation: the ADD principle.

Some argue that COVID has accelerated the pace of significant resignations, attrition, and employee turnover.

But the truth is, there has been a gradual march in this direction since the 1950s. Companies that don't move with the times will lose their permanence and fade into irrelevance.

Many already have.

Consider this progression. Where is your company located? What changes can you make?

In the third part of this book, where we look at Systems of Permanence, we will return to this principle and learn how to build this into your team. But speaking of teams, how do we incorporate these values into the team while maintaining their sense of ownership, self, and diversity?

We have discussed the rapid acceleration of change in the last two decades.

But what we fail to talk about is what has stayed the same.

The last decade or so has seen a massive intensification of divisions and calcifications of opinions, which threaten to destroy the fabric of communities we seek to build in our organisations.

One of the professionals in one of the small businesses I worked in was a flat-earther. He was loud and boisterous about it, alienating many of his colleagues.

A whole NGO organisation on the High Street nearly collapsed because of a dispute over same-sex marriages.

I watched, in another SME, as an employee was driven to tears because of a disagreement over party alienation.

How do we handle such fierce disagreements to enable businesses to work harmoniously?

The answer, controversially, is found in a simple, timeless tool used across cultures for millennia.

The Bucket.

I call this the Principle of The Bucket.

In my young days in Ghana, West Africa, we were plagued by a lack of clean running water, even in the capital city, Accra.

When the taps went off, which was very common, my parents used to send us with buckets. We would walk for hours to get clean water, which we stored for weeks at a time in large barrels. If we were lucky and the rain fell, we devised ingenious methods to collect the rain from our corrugated roofs into specially made barrels to store.

The buckets were separated according to the cleanliness of the water. Clean drinking water was stored in special buckets or tanks for drinking and cooking.

We also had not-so-clean buckets of water used for washing clothes and apparel.

Even when it came to washing clothes, we had different buckets for whites, different buckets for coloureds and different buckets for dark colours.

One day, as I looked at many SMEs, I realised how crucial the bucket principle was.

The Principle of the Bucket means identifying the very few things that will remain eternal and never change in your company or your industry.

This boils down to the values and mission of the company.

These should go into what I call **the primary bucket.** Like the whites in our bucket in Ghana, they cannot be contaminated, updated, or changed.

The company's fundamentals – its core values – lie in this bucket. Everyone from the CEO to the new apprentice has to sign up in unity for this first bucket, which forms the basis for the company. These distinguishing values and missions determine why the company exists.

No flexibility is allowed.

Then, we have what I call **the secondary bucket.**

The secondary bucket consists of all the different ways the business fulfils its mission, core values, and purpose. We come to different conclusions about these, and some differences are allowed. A company will never unite on all things and perspectives.

No company employee will ever agree with everyone else on every issue.

Things that will go into a secondary bucket could be:

- Religious affiliation
- Political issues and affiliation
- Cultural norms

These are important and, I'll argue, even crucial elements. And these are issues that people do (and should) hold passionately to.

However, these are not the tenets intended to bring people together in the company. As you note, these issues have constantly changed over the last 100 years, some for the better (and possibly some for the worse). However, the key to maintaining stability and a strong team is each employee's ability to respect, hear, and sometimes celebrate these differences.

Problems come in when second-bucket issues are elevated to become first-bucket issues.

It occurs when the leader of a software SME tries to persuade everyone to vote for the Republican or Conservative Party.

It's when the leader of a pharmacy chain tries to get his employees to support Brexit.

These are all second-bucket issues. They are essential but not crucial to the company's functioning.

Then there is the **third bucket.**

Things that may go into the third bucket could be personal preferences, such as hobbies, support for a particular football or sports team.

However, it should be noted that the different buckets will not be the same for every organisation.

For instance, a company working for a football team must commit to that team for its first bucket.

Let me illustrate this Principle of the Bucket with a sport I dearly love and participate in: the Half Marathon.

- *First bucket:* We have all come together to run the marathon on 5 May 2023 on this particular route. That is why all 10,000 of us are here. We all agree on the rules: we should all have numbers, start at a specific time, follow a route and so on. Failure to adhere to this would mean disqualification from the race.
- *Second bucket*: Although we are all here to run the marathon, we recognise that people choose to run it for different reasons: one may be because they are a professional runner, one to raise money for a charity, one to remember a loved one who has passed, or one may be representing a running club. So, even though we are all running the same race, it is allowed for people to have different reasons to complete that goal.
- *Third bucket*: Personal preference. We may all be running the same race for different causes, but I have a personal preference within that race and that cause. So, even though I may be running for a charity to raise money, I may personally decide to wear Nike shoes, a clown outfit, or dress like Father Christmas.

The problem is when companies elevate the third or second buckets to the first bucket.

It's when the runner dressed as Father Christmas tries to get his fellow charity runners to all don Father Christmas outfits.

Or, for the runners running for breast cancer, try to get all other charity runners in the race to ditch their careers in favour of breast cancer.

When a company leader refuses to get vaccinated, he tries to coerce his employees into following his example.

When the leader or CEO of a secular company tries to impose his cultural or religious principles on the members of his staff.

Chaos, divisions and unnecessary friction result.

But after the foundations and priorities have been set, how do you ensure your employees' well-being and job satisfaction?

The Third Determinant: Human Capital   89

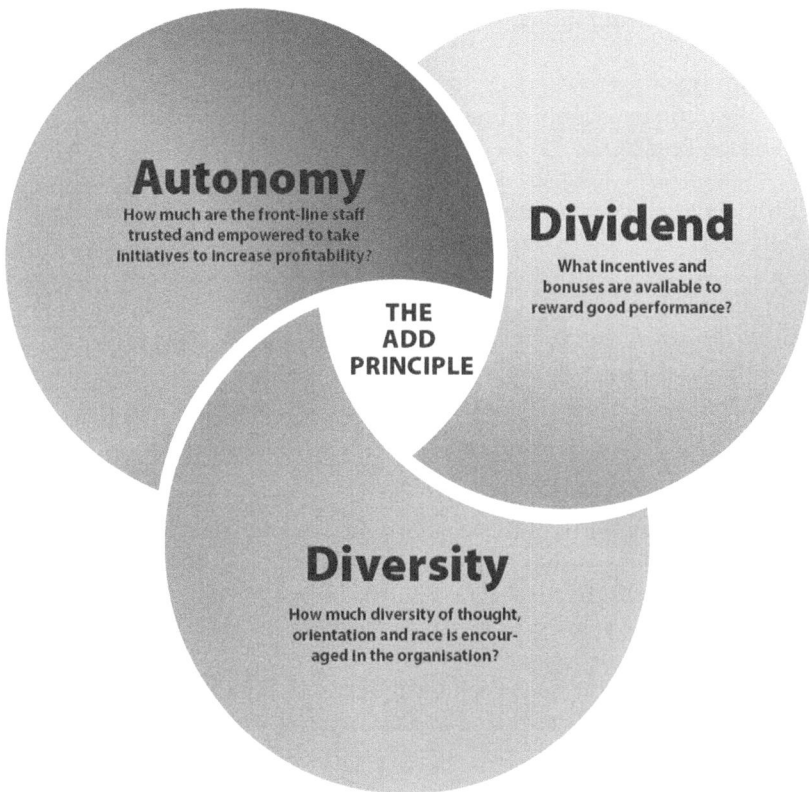

Figure 10.3 The ADD Priniciple.

It's not enough to hire the right people; it's also best to aim to keep them.
To this, CEOs need to add to the employee's positive experience, not make it worse.
But how?
Welcome to my **ADD principle®**.
I called this the ADD principle for two reasons:

1. The first reason was that it's a brilliant acronym for what we need to do to our employees: enhance their positive experiences rather than make them worse.
2. The second reason is what the principle stands for:
   - **A**utonomy,
   - **D**iversity,
   - **D**ividend

Let us start with autonomy.

Autonomy:
In illustrating autonomy, I had an exciting encounter with a manager of a Timpson branch.

> *We've managed to keep going by making sure we fill the business with amazing people and just letting them get on with it.*
> James Timpson, CEO, Timpson

> '*How much does this cost?*' *I asked the Timpson's store manager.*
> '*Well, how much do you want to pay?*' *he asked.*
> *I was taken aback.* '*You mean you want me to set a price?*'
> '*Yes,*' *he said.*
> '*Huh?*' *I fumbled.*

This is what is meant by autonomy.

Micro-managing infers a lack of trust, primarily due to the leader's insecurities rather than the manager's ability.

One of the best ways to motivate employees is to grant them autonomy, not abdication in their jobs.

We hear a lot of talk and coaching about autonomy these days.

But it is constructive to define what autonomy is not before we focus on what it is.

1. **Autonomy is different from abandonment.**
   Abandonment occurs when employees are left to their devices without proper training, continuous professional development, or a clear definition of role expectations. In my opinion, abandonment (or what James Gerber calls abdication) is one of the greatest demotivators of employees – they feel uncared for, neglected, or misused, leading to high attrition.

   I chatted with Mark Fallick, the area manager of Timpson for the South West, whom I mentioned earlier. He talked about regularly visiting his stores to chat, learn what the store managers needed, and find out how to support them in any way he could. But autonomy functions best within a pre-specified framework.

2. **Autonomy does not mean a lack of boundaries.**
   Autonomy works best when the employee is given a clear, achievable, realistic role or goal. It fits best when the right people are given the right goals and roles and receive regular, consistent, and constructive feedback on their progress in achieving that goal. It also works best when they are adequately equipped and trained to the highest standards to execute the role to the best of their ability.

3. **Autonomy is not stagnated siloing.**
   No man is an island. The parts cannot function properly if they are not part of a whole. Genuine autonomy begins when employees realise that what they do fits into a larger purpose. This involves working with other teams and individuals in a coordinated way to help achieve the company's goals and continually creating opportunities to learn, improve their skills and capabilities, develop new ones, and learn from each other.

> To simplify, once the right person is hired according to the company's values and mission, they are given the proper role according to their purpose and passion. They are trained to the correct requirements and skills needed for the job, and clear, transparent and achievable goals are set; they are left alone to craft their careers to meet those goals as they see fit.

Timpson have only two rules: put the money in the till and dress to look the part.

In other words, autonomy means the workers are given actual ownership of those goals. The leader/founder's job is then like that of a coach: provide clear direction, focus on development and growth, and ensure the well-being of their workers through inspiration. They also ensure they are compensated fairly and competitively, trust, and give regular, constructive, and fair feedback on strengths, areas for growth, and other opportunities.

Suppose the coach is a good judge of character, fair, and focuses on growth and development (as opposed to promotion and perks), communicates well, and the worker has been hired according to the company values. In that case, they will do a great job if left alone.

Rewarding them appropriately does not always involve an increase in salary or monetary compensation, though these are undeniably important and even crucial.

Autonomy goes way beyond this.

Morris Evans, the biographer of James Daunt, states:

> *James Daunt defied every advice and refused to close failing stores amid the worst of Waterstones' financial troubles. Rather, he trusted local managers' in-depth familiarity with their areas and gave them the reins. This audacious move proved that the best approach is often listening to the quietest voices, as stores grew and doubters became believers.*[15]

No wonder James Daunt has been chosen as one of the world's top 50 leaders for 2024 by the Thinkers50 organisation.

In awarding him this prestigious accolade, the organisation wrote:

His leadership style, grounded in trust and autonomy, empowers local teams to take ownership of their stores and respond creatively to their unique markets. This decentralised approach has fostered a strong sense of purpose and loyalty among employees, customers, and the wider literary community.

James Daunt shows what 21st-century leadership looks like: give people the freedom and responsibility to serve their customers. By trusting and equipping local teams to run their stores as community bookshops rather than corporate outlets, he transformed Barnes & Noble from a failing chain into a thriving business. His example proves that the best leaders succeed not as controllers-in-chief but as social architects.[16]

Authentic leadership by autonomy involves less direction and more elevation.

In a survey conducted by the McKinsey group and quoted by the World Economic Forum, the primary reason why people quit their jobs in 2021/22 (46%) was due to a lack of career development and advancement, and not far behind was lack of meaningful work (31%).

Room to grow.

As quoted in the Yoga Sutras of Patanjali:

When you are inspired by some great purpose, some extraordinary project, all your thoughts break their bounds. Your mind transcends limitations, your consciousness expands in every direction, and you find yourself in a new, great, and wonderful world.[17]

And room to grow could be either vertical or horizontal.

We usually emphasise vertical growth, a higher position, and a higher title, corresponding to increased monetary and financial benefits.

But horizontal growth is just as significant.

A significant new role was recently advertised in my native city, Plymouth, for one of its best schools. The role involved a major advancement in responsibility, significant adjustments in work-life balance, and zero pay or bonus benefits.

It got oversubscribed.

This is a horizontal career advancement, and it's more common than we realise.

We will come again to this topic of autonomy when we tackle the fifth determinant, strategy.

But there is the second tenet of the ADD principle where our differences are acknowledged and celebrated:

Diversity:
'Just a job.'
'I'm just a number.'
'I wasn't even acknowledged as he walked past.'

To make things even worse, this situation has not improved in the last twenty years. Diversity and inclusion are paradoxical topics, but they are among the most critical to the success of small businesses.

Diversity implies differences, uniqueness, and individuality, while inclusion signifies togetherness. Recent research shows that there is more bark than bite.

For instance, in an article written for *Harvard Business Review* on June 15, 2022, Robert Ely and David Thomas write about how organisations have largely failed to adopt a learning orientation toward diversity and are no closer to reaping its benefits. Abundant research has now made it clear, they write:

> *Increasing the numbers of traditionally underrepresented people in your workforce does not automatically produce benefits.*

They further write:

> *Increasing diversity does not increase effectiveness alone; what matters is how an organisation harnesses diversity and whether it's willing to reshape its power structure.*[18]

A similar article, written by Peter Bregman in 2012 for the same magazine, in the March 2012 edition, has a similar headline: *Diversity Training Doesn't Work*. Frank Dobben and Alexandra Kalev's *Why Diversity Programs Fail* (2016)[19] also suggests that we have made almost no progress for ten years.

Jabo Butera, CEO of the Diversity Business Incubator, says:

> *The opposite of belonging is not exclusion – it's the word 'belittling.'*
> *Any form of exclusion is just belittling. We don't respect their uniqueness and value; we believe they have little to offer.*[20]

Why is this the case?

From my research and working with small businesses across the UK, there are typically three levels of inclusion and diversity, which I have explained in the diagram below:

The 1st degree of inclusion: Tolerance.

She lay in bed in the city's biggest hospital at the point of death.

Figure 10.4 The Three Levels of Inclusion: Tolerance, Acceptance, and Integration.

Azi Aman had just tried to kill herself.

She was saved, literally, by the alertness of her family and the expertise of the healthcare professionals.

On the face of it, it was shocking.

Azi Aman was a second-generation British citizen whose parents had relocated to the UK after escaping the constant discrimination they faced as Kurds living in Iran.

She attended one of the best comprehensive schools in the city. After graduating, she was excited to be interviewed for her first job: a healthcare assistant in a growing chain of retail health shops in the South West of England.

She felt welcomed because in a city that was 95% white, the leader was also of an ethnic minority.

She was happy and fulfilled and was progressing until the BAME leader left.

Then it started.

She was pushed into a field she had not been trained in. And any time a foreigner who looked remotely like her came in, she was pushed out to greet them even though they had nothing in common. Then came the microaggression. The gossip. The exclusion. Her mental state got worse and worse.

Then she left to have a baby.

But the trauma and effects of the racism lingered. She began to have palpitations, paranoia, hallucinations, and started hearing voices. This was aggravated by the post-traumatic stress of having a baby and witnessing the racial persecution she suffered before coming to the UK.

She looked fine on the surface. She had a lovely smile, a hard-working husband, a beautiful baby, a gorgeous house, and supportive parents and family.

But, like the proverbial swan, she was struggling underneath.

Things came to a head when they found her on the floor.

That was the moment they rushed her to the hospital—the moment she nearly died. That's when she nearly died.

I was on the team that hired her but I had left the organisation years before.

Yes, she lived, but something in her died. I could see it in her eyes.

As she told me her story, I realised that, yes, really, we haven't moved on. People know the right things to say and how to behave on the outside, but their true feelings come out when no one is looking.

There is now a certain inevitability to inclusion. The law in most countries prohibits discrimination based on gender, race, and sexual orientation. So many companies grudgingly accept the law and hire employees who fall into minority groups simply because they have to.

However, the law offers a baseline, a foundation and so many companies stop at just fulfilling the law; they do not make an effort to include minority groups in day-to-day decisions and these groups feel constantly belittled and facing microaggression. They are left on the fringes of the organisation.

This happens much more often than you'd expect. The true story of Azi Aman is all too common. I know this because I hired her and have seen it many times.

Tolerance creates what author Catherine Garrod terms 'the illusion of inclusion.'[21] This means that if companies can get away with bias against inclusion, they will. And even if some BAME workers make it through the door, they face stories like Azi's.

This is not limited to race. I have met and worked with members of the LGBTQ+ community and those with various levels of disability who have faced the same kind of discrimination.

However, this is just the first level of inclusion. There is a second, more profound level, albeit still shallow.

The second degree of inclusion: Acceptance.

On the 16 August 2024, one of the nation's top health and beauty High Street chains, Boots, was fined £58,000 for racially profiling an employee professional pharmacist of Black origin who had many years of experience.[22]

Having BAME pharmacists and staff is commonplace for a company like Boots, so one may argue that this may be an isolated incident. However, this issue was not racist behaviour per se, rather it was how the whole issue was handled by upper management.

The judge gave a devastating criticism of Boots in his judgement, surmising that:

The Grievance Manager was 'not equipped' for an enquiry of this nature, with no specific training on conducting grievances into severe allegations of discrimination.[23]

This is the most common degree of inclusion in companies: diversity is accepted, hence half-hearted token gestures are made to face this reality. This forms the typical 'tick-box' or what many minorities call the 'trophy syndrome' – because the prevailing idea of inclusion is that it 'looks good' on the company CV, many minority members of companies are hired as trophies, signalling that the company is 'inclusive.'

Many even send some of their employees on 'diversity and inclusion programmes,' which study after study have proven to be ineffective. Some go even further to hire a 'DEI' or Inclusion Head, and there are token gestures, such as a photo op for Black History Month, International Women's Day or festivals such as Diwali or Eid. Such companies herald their diversity credentials, but true inclusion is still at the fringes. BAME members may even have a seat at the table or be given a say in the organisation's running.

On an individual level, there may be the occasional chat and handshake, but usually, BAME and minorities have two lives – their lives at work and those at home. These two lives are wholly compartmentalised, and they put on what I call the 'mask' where, just before they enter the workplace, they pause internally, put on the mask, and join as a completely different person, leaving their authentic self at home. On the surface, they appear integrated, happy, and fulfilled, but they know their place. They are there to do a job to the best of their ability; they may even get a promotion, a nice bonus, or climb the ladder if they play by the invisible rules. In my work and research, most companies operate at this level but they lose the massive potential they could draw from their BAME colleagues. They miss out on the next level of inclusion – integration.

The third degree of inclusion: Integration.

Benaee had interviewed for dozens of healthcare companies when she moved to England from Kurdistan. She was a devout Muslim who had endured domestic abuse yet had mustered the courage to walk out on her husband who lived 120 miles away, and travel down to the South West to find a new life and a new job.

She managed to get housed in a leaky, damp flat in one of the city's poorer suburbs and was kindly accepted by a professional in the city to complete her healthcare training. She passed her exam and had years of experience in her home country.

But she could not find a job in the city, which was 96% white. After almost a year of searching, she nearly gave up until she was recommended to a manager. She spoke very little English, proudly wore her hijab, prayed five times a day – and she had no English friends. You could sense the apprehension from both sides as she started her first day at work. The manager worked hard to integrate her into the team. She was allowed and encouraged to pray in a secluded part of the organisation. She was exempted from answering the phone for two months until her English improved. She was encouraged to wear her hijab. When it was time for the Muslim fast during Ramadan, she was exempted from heavy duties and was supported by team members. The leader actively sought ways to encourage her, banning all microaggressions and encouraging her friends and family to visit. The team booked meals in a Kurdish restaurant for the Christmas office dinner and refrained from buying alcohol when she was present.

It was hard work and there was a lot of groaning and complaints of favouritism along the way. But it paid off.

Massively.

She began to invite her community to patronise the services of this health community. She took the lead in meeting members of her community and other Muslims. She made friends with the team, even inviting them to her wedding. She cooked Kurdish food and shared it with members of her staff – and they responded. Real bonds began to form. She showed videos of some of her family members escaping on small boats from violence in her home country. The videos were harrowing, but the other staff members' perceptions began to change.

The company also benefited. During COVID, Benaee played a massive role in encouraging community members to get the vaccine. She trained as a vaccinator and gave more than 20,000 vaccinations to community members. She was kind, hard-working, and conscientious. Her jokes made everyone laugh. Community members began to warm to her, even asking for her when they came for their health needs.

Yet, she was encouraged to stay true to her devout Muslim faith, and her boundaries were respected.

In return, she gave her all. And so did Chloe.

Chloe was a bisexual member of the staff who joined later. She wore her badge promoting the LGBTQ+ community. Situated near the city's university, the company began to see an increase in the number of customers who were members of the LGBTQ+ community.

The result: the company went from imminent shutdown and bad reviews to the best healthcare provider in the city. It began to turn a profit after years of losing money. The staff had become more educated and eager to help members of the minorities with open arms.

The company was transformed.

And the biggest takeaway? The team included someone on the spectrum, a single mother, an openly gay member of staff, two Muslims, a black Christian, and a teenager.

Of course, there were arguments, but the leader worked hard to maintain a strong culture of openness and hard work.

A symbol of third degree (integrated inclusion) is when the distance between the private life and public life of the minority is collapsed. The more their private life shows up in the workplace, the more authentic they become, and the better their performance – not in the sense that they have to divulge their whole personal lives, but just that they don't have to put on the 'mask of work' when they enter the workplace.

The key to a better third degree is simply a question of authenticity and leaders and management need to create the environment for this authenticity to happen.

This is what the third degree of inclusion looks like. In an article I wrote for a leading leadership magazine, *Brainz,* I suggested eight ways that may give food for thought on how this can be replicated in any organisation:[24]

1. **Search your heart and brutally confront your prejudice against diversity**: As the CEO or leader, the buck stops with you. And your employees aren't stupid – they will see through the tick boxes, the empty trophies, the *'flowers, flags and fun'* as diversity expert Dr. Jonathan Ashong-Lamptey says, and consequently, they will not bring their authentic selves to work. We all need to do some serious soul-searching and openly confront the brutal truths hidden deep in our subconscious on racism, sexism, faith and religion.
2. **Be open to learning and avoid stereotyping:** This flows from the previous point. As I keep returning to, the word is 'personalisation.' As an example, in an article in *Harvard Business Review, How to Better Support Muslim Women at Work*, Hira Ali writes: *'Instead of assuming all Muslim women are the same – ask (and observe) how your colleague wants to be greeted at work – a hug? a handshake? or a simple good morning?'* Regarding my own experience, you already have the best FREE resource: your employees.
3. **Make reasonable adjustments to foster authenticity**: Devout Muslims pray five times daily. Single mothers with young children may need time to pick up their children, check on them during working hours, or be on standby. We offered to give our gay employees paid time off during a local Pride parade. Neurodivergent employees may need exceptional

help or should be put in roles that complement or enhance their nature. To facilitate third-degree inclusion and integration, we need to make reasonable changes to allow this.
4. **Ruthlessly police and eliminate any form of racial bigotry, bias and sexism right from the beginning:** An oft-forgotten rule of enhancing a good culture is that it must be rigorously and ruthlessly policed. In his New York Times bestselling book, *The Earned Life*, Marshall Goldsmith introduces the concept of referent groups. Referent groups describe the phenomenon where sometimes people act the way they do despite all logical reasons to the contrary. It is the principle that each of us feels emotionally and intellectually connected to a specific population group. Knowing a person's referent group – who they want to impress or whose respect they crave – is crucial to understanding why they talk, think and behave the way they do. The key is that whilst you don't have to agree with their referent group you can still fiercely protect and guard their right to adhere to those groups (as long as they don't contradict the company's values). Your job as a leader is to drive company performance and ensure every single employee can bring their authentic self to work. And a big part of that is ensuring every employee's allegiance to their referent group is heard, understood, empathised with and respected.
5. **Embrace the culture, language and milestones of each employee:** The culture in the office needs to foster an atmosphere of genuine, non-judgemental curiosity; curiosity about their religion, culture, background, and values. Essential festivals like Eid, Diwali, and Christmas should be actively celebrated and acknowledged. This is what I call the power of the AND – minorities should not be made to choose between their allegiance to their place/demographics of work, religion, sexual orientation, gender, family status and their homeland, there can, instead, be an 'AND.' If there is an issue, they will likely bring their authentic selves to work and inadvertently serve as a brand ambassador to the organisation, where other minority customers, clients, and patients feel welcome, patronising services more readily.
6. **Encourage 360-degree integration:** The inclusion debate must also consider the responsibility of the minorities themselves. One thing that kills company culture quickly is allowing subcultures to form within the organisation. I mention Marshall Goldsmith's referent groups in point 2 and whilst it is natural for people of a particular referent group to 'huddle' together, leadership must try to integrate all groups under one banner: the organisation's values and mission. This is what I call 360-degree integration. Minorities are also responsible for reaching out, integrating, and actively complementing leadership's integration efforts.

7. **Recognise your base:** I gave an example earlier under Mindset of why Japan's buildings are so resilient to earthquakes. This same principle applies to healthy, inclusive, resilient cultures within organisations. For diversity to work, the company's foundation must be universally rooted in respect, transparency, openness, and love. Respect for the ideals of the company and the society in which the organisation is based. So, paradoxically, a robust and uniform foundation rooted in values is the only way to establish true diversity. I spoke about this earlier in the Principle of the Bucket.
8. **Unity does not imply Uniformity:** Unity signifies the singularity of purpose within an organisation or community setting. Uniformity is not necessary to achieve unity. Forcing uniformity in thought, actions, and deeds is a sure one-way street to inauthenticity and, by extension, resentment, which will inadvertently affect performance. As Jeff Gennette, CEO of Macy's (who is openly gay), said in an interview with *TIME* magazine:

> *Equity is an essential component of how you get to an inclusive environment. An executive team is like a stadium. Who's on the playing field making the calls and driving strategy? It would be best to have an inclusive environment where everybody feels like 'I'm showing up with all my ideas and experiences.' Until everyone feels valued, you're not going to maximise the potential of your brand that's serving the most diverse population the country has ever had.*

True diversity drives creativity and innovation.

The last subset of the Diversity principle (the second 'D') of the ADD principle features what Jim Collins says about *'getting the right people on the bus.'* [25]

In my work with SMEs across two decades, I have seen four kinds of people:

The Hunter: The hunter within the organisation is the entrepreneur, or as has become commonly known, the 'intrapreneur.' The entrepreneur within the organisation is the one who is continually biased towards trying new ideas, shaking things up, finding new revenue streams and disrupting the usual way things are done. They are great at change, diversification, and creativity and usually have the 'shiny object syndrome.' They typically are great at what Professor Alex Hill, in his book, *Centennials*, calls 'the disruptive edge.'

The Gatherer: The gatherer within the organisation is the stable core – they insist on maintaining order, stewarding losses, supporting systems and processes, and keeping things ticking. They usually work in the background and within an operational setting.

People-oriented: These employees tend to build relationships with customers and clients, and their primary work orientation involves people. They thrive and are energised when given tasks that revolve around people. They can be either hunters or gatherers.

Task-oriented: These employees are motivated by processes, systems, tasks, and operations. They feel more fulfilled when their work involves maintaining or introducing quality standards, standard operating procedures (SOPs) and typically back-office procedures. They function best when they are not client-facing. Again, they could be either hunters (continually trying to improve, disrupt, and find new ways of working) or gatherers (geared towards maintaining the status quo and ensuring that agreed-upon systems are running as they should).

With these four types, we could form a four-way grid:

People Hunter: These employees combine an entrepreneurial bent with a natural disposition to work with people outside the organisation. They are typically great at customer-facing positions and getting new business for the company within a sales or new customer framework. The problem is, because of their entrepreneurial mindset, they are sometimes driven to 'shake things up' to provide better services for the organisation and hence may ruffle some feathers – mainly because they embrace change and are not hesitant to say so. They are also not very good at maintaining and managing

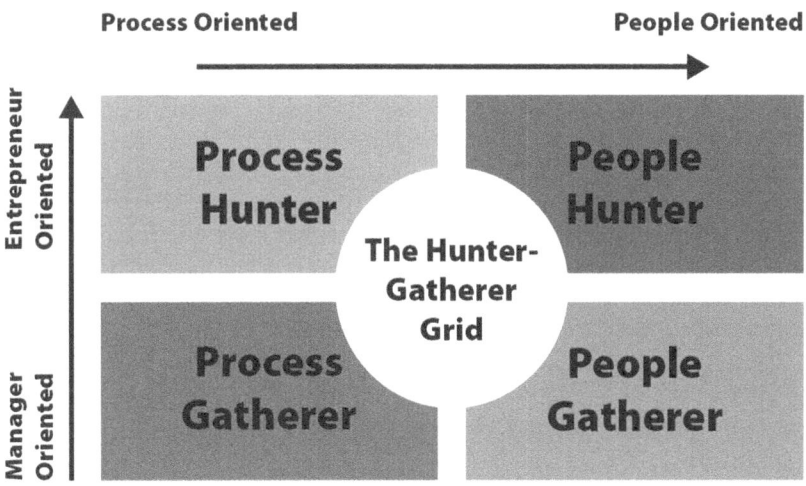

Figure 10.5 The Hunter Gatherer Grid.

the status quo and get bored quickly, especially with processes. Admittedly, some of my most significant challenges as an SME leader, manager and consultant have been with People Hunters (possibly because I am one myself). They ruffle my ego and sometimes drive me the wrong way, and I have to pause, breathe, and separate the emotion from the truth. People Hunters must improve their EQ (Emotional Intelligence Quotient) to bring to staff when they make changes to benefit their customers and clients.

Process Hunter: These employees combine an entrepreneurial mindset with a natural disposition to work with operations, systems and processes. They are typically great at tinkering with processes and finding new ways to do things better and achieve better results and effectiveness – new ways of doing things. They focus on getting things done better and more efficiently, typically at the organisation's back end. Again, their embracing of back-end change and continual desire to break and improve things creates a problem similar to that of the People Hunters, possibly even more so because people get used to specific systems, operations, and procedures. We'll discuss systems and operations in part 3 of the book, Systems of Permanence.

People Gatherer: These employees have a managerial mindset and work best in a human resource position. They are great at looking after the wellbeing of people within the organisation, according to established norms or working with people outside the organisation to follow on from the work of the People Hunter.

Process Gatherer: These are the employees who keep things ticking over, possibly what I call the 'enforcers.' Once the rules, SOPs, and culture are set, the process gatherer is responsible for ensuring the SOPs are followed, quality is maintained, the rules are followed, and everything in the company is 'ticking over.'

My spouse, Dela, is a typical Process Gatherer. Her main irk is when processes and standards are not followed, quality seems to be dropping, and protocols are not being valued. As a teacher, she loves her students. Still, she will instantly notice when they are wearing the wrong earrings, haven't dressed appropriately, when her colleagues are not following protocol, when discipline is lacking, and when agreed-upon guidelines are being ignored. She is not keen on setting the procedures but rather on enforcing them once they are 'signed into law.'

These four types of employees are essential for the successful running of any organisation, and even though I wouldn't say I like putting people in boxes, this grid is an easy way to assess staffing needs and hire or adjust appropriately.

Of course, the proportions depend on the type of business, environment and market. In more controlled and regulated SMEs such as High

Street pharmacies and governement institutions, we will need more People Gatherers and Process Gatherers, perhaps more than People Hunters.

So, when hiring, it is essential to look at which vacancies you need to fill and hire appropriately with the right questions. A Hunter-Gatherer questionnaire grid is given for free at www.stevenadjei.com

Wrong fits could have massive consequences, as the story below illustrates.

We decided to upgrade our bedroom and, on recommendation, chose a 100-year-old, mid-sized family company from the High Street with a history of fitting furniture for homes and offices.

They are in direct competition with UK market leader Sharps.

However, I saw first hand how the company needed to utilise the Hunter-Gatherer Grid properly.

The initial salesman (People Hunter) was great. He was friendly, approachable, and good at his job. After his visit, we were convinced.

Then came the surveyor (People Gatherer). He was introverted and disliked spending time with people – all we ever got out of him were grunts. He was brilliant at putting our dreams onto paper, but his people skills needed to be improved; he was good at processes but bad with people.

Then came the actual installation (Process Gatherer). This was a young apprentice who showed up with the tools, spoke to no one, and got on with the job. But in the end, he left us with many mistakes and forgot to add some vital additions, which meant that the furniture looked lovely, but was utterly useless. The company had to send another, more experienced, People Gatherer to apologise and to rectify the situation.

After further research, we realised the problem had arisen when a back-end operational manager (Process Gatherer) inserted the wrong key into the company software, crashing the whole system. Thus, the job failure stemmed from the inability of the back-end operations (Process Gatherer) to perform its duties. This impacted the installation process, costing the company hundreds of thousands of pounds and causing many dissatisfied customers.

Finding the right fit for the right job and appropriately rewarding employees is crucial – the last D of the ADD principle.

Dividend:

Dividend refers to the benefits the employees accrue when they work for the company.

Employees need to be paid fairly and comprehensively for their work, and their salaries to be competitive with those of companies in the same or similar sectors.

Holiday pay, sick pay, pension and sickness benefits should all be as competitive as the company can afford.

Bonuses that reward meeting aspirational-specific KPIs should also be given.

Shockingly, several companies fail to meet this foundational dividend. Seeing the CEO enjoying the trappings of wealth will not encourage employees to put their best foot forward for the company, especially when they feel underpaid.

Using Glassdoor, LinkedIn, Indeed and many other similar employment and recruitment platforms, it is now straightforward for employees to find out how much employees in similar firms are being compensated.

The foundation of reasonable company compensation is a good, competitive salary.

What exactly do we mean by compensation?

It's not just about money, as many tend to assume.

What is the hourly rate? How many holidays do I get? What is the pension like? Are there any work-related bonuses?

But yes, monetary compensation is crucial – bills need to be paid, and families need to be fed. However, I have noticed one continual trend across my two decades of personal experience and research.

Companies that pay the best don't necessarily retain the best employees – meaning that appreciation and dividends go beyond just money,

In 1992, Gary Chapman wrote a life-changing book on marriage, discussing the Five Love Languages for romantic relationships.[26] The book spent over 297 days on the New York Times Bestseller list and sold over 13 million copies. The book lists five ways romantic couples give or receive love.

Dr. Chapman listed them as:

- Words of appreciation
- Gifts
- Acts of service
- Time
- Physical touch

This was thought to apply only to romantic relationships for a long time, but it was later expanded to include platonic and family relationships.

In 2019, author and researcher Dr. Paul White approached Dr. Chapman, and together, they co-wrote a variation of this book to cater for the workplace called *The 5 Love Languages of Appreciation in the Workplace*.[27] The book expands the concept of love languages to include how employees will likely respond to appreciation for their work.

I have also expanded this concept based on research I have done within the NHS in the UK. I have combined the reasons for the Great Resignation with how employers can use principles from the five languages to address this phenomenon. The following few pages distil these findings while pulling facts from Dr. Chapman's iconic book.

My take on this is that you can learn a lot from your employees and what means a lot to them, from their complaints.

While Dr. Chapman uses these principles to honour and appreciate employees, I want to conclude how they could also be used to tackle the phenomenon of the Great Resignation.

If an employee continually complains that they are not shown any appreciation, or if nobody says 'please,' 'thank you' or 'what a great job you're doing,' that may be a sign that their love language is words of appreciation.

If an employee constantly asks for 5 minutes of your time to 'have a quick word,' that may signify that time is their love language.

It is thus fair to surmise that the lack of appreciation and poor compensation for these personalised traits drives the bulk of the Quiet Quitting or Great Resignation we see today.

Let's delve a bit further.

1. Time

One day, Emily Smith had had enough.

She worked for a small IT company in the South West of England and was in her early twenties.

She was brilliant at her job and extremely popular with colleagues and clients.

She met her husband during her second year at this firm and after getting married, Emily became pregnant.

That's when the discrimination started.

She was accused of knowingly getting pregnant when she took the job so she could benefit from maternity leave. Because she needed the money, she kept her mouth shut and after her maternity leave, she dutifully returned to work. But with her husband working and the UK having one of the highest childcare costs in the world, they were struggling to make ends meet.

So she approached management for help with flexible hours – working from home, working part-time in the office, and flexible hours to support her family.

She needed appreciation and support around time.

The management disagreed and things came to a head.

She resigned and is now looking to start her own business.

Jennifer is the supervisor of a medium-sized healthcare facility chain in the UK. Every two to three months, the chain owners would organise a flying visit where they would visit each of their 15 or so branches. She wanted some time with the senior management to voice her concerns and have them recognise her hard work – to spend some time with her.

All she ever got was 5 minutes and the occasional Zoom call. When they spoke to her, the managers did not even look her in the eye. All the 'well done' bonuses and appreciative emails did not mean much to her because they meant nothing if they could not give her 15–30 minutes of undivided attention.

She felt underappreciated and ended up leaving the company.

She needed appreciation and support around time.

After the COVID pandemic, an SME management consulting company allowed its employees to work from home three to four days a week.

Ali Mohammed gladly accepted the offer because he had a young family. However, he was struggling with depression and loneliness and a breakdown of his marriage. He had pictures of his girls all around the room/office and he half expected his senior manager to ask about the photos of the girls and spend 5 minutes before meetings to enquire about how things were going with him – but, no.

All the leader wanted to do was work.

He could feel himself spiralling and, partly due to his cultural background and gender, he felt unwilling to discuss his problems with friends, family or a healthcare professional.

In her brilliant book, *Your Resource Is Human*, Melissa Romo explains how issues like guilt, depression, and loneliness could impact productivity for remote workers and gives tips on how remote leaders could spot the signs and intervene:

> *My personal experience has taught me that hearing from a leader, knowing they are thinking about you, and supporting you through a difficult time can make all the difference, even though they cannot realistically do anything.*[28]

And this is only possible with the investment of time.

2. Gifts

'They came from London and they didn't bring any gifts – even the pastries they brought us were nearly out of date.'

'All the hard work we did, and we didn't even have a cent to show for it.'

Moving between jobs has now become the norm. Most people, especially in the financial and technology sectors, stay for an average of four years before moving on to another job.

But gifts are not just about money.

Some employees feel appreciated when small, but meaningful, gifts such as cards or personalised cups are given.

3. Words of Appreciation

Sometimes, a 'thank you' or 'you're doing a great job' is all it takes. People want to be noticed, appreciated, and told they matter.

According to a recent study involving more than 2000 employees, 70% reported they would work harder and feel better about themselves if their boss was more grateful, and 81% said they would work better for an appreciative boss. This is what is termed a 'gratitude gap' where, in their whole lives, work is where they are less likely to experience it. Genuine gratitude at work is surprisingly rare, especially from those in power and mainly when things are tough, just like they are on the High Street.

4. Physical Touch
In one of Britain's most watched TV programmes, *The Great British Bake Off*, frontman and veteran baker Paul Hollywood gives his famous 'handshake' – reserved for the best of the best bakers in a particular genre.

It was his way of saying 'well done.'

This physical touch can range from a tap on the shoulder, a handshake, to a bear hug.

(bearing in mind cultural and gender sensitivities)

5. Acts of Service
Another way to show appreciation is through acts of service, such as when a leader comes in and makes a cup of tea for the staff, sweeps the floor, or empties a bin.

These five ways come down to the same principle I return to, again and again in this book:

Personalisation
Leaders need to know their staff individually, right down the pyramid:

Pyramid by:
1. **Building a culture of appreciation:** Day Lewis and Timpson run a 'Happy Index,' which measures, in tangible terms, how fulfilled employees are in their jobs. They use open strategy techniques to discover genuine ways to improve their fulfilment, including training and promotions.
2. **Mentoring and training:** Training and mentoring can embed these values of appreciation in the organisation. We discuss this further in Part 3 of the book, under Scalability.

James Timpson makes the same point:

> *Whereas most businesses measure profits and margins, we measure colleague happiness. The company conducts a weekly morale survey for every colleague and an annual 'Happy Index.' Everyone in the business gets their birthday off and an additional day of leave when they become a grandparent or when*

their child has their first day at school. Staff are also granted pet bereavement days.[29]

Julian Richer, in his Sunday Times column, beautifully summarises the principle of dividends, which addresses these five kinds of appreciation:

When it comes to colleagues, I concluded many years ago that staff motivation has five key components:
1. Work should be as enjoyable as possible.
2. Staff deserve systematic recognition – straightforward ways to compliment them on their performance.
3. Effective communication is essential, both upwards and downwards.
4. Rewards should be relevant and linked to achievement.
5. Finally, bosses should be loyal to their workforce.[30]

And to further reinforce this point, it is worth noting that James Timpson, CEO of Timpson and a close friend of Julian Richer who shares these same values, took over writing this column in the Sunday Times the following year.

LUSH. Day Lewis. Timpson. Richer Sounds. Companies on the High Street that succeed truly believe in (and embody) their values so passionately that they are willing to shout them from the rooftops for all to hear (or see).

However, no matter how satisfied your workforce may be, threats are always looming, especially on the High Street. In the following chapter, we will explore various threats and how High Street businesses can prepare to handle them, starting with a major catastrophe that nearly bankrupted one of our selected High Street companies.

Notes

1. TED. The Anti-CEO Playbook, Hamdi Ulukaya: www.ted.com/talks/hamdi_ulukaya_the_anti_ceo_playbook
2. TED. The Anti-CEO Playbook, Hamdi Ulukaya: www.ted.com/talks/hamdi_ulukaya_the_anti_ceo_playbook
3. TED. The Anti-CEO Playbook, Hamdi Ulukaya: www.ted.com/talks/hamdi_ulukaya_the_anti_ceo_playbook
4. Bersin, Josh. *Irresistible: The Seven Secrets of the World's Most Enduring, Employee-Focused Organizations*, IdeaPress Publishing, 2022.
5. Julian, Richer. Treat workers well, and ignore accountants at your own peril, *Sunday Times*: www.thetimes.com/business-money/entrepreneurs/article/treat-workers-well-and-ignore-accountants-at-your-peril-t0dtxdr2z, June 5, 2022.
6. Bersin, Josh. *Irresistible: The Seven Secrets of the World's Most Enduring, Employee-Focused Organizations*, IdeaPress Publishing, 2022.

7 Rai, Mandeep. *The Values Compass: What 101 Countries Teach Us About Purpose, Life and Leadership*, John Murray Business Books, 2022; Bersin, Josh. *Irresistible: The Seven Secrets of the World's Most Enduring, Employee-Focused Organizations*, IdeaPress Publishing, 2022.
8 For the full list of values, see Day-Lewis. Core Values: www.daylewis.co.uk/about-us/core-values.
9 Heath, Chip and Dan Heath. *Made to Stick: Why Some Ideas Take Hold and Others Come Unstuck*, Arrow Books, 2008.
10 Heath, Chip and Dan Heath. *Made to Stick: Why Some Ideas Take Hold and Other Come Unstuck*, Arrow Books, 2008.
11 Adjei, Steven N. *Pay The Price: Creating Ethical Entrepreneurial Success Through Passion, Pain and Purpose*, BlueCloud Publishing, 2022.
12 Richer, Julian. *The Ethical Capitalist: How to Make Business Work Better for Society*, Random House, 2018.
13 Gartner. Employees seek personal value and purpose at work. Be prepared to deliver. www.gartner.com/en/articles/employees-seek-personal-value-and-purpose-at-work-be-prepared-to-deliver, March 29, 2023, accessed November 15, 2024.
14 Francis, Ali. Gen Z: The workers who want it all, *BBC Worklife*, June 17, 2022: https://www.bbc.co.uk/worklife/article/20220613-gen-z-the-workers-who-want-it-all.
15 Evans, Morris. *James Daunt Biography: How a Passion for Literature and Strategic Acumen Revitalized Iconic Bookstores Across the Globe*, Independently published, 2024.
16 Thinkers50. Leaders50: A uniquely curated biennial listing of 50 inspiring leaders from organisations worldwide: https://thinkers50.com/leaders50
17 Onejourney. Patanjali Quote: "When you are inspired by some great purpose…": https://onejourney.net/patanjali-quote-when-you-are-inspired-by-some-great-purpose
18 Ely, Robin J. and David A. Thomas. Getting serious about diversity: Enough already with the business case, *Harvard Business School*, November/December 2020: https://hbr.org/2020/11/getting-serious-about-diversity-enough-already-with-the-business-case.
19 Dobbin, Frank and Kalev Alexandra. Why diversity programs fail, Harvard Business Review, July–August 2016: https://hbr.org/2016/07/why-diversity-programs-fail. *Harvard Business Review*, July-August 2016.
20 Butera, Jabo: Quote used by personal permission.
21 Garrod, Catherine. *Conscious Inclusion: How to 'do' EDI, One Decision at a Time*, Practical Inspiration Publishing, 2023.
22 The Pharmacists Defence Association. Boots ordered to pay £58,000 following racial harassment case: www.the-pda.org/boots-pay-58000-in-racism-judgment, August 16, 2024, accessed November 16, 2024.
23 The Pharmacists Defence Association. Boots ordered to pay £58,000 following racial harassment case: www.the-pda.org/boots-pay-58000-in-racism-judgment, August 16, 2024, accessed November 16, 2024.
24 Adjei, Steven, N. Eight ways to successfully unlock diversity potential in your business, *Brainz Magazine*, August 2022: www.brainzm agaz ine.com/post/eight-ways-to-successfully-unlock-diversity-potential-in-your-business.
25 Collins, Jim. *Built to Last: Successful Habits of Visionary Companies*, Random House Business, 2005.

26 Chapman, Gary. *The 5 Love Languages: The Secret to Love That Lasts*, Moody Publishers, 25th-anniversary edition, 2015.
27 Chapman, Gary and White, Paul. *The 5 Languages of Appreciation in the Workplace: Empowering Organizations by Encouraging People*, Moody, 2019.
28 Romo, Melissa. *Your Resource Is Human: How Empathetic Leadership Can Help Remote Teams Rise Above*, London: Practical Inspiration Publishing, 2023.
29 Timpson, James. *The Happy Index: Bestselling Practical Leadership Advice for a Happier Workforce and Better Results*, Harper North, 2024.
30 Richer, Julian. Customers and staff should be like your children – equal, *The Sunday Times*. www.thetimes.com/article/customers-staff-treated-equality-comment-027lttdhs, accessed January 5, 2022.

Chapter 11

The Fourth Determinant
Risk and Resilience

2022 could have spelt doom for Waterstones[1].

Despite a summer sales boom of £452.5 million driven by the popularity of bookstores and the acquisition of Blackwells, Waterstones had upgraded its stock distribution to meet demand by contracting Blue Yonder, a leader in supply chain management, which promised a 'synchronised end-to-end solution.'

Things went awry when a software glitch delayed orders for up to six weeks, causing local stores to run out of stock and complaints to soar. Trust in the head office plummeted, frustrating authors and resulting in £13.5 million in losses. Despite rising sales to £452.5 million in 2023, profit after tax fell to £12.0 million, down from £42.1 million. Nevertheless, the company survived and a spokesperson emphasised the team's resilience, noting that 13 new shops had successfully opened despite the disruptions[2].

All High Street businesses and SMEs face similar challenges, and their responses define their success or failure.

But before we get to this, we must discuss the risks themselves.

In this book, I identify two classifications for risk:

- Yossi Sheffi's Quadrants of Catastrophes for his landmark book *The Power of Resilience*
- My classification of the response to pain – The Pain Flag Response Model from *Pay The Price*

With these risks in mind, I want to discuss a famous speech given at a press briefing on February 12, 2002 which, a decade later, became the basis for a New York Times #1 bestseller.

Known and Unknown.

At a press briefing, the late former US Secretary of State, Donald Rumsfeld, mounted the podium at the Pentagon to give a famous speech that has now gone down in history.

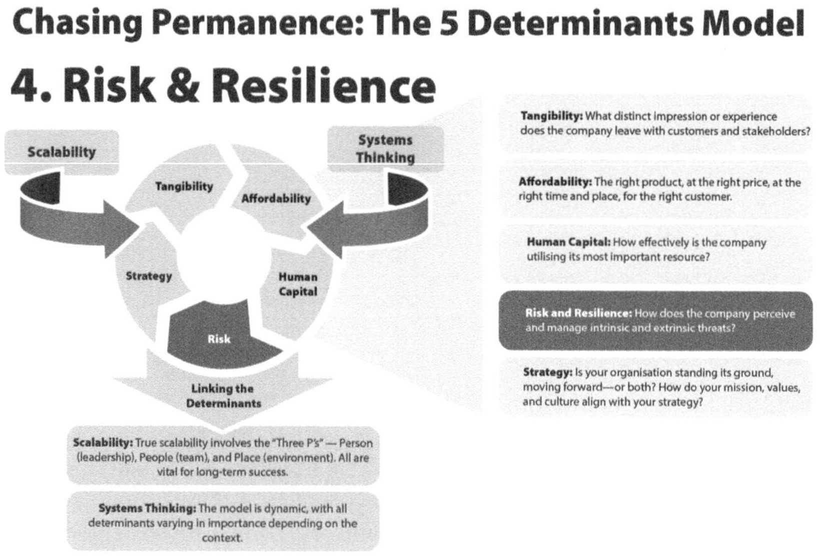
Chasing Permanence: The 5 Determinants Model
4. Risk & Resilience
Scalability
Systems Thinking
Tangibility
Affordability
Strategy
Human Capital
Risk
Linking the Determinants
Tangibility: What distinct impression or experience does the company leave with customers and stakeholders?
Affordability: The right product, at the right price, at the right time and place, for the right customer.
Human Capital: How effectively is the company utilising its most important resource?
Risk and Resilience: How does the company perceive and manage intrinsic and extrinsic threats?
Strategy: Is your organisation standing its ground, moving forward—or both? How do your mission, values, and culture align with your strategy?
Scalability: True scalability involves the "Three P's" — Person (leadership), People (team), and Place (environment). All are vital for long-term success.
Systems Thinking: The model is dynamic, with all determinants varying in importance depending on the context.

Figure 11.1 The Five Determinants Model: Determinant 4: Risk and Resilience.

> *There are known knowns; there are things we know we know. There are known unknowns; things we know that we don't know. Then there are the unknown unknowns – things that we don't know that we don't know.*[3]

This speech has been used to explain everything from energy efficiency to tools for starting a strategic process to cybersecurity.

But the most critical application of this speech is found in quantifying risks used by Yossi Sheffi, in his excellent book, *The Power of Resilience: How the Best Companies Manage The Unexpected.*[4]

Sheffi classifies risks along a likelihood matrix against impact and high likelihood. He calls this the 'quadrants of catastrophes.'

In general, Yossi Sheffi postulates that the impact and likelihood of risks largely follow the power law or the Pareto Principle – namely, that 80% of events would be frequent and minor, and only a rare, small percentage, around 20%, would generate a significant impact.[5]

Sheffi shows that many disruptive natural events, such as earthquakes, volcanoes, hurricanes, epidemics, and even artificial ones, such as terrorist activities, cybercrimes, wars and considerable price fluctuations, follow this law.

Of course, these fluctuations are also dependent on the region of the world where your business(es) are situated – the likelihood of tornados and hurricanes in some parts of the US, government unrest in some parts of Africa and the Middle East, and earthquakes in Japan, for example, could be more or less likely.

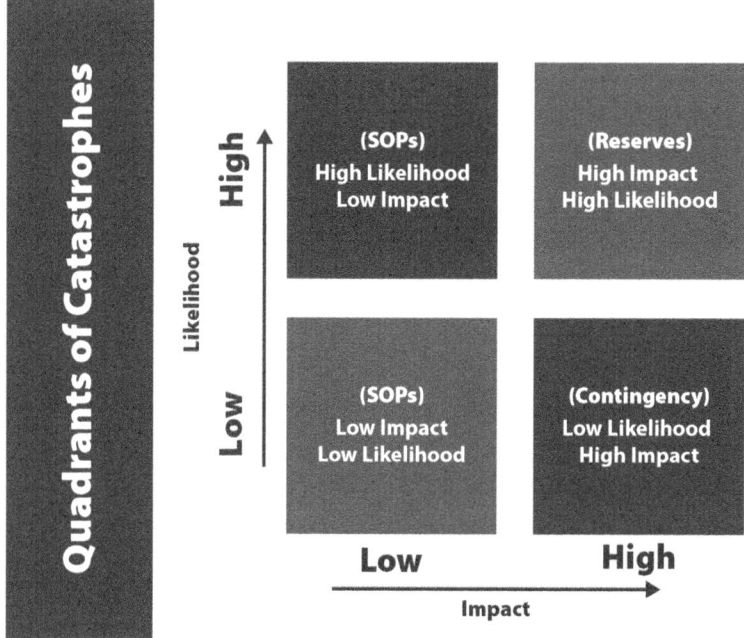

Figure 11.2 The Quadrants of Catastrophes: Likelihood vs Impact.

This phenomenon introduces another element to this neat table: detectability, which we will introduce later.

But for now, let's examine the four kinds of risks Sheffi discusses in more detail.

Low Likelihood, Low Impact

Chaos erupted suddenly in a community pharmacy healthcare facility that was part of a London-based SME. The facility had been running more or less smoothly for the past four decades on the High Street of a medium-sized city in the UK.

Due to changes in the law and reductions in remuneration, most of the competition within a 5-mile radius of the healthcare facility had suddenly decided to close down. These facilities were all owned by a significant High Street healthcare chain that had suddenly decided to diversify out of community pharmacies.

Almost overnight, footfall at this healthcare facility quadrupled. The management was taken aback by the surge and realised that staff training, facilities, inventory, and overall capacity needed urgent enhancement to accommodate this sudden increase.

This facility, consistently rated among the top three pharmacies in the city, was suddenly overwhelmed. Staff members began to fall ill with stress and absenteeism skyrocketed. They were fighting for breath, trying to manage the sudden increase in demand.

Management took drastic steps, immediately increasing the opening hours, recruiting more qualified staff, reducing non-essential services, and alerting customers to the long waiting times.

Within a month, things had begun to settle.

Profitability increased.

This is an example of a low likelihood, low impact scenario. Together with the following scenario (high likelihood, low impact), it can be managed tactically or strategically through SOPs, routine business processes, and day-to-day operations that do not constitute an existential threat to the business.

High Likelihood, Low Impact

High likelihood, low impact risks include everyday '*dribble of micro- disruptions*'[6] from supply issues, workplace incidents, problems with equipment, and staff issues that may affect customer commitments and efficiency but do not pose an existential threat to the company or its day-to-day functions.

It is not uncommon for retailers to see out of stock items, delays in delivering solutions to customers, disruptions caused by weather incidents or employee sickness that slow project execution. Even moderate issues such as power outages, communications failures or weather disruptions can derail a company's operations for up to a week or two.

The hope is that the day-to-day operations of management and leadership can smooth out the disruptions and, even more importantly, prepare the teams in resilience procedures and detectability to weather the more significant storms. These are the storms that threaten the very existence of these firms.

High Likelihood, High Impact

The difference between high likelihood and low likelihood is the ability to plan.

The Waterstones example at the beginning of this section is an example of a high likelihood, high impact scenario.

Companies can factor in the possibilities of this happening, insurance companies can factor this into their calculations for insuring a company, and staff can be trained in these kinds of risks because the likelihood is within the realm of possibility.

For example, stress tests conducted by Waterstones before implementing the new technology indicated that the company could withstand losses of up to £20 million in the worst-case scenario.

COVID-19 is another typical example. Pandemics have been relatively common and experts have been predicting them for a while. There have been various recent outbreaks of SARS and Ebola, so a world with pandemics is within the realm of possibility. As the world becomes more global and our lives become more intertwined, the likelihood of another pandemic becomes increasingly possible and failure to plan for these 'eventualities' virtually guarantees failure.

Low Likelihood, High Impact

Like millions of other ships before it, the 400-metre Ever Given was carrying close to 20,000 tonnes of cargo through the Suez Canal in March 2021 when, apparently due to human and technical errors and an unfavourable wind current, it became stuck, with its bow and stern at opposite ends.

It completely blocked the canal, trapping 349 ships behind it. Egyptian, Dutch, and Italian tugboats worked for six days and millions of dollars was spent in order to free the vessel.

This caused an estimated loss of $9.6 billion in world trade and resulted in significant supply chain issues across the Western world.[7]

This was a risk that was unfathomable and unimagined.

In 2015, my family and I went on a cruise through Devon, England, and decided to spend the day in a quaint town called Dawlish.

In the middle of the town runs a small stream populated by an unusual occupant I had never seen, but who had made the city famous throughout England.

A black swan. A highly improbable bird located in a highly improbable part of the UK.

This reminded me of Nassim Taleb's groundbreaking book of the same name,[8] which is widely credited with predicting the financial crash of 2008.

As Naseem describes them, black swans are events that have been thought impossible but do happen.

The above event is a black swan event.

The financial crashes of 1930 and 2008 were also black swan events. Even though there were isolated predictions, nobody saw it coming.

The difference between low likelihood and high likelihood impact lies in two things:

- Detectability – how quickly the company realises the impact
- Response time – how quickly and to what degree the company can respond to the impact

We will discuss this after the second risk classification, the Flag Response system, which I comprehensively explained in my first book, *Pay The Price*[9].

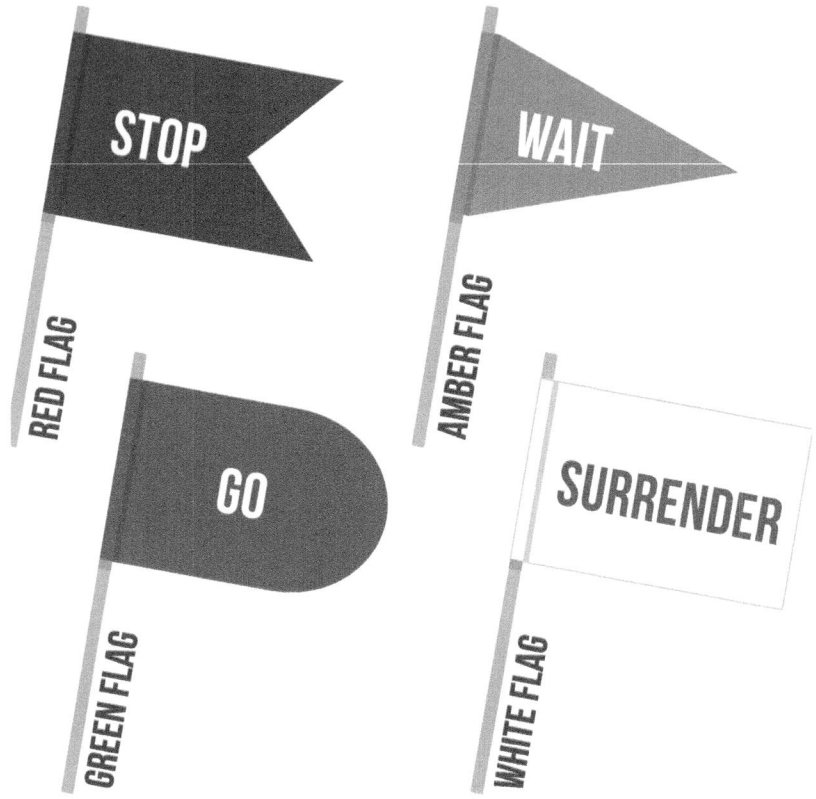

Figure 11.3 The Flag Response Model of Risk.

The Flag Response system applied to risk

In *Pay The Price*, I talked about pain in business, which is related to the sources of pain and how to address them. In this book, I apply this same classification to that of risk. Whereas the Quadrants of Catastrophes are related to impact, the Flag Response System addresses risk from an apparent angle:

The Source.

Let's look at this in turn:

The Red Flag of Risk: The Red Flag depicts the risk of self-sabotage. It reminded me of a trendy, small-medium restaurant suddenly closing on our High Street in Ebrington, Plymouth.

It was ideally situated across the road, with available parking, lovely food, a buzzing atmosphere, and friendly staff embedded in the local community. Then, one day, the unexpected happened.

I had invited a client for a meal at the restaurant but as I met her, the staff walked outside aimlessly and then sat down. The doors were firmly locked and a sign read:

DO NOT ENTER

The restaurant had gone bust.

The owners had not been paying their bills and were secretly siphoning off the profits for their own gain.

Like this example, we've all heard of businesses that have just gone bust for totally avoidable reasons, and have often self-sabotaged.

These usually happen when no robust accountability processes are in place and this is more likely to occur in SMEs.

Why a red flag? Because they are manageable risks to spot: not treating your staff fairly, flouting government and safety regulations, and a lack of financial discipline. These are easily avoidable risks, but they form the majority of companies going under.

The solution is simple: Stop. Thoroughly and regularly audit the company, find out where self-sabotaging is rife or latent, and deal with it before it deals with you.

As a CEO or leader, are there habits or character flaws that pose a risk to you or the business in general? The quality of the CEO's character and performance is crucial and as reiterated in Part 1 of this book, the succession issue is critical.

A CEO's fall due to red flag pain can bring the whole business down, tarnish its reputation and destroy its trust, particularly in this day and age, where social media and 24/7 news allow information to travel like wildfire.

The antidote to this is found in one word:

Accountability.

Strong governance structures: a good advisory board, mentorship, accountability partner, or coach are indispensable. A robust check-and-balance system must mitigate this red flag risk and ensure continual success.

The Amber Flag of Risk: This risk is common where there is a misalignment of the timing of the market with the business. Adaptability is key. I talked about customer agility as one of the fulcrums of tangibility. Timing of market adaptability is critical to avoid this kind of risk. The rise of AI is one such example – everybody is jumping onto the bandwagon of AI and threats abound, warning that businesses that don't hop on immediately are doomed. But is your business ready? Is it necessary at this point? Or are you lagging? There are times when companies use the 'first mover advantage' as a strategic competitive advantage, but this may not always be the case – for instance, check out Apple Watch, which entered its market late but has now captured a sizeable share.

Rushing too quickly ahead of the market can spell disaster, waste resources, or both. Timing is everything. Amber at a traffic light signifies wait.

But moving too late and rushing to the stable after the horse has bolted is equally damaging. One primary reason is that companies get stuck in a rut, fail to adapt to evolving customer changes and get left behind.

The White Flag of Risk: These are risks over which the business has no control. These will fall in the high impact category (whether low or high likelihood). The only way is to surrender to these risks and develop appropriate resilience mechanisms. The key here is more of the response than the preventability. The White Flag of Risk is similar to the high impact, low likelihood (and in some cases the high impact high likelihood) risks described under Yossi Sheffi's categorisation above and exemplified by the incident in the Suez Canal.

The Green Flag of Risk: In October 2008, a rumour circulated that Apple CEO Steve Jobs had suffered a major heart attack.

Although the rumour was eventually debunked, its swift spread and initial acceptance as truth by investors led to a significant $9 billion loss in market value.[10]

Recently, a hoax regarding a McDonald's sign claiming that African Americans would be charged an extra $1.50 to be served sparked widespread discussion on X. McDonald's was compelled to refute the claims, labelling them as a 'senseless and ignorant hoax.' How can such outrageous claims inflict so much harm?

Researchers like Dubois provide insight:

How does a rumour become accepted as fact as it circulates among consumers? We suggest that consumers' confidence in their beliefs (attitudes, opinions) is often overshadowed by the beliefs themselves, rendering their certainty information more vulnerable to loss during communication. Accordingly, current studies show that while consumers convey their core beliefs to each other, they frequently do not pass along their level of certainty or uncertainty regarding those beliefs. A belief that starts with high uncertainty tends to lose that uncertainty as it spreads.[11]

A colloquial English term for this process is 'Chinese Whispers.'

This risk has significantly affected the High Street, with the press playing a significant role.

A recent survey led by data analyst Laura Harris, founder of the High Street Positives community, in partnership with Find Out Now, gathered over 54,000 responses and confirmed what many of us already sense – the stories people hear shape where they choose to shop. When exposed to positive media, 85% of people say the High Street is worth visiting. But among those who see only negative coverage, that number drops to just 35%.

The more people hear about decline, the less they show up. And as footfall falls, so does confidence. Businesses hesitate, landlords hold back, and the cycle continues.

As Laura rightly points out, boardrooms are made up of people. If all they hear is failure, why would they choose to invest?[12]

Homebase, a DIY garden store chain primarily located in out-of-town retail centres, recently went into administration. The Mirror reported this.

Homebase has put 74 of its stores up for sale just days after collapsing into administration, delivering a major blow to the High Street.[13]

Birmingham Live also reported:

More High Street stores close before Christmas as Homebase shuts its doors.[14]
The High Street continues to face intense pressure, and Homebase is just the beginning.

And from the *Big Issue* of December 2024:

Can Christmas save Britain's High Streets? It's complicated, experts say.
Some of the country's most prominent retail players have had a challenging year. Will Christmas help save them?[15]

Stories like these, prevalent in the press, contribute to the perception that the High Street is becoming an 'endangered species' and perpetuate the misleading narrative that it is on the verge of collapse.

In his insightful 2023 book, *Build for Tomorrow*, author and editor-in-chief of the *Entrepreneur* magazine, Jason Feifer, interviews Amy Orben, a specialist on social media's influence on youth, who introduces the concept of the Sisyphean Cycle.[16] She describes the typical response to what Jason terms 'the drumbeat of panic,'[17]

1. Something feels different
2. Politicians (and influencers) step in
3. Scientists (and researchers) accelerate their efforts, eager to capitalise on the publicity (and funds that follow)
4. Information becomes viral, panic ensues, and chaos follows. 'If it bleeds, it leads'

This phenomenon can be viewed as the Green Flag of Risk. The rise of review platforms like Trustpilot, Amazon, Google, and Facebook reviews has heightened this risk – a single negative customer experience, whether real or perceived, can severely harm a brand, especially for small and medium-sized enterprises on the High Street.

I previously discussed Customer Agility under Tangibility, emphasising the importance of customer-facing staff being equipped and empowered to recognise and address potential customer risks quickly and effectively, saving High Street businesses millions in brand damage. I used Timpson as an example, where staff are authorised to swiftly resolve customer complaints at the cash register, up to £500.

A glance at Trustpilot reveals that they boast a 71% rating of four or five stars, and a dedicated customer service team promptly addresses every negative review within 24 hours.[18]

Thus, we observe two distinct types of risk development here. However, recognising risks and understanding their evolution is only part of the challenge.

The other half is how we deal with these risks.

It all comes down to building **resilience.**

And as Peter Drucker wrote:

Risk is of the essence, and risk making and risk taking constitute the basic function of the enterprise.[19]

The current risk profile of today's world has been summed up in one word: Polycrisis.

The World Economic Forum's Global Risks Report 2023 uses the term to explain how,

Present and future risks can also interact to form a 'polycrisis' – a cluster of related global risks with compounding effects, such that the overall impact exceeds the sum of each part.[20]

The WEF pooled 1,200 experts and summarised their findings, resulting in 10 short-term and long-term risks likely to affect the world as we know it. The first five short-term risks include the current cost of living crisis and involuntary migration.

So even though the tables and charts I have written about fall neatly into separate categories, the reality is much more intricate and complex. For instance, wars force up energy and commodity prices, exacerbating the cost of living crisis, leading to civil unrest and strikes that accelerate the risk of the erosion of social cohesion and societal polarisation. (The cost of living crisis and societal polarisation make the top 10 list of the 2023 risk report, by the way).

A PwC report in March 2023 lists the three main risks likely to affect businesses in the current era: cybercrime, supply chain and climate.[21] They have come up with three main factors which, for them, will serve as a basis for tackling risk and building resilience:

- **See it:** Start with what matters most
- **Share it**: Collaborate to eliminate blind spots
- **Sort it:** Turbocharge solutions with technology

Figure 11.4 The Risk-Resilience Cycle Model.

Considering this, I have developed a model for identifying and managing risks, which is especially useful for High Street SMEs.

I have called it the Risk-Resilience Cycle.

It consists of four elements:

1. Reserve
2. Detect
3. Act and Adapt
4. Integrate.

Let us take each in turn…

1. Reserve – minding the gap:

The first step in the Risk-Resilience Model is the principle of Reserve. It is nearly impossible to react and prepare for any eventual risk (as shown in the profile above). In times of polycrisis – especially on the High Street – SMEs tend to be the first to take the hit and are likelier to go under. Businesses must build the spare capacity needed to withstand shocks when they occur.

Reserve means adequate preparation beforehand to collapse the gap between risk and resilience and doing what is within its circle of control.

Regarding the impact versus likelihood scenario, Yossi Sheffi describes two foreseeable ways organisations can build a reserve: reducing the likelihood and the impact.[22]

Likelihood: A company can reduce the probability of disruptions by just being a 'good citizen' and implementing several of the principles we discussed in previous sections: addressing concerns such as designing and implementing up-to-date SOPs, which we will talk about in more detail in section three, maintaining good intra and inter labour relations by looking after their staff well, complying fully with regulations, and choosing suppliers carefully. Other reserves are implementing up-to-date, resilient and reputable cybersecurity and infrastructure, proper quality, safety and security measures, collaborative measures, and good relations with related industries and competitors.

Other modern ways include facilitating collaboration between different branches and departments (see collaboration) and building leadership capabilities for as many people as possible within the organisation. We will return to this in the next section of this book, under scalability.

Impact: Another way to build reserve is by implementing measures to mitigate the impact of potential risks, since it is impossible to fully prepare in advance for 'black swans' or the mixture of different crises that build up simultaneously. For these kinds of crises, Yossi Sheffi, in *The Power of Resilience*, outlines two ways to build reserve:

- Building Redundancy
- Building Flexibility

Let's use my speciality, community pharmacy, as an example to explain these options.

- *Redundancy:* 2023 marked a severe shortage in the supply of medicines throughout the UK. An article in the Guardian[23] and a documentary on Britain's ITV channel documented these challenges. According to reports by Community Pharmacy England, there were over 110 medicines in short supply, up from 56 in January 2022. Additionally, 87% of community pharmacists reported that patient health and safety were being put at risk.[24] This was not just a UK-wide phenomenon; it also extended into Europe – affected by the Suez Canal crisis, the impact of the Ukraine War, and a delay in supply due to attacks on the Red Sea and an increased volume of paperwork. However, these shortages were more pronounced in the UK due to the falling price of the pound (making medicines more expensive in the UK), Brexit, and the government's decision to cap drug spending. Successful businesses such as Day Lewis were able to weather the storm by diversifying their supply chain, increasing collaboration between different branches and competitors, improving collaboration between GP practices, increasing their inventory of items that are more likely to go out of stock, and establishing better communication with patients to find mutual ways to lessen the impact. These measures were instrumental in weathering the supply chain risks, leading them to increase their market share at a time when more established chains struggled to cope, sometimes leading to unprecedented closures or some companies having to completely exit the market altogether.

However, lack of purchasing power and space, as well as availability, meant that there was an upper limit on stock inventory that could lead to the following ways to mitigate risks.

- *Flexibility:* Flexibility implies exhausting the different uses of a given asset to maximise its profitability, putting less strain on other assets which are mostly affected by the occurrence. The UK government has used this effectively in relation to the current NHS increased waiting lists and GP shortage: flexibility has been achieved to lessen this load, for instance, by allowing pharmacists to supply hard-to-obtain medicines without a prescription, supply antibiotic medicines for common acute conditions, train dispensary staff to take up old traditional pharmacist roles and extend opening hours. 93% of community pharmacies took up this offer, and over 3,000 consultations were done in just the first three days.[25] The same principle could be used in SMEs by shifting demand to other stores with less capacity, collaborating with other enterprises, and upskilling training to equip staff to undertake more specialised tasks in case layoffs are required.

Flexibility and redundancy should be used together, and the best-performing SMEs would have some reserve (just-in-case scenarios) for both, before the risk occurs. However, reserves alone cannot build resilience if nobody is set, empowered, or trained to spot what's coming.

2. Detect – spotting the risks:

No matter how much redundancy and flexibility an organisation builds into its structures, or how it mitigates risk, what matters is how quickly it detects the problem and reacts. Detection time is measured from when a company realises it will be hit to when the disruption occurs. Detection time can be zero (such as in a fire), negative (after the damage has already been done), or positive (when you can see it coming).

As detailed previously, the company would have to rely heavily on its reserves in zero- and negative-time situations.

Some risks or trends can be detected months or years ahead, such as the current cost of living crisis (inevitable after COVID), the current ageing population in the West, the disruption caused by Brexit, the instability in the Middle East, or the rise of AI.

Other examples include suppliers' viability, crucial shipment equipment errors, and changes in government policies.

Others, like weather updates, potential customer or staff unrest, cash flow, or pandemics, have shorter detection times, but they can still offer time to detect.

Adequate business insurance is crucial for two main reasons: first, some insurers provide early risk warnings, helping businesses anticipate potential issues. Second, they ensure that the business has sufficient coverage – alongside redundancy and felxibility – to effectively mitigate any possible risks.

There are three things every company should have in place to enhance detection:

a. **The playbook:** Depending on the organisation, experience and regular drills are essential to reducing detection and response times. The most familiar example is the fire drill, but such exercises can – and should – be extended to cover a wide range of risks, including supply chain disruptions. These drills are particularly effective for high-likelihood events, regardless of their impact level. For SMEs on the High Street, which often have limited resources to anticipate every possible risk, the best approach is to identify and prioritise those risks most likely to cause significant harm to clients and the business. The playbook should then focus on these critical areas. Furthermore, these risk scenarios and responses should be regularly reviewed and adapted in line with changes in business strategy and the broader risk environment (see below).
b. **A collaborative approach:** In large parts, the staff who are most likely to detect risks are the ones who are *least likely* to have the empowerment to activate levers of detectability. Those often quick to detect are not top management but are on the shop floor with their ears to the ground. This was covered in depth under tangibility. Collaboration to increase detectability is also needed outside the organisation – government agencies, partners, and competitors. Companies can learn from each other, even those in seemingly unrelated fields (such as collaboration between Day Lewis and Timpson, for instance).
c. **Technology:** Technology, particularly AI, is becoming increasingly effective at identifying risks. From simple tools such as smoke alarms to advanced systems powered by AI, organisations can leverage technology to strengthen the first two strategies.

However, to further build resilience, the company needs to implement what may be the most important – acting on the information and adapting.

3. Act and adapt:

Sometimes, in high-stakes situations, there can be what is called 'paralysis analysis.' Sometimes, for companies, the problem is not to reserve or to detect – the problem is to act.

Most management books on resilience written in the last five years talk about the same principle:

In his book *Centennials*[26] Dr. Alex Hill discusses successful 100-year-old companies having a 'stable core' and a 'disruptive edge.'

In his new book, *Change*, John Cotter discusses the 'dual system' of successfully run businesses.[27]

Day Lewis takes this dual approach, calling it a 'change team' and a 'run team.'

The run team was responsible for the business' central managerial ethos: it was in charge of systems, policies, SOP processes, etc.

The 'change team' was responsible for all things innovation. They had informal links throughout the 250-odd stores and reported directly to the CEO and senior management.

We will cover this in more detail under strategy, but the main point is that some organisation members are working in tandem. Organisations that run under this 'change' and 'run' system are more likely to detect risks and report directly, bypassing the managerial hierarchy to enable senior management to 'turn the ship around quickly' as it were to mitigate and manage the risks.

For zero and negative response times for detectability – and even favourable response times in some cases – the goal is to build stronger resilience to enable the organisation to weather similar storms. This brings us to the final cog in the wheel: building resilience to risks.

4. Integrate:

In his classic book, *The Fifth Discipline*,[28] Peter W. Senge quotes from the legendary management guru Dr. W. Deming:

> *Our prevailing system of management has destroyed our people. People are born with intrinsic motivation, self-respect and joy in learning.*

Peter Senge says that the only way to build a consistent strategic, sustained competitive advantage is through continual learning and what he calls 'reflective conversation.'

The lessons learned from exposure to risk and its detectability will do the organisation no good until there are quantifiable, tangible and natural ways to integrate lessons learned into the fabric of the organisation's practice and adapt the organisation's culture to make this possible.

The key to integration is to develop mechanisms for codifying, recording, and integrating lessons learned after exposure to the risk, particularly from the first three points, into the organisation's culture and processes.

The easiest way to do this is to build a culture and process of learning and respect, where lessons learned from risk management are integrated into strategic and risk assessment decisions for the future, as discussed under values and culture previously.

This is where technology and AI can be most helpful. Once the learning process is integrated into systems, technology can turbocharge the systems to make integration faster, especially systems that run with minimal human intervention. This leaves humans and leaders to do what they do best – the tangibility aspects on the organisation.

Speaking of humans and leaders, investing in community, relationships, and team culture is one of the most effective buffers against the detrimental effects of stress. Integrating lessons learned under the above loop is more likely to stick if there is a sense of trust, support and community.

Being in a community where we feel a sense of trust and support acts as a buffer against the detrimental impacts of stress, lack of agency, and scarcity. This is why investing in community and relationships is so important. Everyone's in it together and can support each other. A sense of community builds natural resilience, making this risk-resilience model even more effective. That's why the first factor – tangibility – is so crucial in building resilience.

Through this loop of: reserve, detect, act, adapt, and integrate, organisations will continue to build more resilience into their cultures, people, and fabric. This will, in turn, incrementally increase their ability to weather (and even thrive) during seasons and times of risk.

In Part III, we will explore this principle of learning the Systems of Permanence more fully.

How can we combine all these to develop an exemplary operation of Permanence? This is where the next (and last) factor comes in.

Before the inevitable shocks happen, what you do determines whether your company will weather the storm. Resilience involves being solid and well-prepared for the inevitable.

However, as John Kotter says (paraphrased):

At the heart of it, the modern organisation is about removing uncertainty and minimising risk, which can lead to a focus on threats or perceived threats ... which leads companies to activate the 'survive' model ... this leads to a default focus on threats over opportunities. However, the key to continued success is maintaining an unwavering focus on opportunity, engaging as many others as possible, giving them permission and air cover to keep the noise down, and celebrating successes along the way.[29]

Risk and resilience, a bit like joy and sorrow, always go hand in hand.

Companies harnessing this risk–resilience model experience the Upshift[30] – a concept Ben Ramalingam discusses in his book of the same name, where businesses and leaders emerge stronger than before the crisis.

As we've just seen, focusing on threats alone, whether real or perceived, can be detrimental. We also need to focus on opportunities.

How do we do this? By turning to the dreaded "S" word – the next and final determinant.

Notes

1 The London Standard. Waterstones profits plunge as warehouse glitch costs £13.5 million: www.standard.co.uk/business/waterstones-profits-plunge-warehouse-glitch-books-retail-high-street-b1138251.html, accessed January 25, 2025.
2 BBC. Waterstones: Book delivery backlog due to technology upgrade: www.bbc.co.uk/news/entertainment-arts-62476802, accessed November 16, 2024.
3 Rumsfeld, Donald. *Known and Unknown: A Memoir*, Penguin, 2012.
4 Yossi, Sheffi. *The Power of Resilience: How the Best Companies Manage the Unexpected*, MIT Press (paperback edition), 2017.
5 Yossi, Sheffi. *The Power of Resilience: How the Best Companies Manage the Unexpected*, MIT Press (paperback edition), 2017.
6 Yossi, Sheffi. *The Power of Resilience: How the Best Companies Manage the Unexpected*, MIT Press (paperback edition), 2017.
7 Wikipedia. Suez Canal Obstruction: https://en.wikipedia.org/wiki/2021_Suez_Canal_obstruction, accessed November 10, 2024.
8 Taleb, Nassim. *The Black Swan: The Impact of the Highly Improbable*, Penguin, 2010.
9 Adjei, Steven N. *Pay The Price: Creating Ethical Entrepreneurial Success Through Passion, Pain and Purpose*, BlueCloud Publishing, 2022.
10 Thomasch, Paul, and Franklin Paul. False Web Report Plays Havoc with Apple Stock, *Reuters*: www.reuters.com/article/technology/false-web-report-plays-havoc-with-apple-stock-idUSTRE49250A, October 3, 2008, accessed August 29, 2025.
11 Dubois, D., D. D. Rucker, and Z. L. Tormala. From rumors to facts, and facts to rumors: The role of certainty decay in consumer communications, *Journal of Marketing Research*, 48(6), 2011, Pgs 1020–1032.
12 High Street Positives. Find Out Now Survey: www.highstreetpositives.org, May 10, 2025.
13 Mirror. Homebase puts huge 74 sites up for sale after falling into administration – see full list: www.mirror.co.uk/money/homebase-puts-huge-74-sites-34172963, accessed August 8, 2025.
14 The Birmingham Mail. More high street stores closing before Christmas after Homebase shuts: www.birminghammail.co.uk/news/money/more-high-street-stores-closing-30590646, accessed November 11, 2024.
15 The Big Issue. Can Christmas save Britain's high streets? It's complicated, experts say: www.bigissue.com/news/christmas-shopping-uk-high-street, accessed November 11, 2024.

16 Orben, Amy. The Sisyphean cycle of technology panics, *Perspectives on Psychological Science*, 15(5), 2020, Pgs 1143–1157.
17 Feifer, Jason. *Build for Tomorrow: An Action Plan for Embracing Change, Adapting Fast, and Future-Proofing Your Career*, John Murray Business, 2022.
18 Trustpilot. Timpson: https://uk.trustpilot.com/review/www.timpson.co.uk, accessed November 16, 2024.
19 Drucker, Peter. *Management: An Abridged and Revised Version of Management: Tasks, Responsibilities, Practices*, Routledge, 2015.
20 World Economic Forum. The Global Risks Report 2023: 18th Edition (January 2023): https://www3.weforum.org/docs/WEF_Global_Risks_Report_2023.pdf.
21 PwC. The Resilience Revolution: PWC'S Global Crisis and Resilience Survey 2023: www.pwc.com/gx/en/issues/crisis-solutions/global-crisis-survey.html
22 PwC. The Resilience Revolution: PWC'S Global Crisis and Resilience Survey 2023: www.pwc.com/gx/en/issues/crisis-solutions/global-crisis-survey.html
23 Boffey, Daniel. NHS medicines shortage putting lives at risk, pharmacists warn, *The Guardian*: www.theguardian.com/society/2024/jan/14/nhs-medicines-shortage-putting-lives-at-risk-pharmacists-warn NHS medicines shortage putting lives at risk, pharmacists warn, January 12, 2024.
24 Community Pharmacy England. Medicine Shortages: https://cpe.org.uk/dispensing-and-supply/supply-chain/medicine-shortages, November 27, 2024.
25 Community Pharmacy England. 3,000 Pharmacy First appointments carried out in first 3 days: https://cpe.org.uk/our-news/3000-pharmacy-first-appointments-carried-out-in-first-3-days
26 Hill, Alex. *Centennials: The 12 Habits of Great, Enduring Organisations*, Cornerstone Press, 2023.
27 Kotter et al. *Change: How Organizations Achieve Hard-to-Imagine Results in Uncertain and Volatile Times*, Wiley, 2021.
28 Senge, Peter. *The Fifth Discipline: The Art and Practice of the Learning Organization*, Second Edition, Random House Business, 2006.
29 Senge, Peter. *The Fifth Discipline: The Art and Practice of the Learning Organization*, Second Edition, Random House Business, 2006.
30 Ramalingam, Ben. *Upshift: Turning Pressure into Performance and Crisis into Creativity*, William Collins, 2023.

Chapter 12
The Fifth Determinant
Strategy

Strategy has now become so overused that it sometimes risks losing meaning. Sometimes, it's worth going back to the basics.

In their classic book *Playing to Win*, Lafley and Martin summarise the evolution of modern strategy as:

> *an integrated set of choices that uniquely positions the firm in its industry to create a sustainable advantage and superior value relative to the competition.*[1]

According to the strategy+business magazine, strategy has now evolved from a top-down directive approach to more of a personal endeavour. Its success will mainly come down to how it changes the way people think, feel, and act. In other words, it must capture not only the logical tenets of the organisation but also the visceral. It boils down to three actions: *refreshing mindsets, adopting new roles, and facilitating a new strategy dialogue.*[2]

Based on these three new actions, eight points for executing modern strategy come to mind:

- **Strategy is not planning:** In my work with middle management and employees, there is a general feeling that a document containing elements of each department's plans counts. It doesn't. Strategy is not ambitious goal setting, visions, or slogans.
- **Strategy is not to-do lists:** Having a to-do list for the day, month, week, or year doesn't equate to strategy.
- **Strategy cannot be siloed**: Strategy that remains in the confines of a few senior management, on the team board, or as a document in a company book remains just what it is: a document. Working with many companies on the High Street, I sometimes had to dig deep to find either the company's overarching strategy or even more frustratingly, its values.

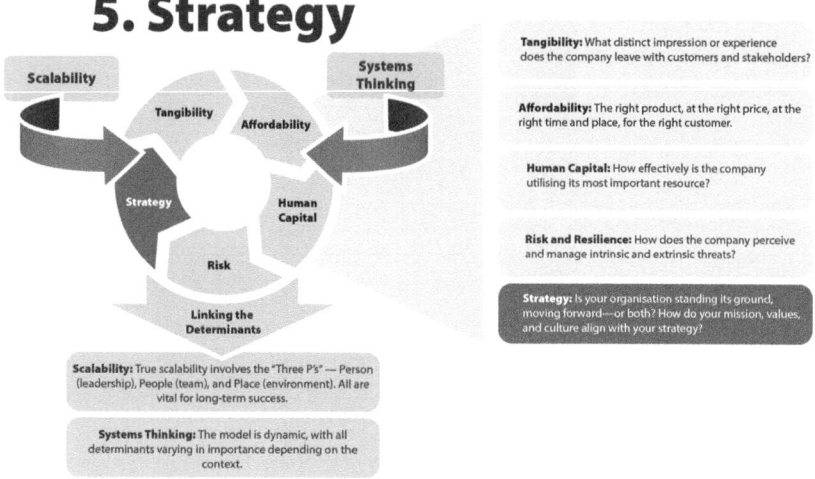

Figure 12.1 The Five Determinants Model: Determinant 5: Strategy.

- **Strategy cannot work on its own:** As detailed below from research on the companies mentioned, strategy, values, and culture go hand in hand: employees, middle management, and senior management work in tandem. You know your strategy, culture, and values have meaning when they are being talked about on the shop floor, discussed in team meetings, lived out by example by management and, most notably, implemented in day-to-day work in the company. This is tough, but as I have consistently found, the most resilient and successful companies mind the gap – and as Dr. Max McKeown consistently says, '*strategy is not a solo sport.*' [3]
- **Strategy must be personalised and agile:** A cursory look at all the companies I have referred to throughout the book, shows that each company's strategy is different and personalised to the company. A strategic document is never final, never complete, never finished. It will have to adapt to the constantly changing circumstances both within and outside the company, Kate Skipper, CEO of Waterstones, said in an interview with the *Retail Gazette*: '*We are very thankful to our bookselling teams who continue to create such welcoming new bookshops, tailoring each store to their local communities.*'
- **The clarity of your strategy depends on the clarity of your vision and values:** One reason most strategies fail is that the company's vision

Figure 12.2 Amy Webb's Futuristic Framework for Strategic Planning.[4]

is unclear; what it is trying to achieve is muddled, or the plan does not align with its values.
- **Strategy must combine short-term specific actions (tactics) with uncertain long-term action (vision)**: Amy Webb of the Future Today Institute, writing in *Harvard Business Review*, talks about Strategy Planning like that of a cone:[5]
- **Strategy is <u>always</u> about people:** Many strategy books, talks, and documents must remember this fundamental truth. Dr. Max McKeown, one of the UK's top strategy thought leaders, surmises:

This is … why there is an over-reliance on strategy documents and under-recognition of the role of people in making strategy fail or succeed.

The percentage of a strategy's success attributable to the document that describes it is relatively low, often around 10–20%, because the actions of people primarily drive success.

He continues:

70–80% of a strategy's success depends on the people who make it work – how they align their efforts, adapt to challenges, and work toward shared goals.

Without commitment, collaboration, and accountability from individuals, even the best documented strategy will fail.[6]

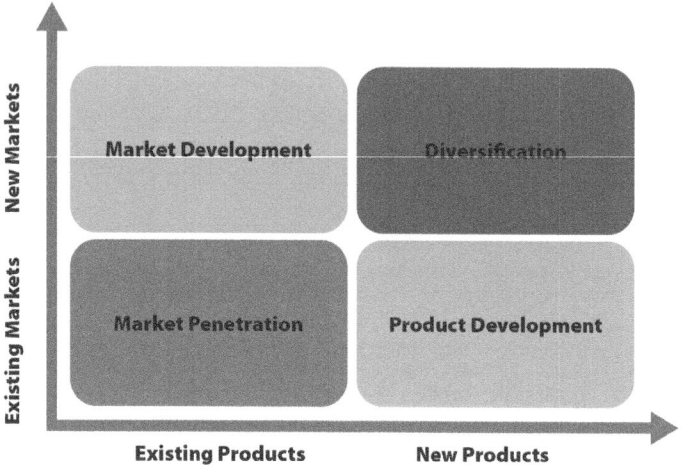

Figure 12.3 The Ansoff Model.

The strategies for all the companies below, differ in this definition. They depend on factors such as the resources available, the environment, competition, and leadership quality.

Does your company know your strategy?

The statistics are shocking. In a recent Gallup poll, a staggering 90% of UK workers felt disengaged from their jobs and were either loudly or quietly quitting.[7]

As Dr. Max McKeown says, why should employees care about the company's strategy if leaders don't care about employee opinions?

This is not limited only to employees. Perhaps more worryingly, middle management doesn't fare that better:

According to a study of 124 organisations by *MIT Sloan Review* in 2018, only 28% of middle management and senior executives responsible for executing strategy could list the top three priorities for their company's strategy.[8] The figure will probably be much lower due to the uncertainty caused by the economic downturn after COVID-19. I confirm this anecdotally with some of the High Street businesses I surveyed.

According to a recent report by consultancy firm McKinsey, over 60% of management's time is spent on repetitive, mundane tasks unrelated to the company's overarching strategy.[9]

For someone who has worked for over two decades in different retail settings on the High Street, I have seen a clear correlation between employee satisfaction, which ultimately contributes massively to company success, and what Christian Stadler calls in his book *Open Strategy*.[10]

The time when the strategy was just a function of the C-suite and stuck in company folders is rapidly becoming obsolete.

Strategy is powerful only when all the employees know what the strategy stands for and even when you use the approach to shape how you think.

In the 2024 edition of *The Strategy Book*[11], Dr. Max McKeown surmises that at its heart, strategy tries to answer six basic questions:

1 Where are you now?
2 Where do you want to go?
3 What's driving you to this point?
4 What's stopping you from getting there?
5 How and what will you do when you get there?
6 How will you measure progress on your journey?

(Dr. McKeown discusses how to use this practically with his Speed Strategy Framework.)

However, for this book, the strategy for High Street businesses is to tie in the knots of all I have outlined four operational models above into one flowing, coherent piece summarising the pathway to remain vibrant, thriving, and flourishing.

For strategy, it is a continuous process of:

1 My Exploit, Explore, Consolidate Model of Growth – Stand Your Ground, or Move Forward
2 The company actively working to stay in harmony with its environment (**the HOW Framework in Christian Stadler's book *Enduring Success***[12]).
3 Constantly aligning strategy and culture to form a harmonious organisation, as described in Charles Handy's four cultures model (from his classic book *Understanding Organisations*.)
4 Communication strategy to employees and stakeholders.

We will take these in turn.

1. Moving Forward or Standing Your Ground:
1a. Consolidate: Stand Your Ground Strategy: Why has Richer Sounds stopped opening new stores?
In their 2004 piece for *Harvard Business Review*, Charles O'Reilly and Michale Tushman discuss the ambidextrous organisation, one of a company's toughest strategic challenges.[13]

Being ambidextrous requires a tricky balancing act: requiring executives to **explore** new opportunities even as they work diligently to **exploit** existing capabilities, what I call 'moving forward or standing still.'

Few companies can balance these two well – many, including GE, Kodak, Nokia, and Boeing, have had trouble.

In my research into the five leading companies on the High Street and dozens of other small successful businesses, I have been impressed at how they have balanced these two tricky extremes – and how a 'one size doesn't fit all' approach has had to be used by each company. For instance In 2022–23, Day Lewis Chemists pressed pause on its relentless acquisition trail. Instead of chasing the next deal, they doubled down on their existing estate – moving stores to stronger locations, merging weaker ones, and letting go of branches where the footfall simply wasn't there. It was a deliberate 'catch-your-breath' moment to keep debt in check while costs were spiralling – a classic Stand Your Ground move that set them up to grow stronger when the winds turned fair again.

This is what I call exploitation in my Exploit, Explore, Consolidate model, which is an adaptation of exploitation before exploration as Ansoff's model showed earlier.

The Stand Your Ground strategy means ensuring the business consolidates and uses all its resources to create the most return possible. The key is to avoid losing market share to physical or online competitors.

It is continually looking at the business, making tweaks to its model, and staying agile to ensure it remains relevant.

James Timpson says:

> *All the time, we're breaking down the bits of the business to see what we can do to increase it – but also recognising that some parts of the company are always doing rubbish.*[14] (Exploit)

In an interview, Josh, the store manager at Richer Sounds, Plymouth, explained the Richer Sounds approach: a classic Stand Your Ground strategy:

> *We have not opened any new stores for a while now, so they are not growing their presence on the High Street, but are consolidating their brand presence online and by telesales – as well as advice over the phone – so our exploration is rather online. In the meantime, we are consolidating our presence by giving more and more power to our employees on the ground. As* [our founder], *Julian Richer, says, 'what goes up slowly, comes down slowly.'*

This is replicated in some form across all five SMEs I have examined.

Further examples include Waterstones, which opened just three stores in 2023, and John Lewis, which has not opened any new stores since 2021.

Day Lewis has also been at the forefront of innovation in pharmaceutical retail, pioneering medicine tills that allow patients to collect prescriptions even when the pharmacy is closed, and exploring the use of AI-driven robotic dispensing. The company has also enhanced freelance resourcing through partnerships with platforms such as Locate a Locum (https://locatealocum.com), expanded its private healthcare services, and continued to grow its nationwide store network through strategic acquisitions.

Yet there is also a warm, almost heroic feeling toward those who choose to strengthen what remains. These are the companies that resist the temptation to chase every new trend or innovation at the expense of their core identity.

There is wisdom in going against the grain—swimming against the current of constant reinvention and fashionable disruption. Sometimes, traditional knowledge is precisely that: genuine wisdom. As Aristotle observed, "Wisdom is knowledge of certain principles and causes," a sentiment echoed by William Magnuson in For Profit, who reminds us that the best businesses balance innovation with timeless fundamentals.[15,16]

Some of the most successful companies on the High Street—John Lewis, Waterstones, and Richer Sounds—embody these time-honoured principles. For them, progress has never meant abandoning their essence; instead, it has meant adapting carefully without overextending.

Trying to move forward and expanding too quickly can lead to overextending the company's resources,.

But sometimes, to stay relevant, this is necessary:

1b. Explore: The Moving Forward Strategy:
This would equate to diversification and market penetration on Ansoff's matrix (see diagram), which involves entering new markets through scalability or developing new products/services through diversification.

Launching into new markets is a critical factor which may determine success and is what Marshall Goldsmith, in his book *The Earned Life*, calls the Principle of Adjacency:

> *The odds of success favour the people who do not stray too far from their expertise, experience, and relationships. That doesn't mean we're restricted to small and incremental life changes. The change can be huge. But it requires adjacency – some connection, however indirect, to our track record of accomplishment.*

An example is the High Street sportswear chain JD Sports, which has recently branched out into gyms, aimed at the market just above the low-cost family fitness centres. JD Sports has also linked sportswear in its shops to discounts in its gyms.

JD Sports starts with an advantage over ordinary gyms because of their High Street presence, brand familiarity, penchant for high-quality sportswear, and market position.

Their gyms have proved very successful and add another dimension to the High Street: fostering community, collaboration, and customer agility, all of which are the ingredients for tangibility.

The same principle applies to HMV. In response to the decline in CD sales, the company adapted its business model by expanding its focus beyond CDs to include band memorabilia and merchandise, while doubling down on vinyl – an area in which it now leads the UK market. Furthermore, HMV has diversified into the broader entertainment sector, notably by hosting live performances in its stores to enhance customer engagement and brand relevance. For instance, UK hip-hop artist Aitch performed live and signed vinyl copies for fans in HMV stores across the country to mark the release of his 2025 album, '4,' as have other artists, some of which are mentioned below.[17]

They have also boldly opened new stores, including a flagship one in Birmingham, in Europe's biggest entertainment store, called the Vault. Spanning 25,000 sq ft across one floor – almost the size of 12 tennis courts – HMV Vault promises to become a 'nirvana for music and film fans' with dedicated spaces for vinyl, CDs and DVDs. In keeping with the theme of collaboration and community, there is also a permanent performance area for live music and performances.[18]

People visiting the store for the first time in 2019 said they had queued since the early hours, ahead of a performance by former One Direction member, the late Liam Payne.

In an even more audacious move, HMV opened another brand new store at its former location on 363 Oxford Street in November 2023, with, controversially, an entire floor dedicated to just books.

Again, this plan involves engaging the community through book signings, literary events, fan meet-ups, and traditional music performances by iconic artists – Madness and Hard-Fi performed at the opening ceremony, and many more have since followed.

According to one Timpson store manager, the key to the company's success lies in diversification:

From working with just shoe repair, we have now diversified into dry cleaning, car key programming, watch repairs and car fob repairs.

Our diversification follows the same formula: small, convenient, one-stop solutions for the customer on the go.

Our agility in diversification has primarily been the cornerstone of our continued growth and our expansion.[19]

They have also moved forward by expanding to 55 more shops right on the High Street. They are experts at copying what others are doing, trying

The Fifth Determinant: Strategy 137

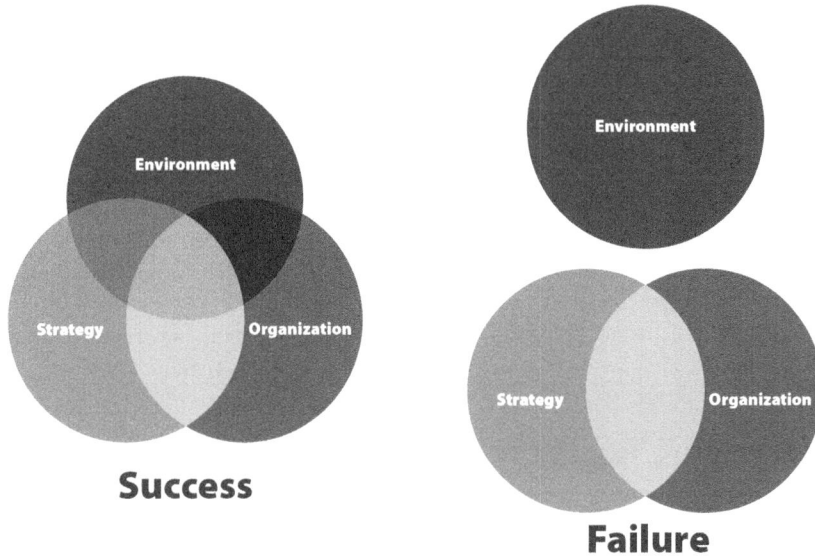

Figure 12.4 Christian Stadler's HOW framework.

them out (exploration), and, if they work, expanding them fast to integrate across all their stores (consolidation/exploitation).

However, adequate consideration of both strategies requires a keen, almost fanatical strategy of continually being aware of (and aligning with) your environment, the topic we turn to next.

2. Harmony with the environment: Christian Stadler's HOW framework:

In his book *Enduring Success,* Christian Stadler says the fate of organisations is not dissimilar to that of communities. If organisations do not ***continually and dynamically*** (emphasis mine) adjust to the communities they serve and are located in, they will soon cease to exist.[20]

I talked about Customer Agility under Tangibility. The HOW framework covers this, but under the guise of the whole organisation. And what is the best way to ensure harmony with the environment?

In their book *Open Strategy*, which talks about how successful companies open up their strategies beyond the C-Suite to all stakeholders, Christian Stadler et al. make this observation:

Open strategy has an astonishing track record: a survey of 200 business leaders shows that although open-strategy techniques were deployed for only 30 per cent of their initiatives, those same initiatives generated 50 per cent of their revenues and profits. This book offers a roadmap for this kind of success.[21]

In his theory of 'upside down management,' John Timpson says:

Several years ago, I realised the only way to provide truly excellent customer service is to trust our customer-facing colleagues with the freedom to serve customers how they know best. This meant turning our management structure upside-down. In doing so, we discovered that we had improved how we serve our customers and found a better way to manage the business.

At Timpson, employees can change stock, change prices, or even pay up to £500 to settle a complaint without authority from the head office.[22]

Michele Zanini, co-author of *Humanocracy*, wrote on the Thinkers50 website about James Daunt's style of CEO,

James Daunt shows what 21st-century leadership looks like: give people the freedom and responsibility to serve their customers. By trusting and equipping local teams to run their stores as community bookshops rather than corporate outlets, he transformed Barnes & Noble from a failing chain into a thriving business. His example proves that the best leaders succeed not as controllers-in-chief but as social architects.[23]

Social architects, according to Wikipedia, can design their spaces to fit in with their environment:

Social architecture is the conscious design of an environment that encourages a desired range of social behaviours that lead to a goal or set of goals ... Building design can refer to the architecture of social spaces such as bars and restaurants.

In social systems, 'social architects' seek to modify human behaviours through carefully designed programmes or workshops involving <u>the members of a population. These aim to improve, for example, the liveability, safety, or environmental impact of their communities.</u> [24]

In Waterstones, employees can stock a book if they feel it will sell well in a particular branch.

In Richer Sounds, sales colleagues can make a swift decision based on a customer's complaint immediately, rather than referring to the head office manager.

The only way to act in tune with your environment is to let those who know best – who are closest to the environment – make those crucial decisions. Then, we need a system where these little decisions across the company – whether one store or hundreds of stores – are fed back to management or the C-suite, influencing decisions and strategy moving forward.

Therefore, the strategy will aggregate all four factors given above: tangibility, risk, human capital, and affordability, to form an all-encompassing learning culture and roadmap.

Many companies fail because they try to align their strategy with their organisation, forgetting the apparent reality of the fast-changing third variable: the environment.

All success is successful adaptation.[25]

3. Aligning Strategy, Vision and Culture: Minding the Gap

As I sat with Yaa (not her real name), a High Street healthcare chain middle manager, I could sense her frustration and anger at top management.

'*What a waste of my time,*' she said.

All the middle managers were invited to a plush conference centre in the Midlands in the UK, where the top management unveiled a brand-new company strategy buzzword, complete with blazing lights, music, and a lot of fanfare.

Sitting amongst the 200-odd attendees, she felt anger. All of the middle managers had yet to be consulted about this. She wasn't sold on the strategy, and if she wasn't, then how was she supposed to communicate this to her team?

How do you make strategy work?

Yaa's fears were confirmed when I later worked as a freelance consultant for this company on the High Street.

She was brilliant with customers, hard-working, and loved her job. On the first day, I discovered that the same strategy document was stuck on the wall. It specified the company's values and strategic plans over the next five years. At the top was that same buzzword that had been so spectacularly unveiled a few years earlier.

Later in the day, I asked her whether she knew what differentiated the company she was working for from the competition – whether she knew what the company stood for and its future strategy.

She had no idea, though it was stuck there, right literally in her face, on the wall.

Imagine my surprise when I asked her next-level manager, who is in charge of 10 branches, and she struggled to answer too – she also had to read the strategy and values off the poster stuck on the wall.

How do you know your strategy is working? In a survey conducted by PwC, 500 senior executives said their overall strategy wasn't well understood, even within their own company.

I touched on this earlier.

As a middle manager once said to me:

I wish I had more control – I love my job, but I don't always love the corporate loopholes made by people in an office so far removed from the people they employ and the customers they try to help.

This is why strategy demands focused energy and thinking time. The idea of this part is to combine all four objectives above – tangibility, affordability, risk and resilience, along with human intellectual capital – into one coherent, flowing, adaptable document that embodies the three variables above. The hard part is communicating and exposing that strategy beyond the C-suite.

Of the five companies I had been researching, I had already read and memorised each company's values and I aimed to find how much those values had trickled down to the shop floor. Irrespective of the company and sector, I consistently found that the employees of the companies could, by and large, tell me the vision and values of their respective companies, collapsing the gap between the values and strategy documents the businesses espoused and what was observed on the shop floor. It also helped explain why Waterstones, Timpson and Richer Sounds were consistently listed as some of the UK's best companies to work for.

What struck me most was how they were able to use stories and everyday language to explain the general strategic direction of their companies, how companies, particularly Richer Sounds and Timpson's strategy, had influenced their culture, and how they were able to use this to form the company's unique identity.

In their article, *Creating a Strategy that Works*, Paul Leinwand and Cesare Mainardi list five ways to make your strategy 'stick.'[26]

Coincidentally, these can be used to tie back to the factors I have already talked about in the Operation of Permanence:

1. Commit to an identity (Tangibility)
2. Translate and align the strategy into the everyday culture (Risk and Resilience)
3. Put that culture to work (human intellectual capacity)
4. Cut away the fat: prune what doesn't matter so your message is clear and straightforward, and you can commit more resources to make it stick (Affordability)
5. Shape your future (Strategy)

In contrast, I spoke to other employees and middle management of some other High Street businesses. Once they could identify the values and strategy, they struggled to see how that fitted into their everyday working lives at the company.

In some cases, the employees felt they were being treated in **direct contradiction** to what they saw or felt the company stood for.

In other words, the company's strategy, values, and culture were misaligned.

As the London Underground blasts out on its platforms:

Mind the gap between the train and the platform.

And as John Kotter states beautifully in his 2021 book, *Change:*

> *This superior approach to strategy starts with the premise that what we typically ask executive committees to do today in strategy formulation and execution is an increasingly impossible task.*
>
> *To deal with all the barriers to change at the needed pace ... it would be best to have diverse masses dedicated to helping you lead change. That means people from all the relevant departments and staff from the top to the bottom of the organisation.*[27]

This is the topic we address next.

4. **Strategic Decisions in Action:**

Mostly, the issue is not formulating the strategy but its **execution** and **communication:**

Corporate strategy is usually only valid if people are engaged in making it work. To gain the leadership team's support, you must explain your strategic ideas, and communication and involvement at all levels are crucial. Selling is often the forgotten part of the process – the part that convinces people that this strategy is a credible and worthwhile way of shaping the future.

At the risk of labouring the point, Professors Markides and Mackennan of the London Business School emphasise the same point in their May 2024 paper, *3 Ways to Communicate Your Company's Strategy:*[28]

> *Employees need to know and understand their organisation's choices to execute their strategies effectively. Unfortunately, even clear communication of these choices is insufficient because communication without context can lead to misunderstandings and a lack of clarity. Since leaders can't explain the full context in which they made their strategy choices, they must find different ways to help their employees understand and appreciate their choices.*
>
> - ***Present the rejected alternatives:*** *This is especially crucial on the High Street. How will the strategy help the company stand its ground and thrive amid many failures and decimation? A good example is to show*

how an initial strategy was used by a competitor on the High Street that either failed or caused damage in a measurable, tangible way.
- **Link to purpose:** Strategic decisions are more digestible if there is a direct link between the 'why' of the organisation and your company's purpose or goal. As the writers say:

Explaining to employees how each choice is linked to the organisation's purpose is a good way for them to quickly understand the logic behind the choice without knowing all the deliberations that went into making it.

Of course, for this to work, the employees must know the company's purpose, values, and mission, which I covered in point 3.

Involve employees in strategy development: *This principle works, even down to the lower levels of management.*

I witnessed this in a role as a freelance locum in a particularly poorly performing branch while on duty.

In this branch, the team leader was 'underperforming' and was 'coerced' to step down.

They then brought in an accomplished team leader from another store to help bring the branch up to speed.

She brought in her team, spent a whole weekend when the store was closed, revamped the store, implemented processes, and brought the branch up to speed in record time.

But in two weeks, the store had fallen back to how it was. The team leader was almost in tears and blamed the staff whom she accused of 'trying to undermine her efforts,' and complained that she had been asked to 'babysit.'

But the truth was simple.

She had not utilised this third point which, incidentally, is the exact point Christian Stadler makes in *Open Strategy*.[29]

She had not brought the old team along for the journey or consulted them for their input, so they did not feel part of the efforts.

As soon as she left, they reverted to their old ways.

It is easy to blame the team leader, but it was an issue of practice training: if she had been trained in the principles listed above by senior management, she would have implemented the same when trying to revamp the failing branch.

I have discussed this at length under *human and intellectual capital*: finding ways to solicit employee feedback, get them involved, and help them find meaning in their work.

So, how does this work in practice?

Using this, the most obvious place to start is a SWOT analysis. This timeless tool is the most popular, and for good reason. But in this case, it is imperative to use the four operation points as a template to pinpoint where the company is at presently:

- Tangibility
- Human Capital
- Affordability
- Risk and Resilience

These can then be combined into a grid framework that employees agree upon at all levels.

This grid needs to answer three basic questions:

1. Where is the company now regarding these determinants?
2. Where do we need to be?
3. What is the quickest time frame we can use to get there?

This framework makes communication and execution much more effective, as all stakeholders can quickly aggregate information into a dynamic document.

To continually stay relevant, a company needs to do two things:

- Be a continually rapidly learning organisation at all levels, for instance, using the risk-resilience model I explained earlier. As Peter Senge says:

In the long run, the only sustainable way of competitive edge is your organisation's ability to learn faster than its competitors.[30]

- To eliminate thinking in silos and develop system thinking.

To illustrate, let's start with the funny but true story of how a notebook, two old friends, and a 1979 Rolls-Royce parked in the wrong spot were the catalysts for a multi-million dollar deal.

Notes

1 Lafley, A. G. and Roger L. Martin. *Playing to Win: How Strategy Really Works*, Harvard Business Review Press, 2013: https://hbr.org/2014/12/playing-to-win-how-strategy-really-works, accessed December 18, 2014.
2 *Strategy+Business*. A guide for practising strategy in an uncertain world: www.strategy-business.com/article/Practicing-strategy-in-an-uncertain-world
3 McKeown, Max. *The Strategy Book: How To Think and Act Strategically to Deliver Outstanding Results*, Financial Times Series, FT Publishing International, 2024: https://thespeedstrategy.com

4   Webb, Amy. How to do strategic planning like a futurist, *Harvard Business Review*: https://hbr.org/2019/07/how-to-do-strategic-planning-like-a-futurist, July 30, 2019.
5   Webb, Amy. How to do strategic planning like a futurist, *Harvard Business Review*: https://hbr.org/2019/07/how-to-do-strategic-planning-like-a-futurist, July 30, 2019.
6   McKeown, Max. *The Strategy Book: How To Think and Act Strategically to Deliver Outstanding Results*, Speed Strategy Edition, Harlow, UK, Pearson, 2024.
7   AoEC. Gallup report calls for action on UK employee engagement: www.aoec.com/knowledge-bank/gallup-report-calls-for-action-on-uk-employee-engagement/?utm_source=chatgpt.com
8   Sull, Donald, Charles Sull, and James Yoder. No one knows your strategy—Not even your top leaders, *MIT Sloan Review*: https://sloanreview.mit.edu/article/no-one-knows-your-strategy-not-even-your-top-leaders/?utm_source=chatgpt.com, February 12, 2018.
9   McKinsey. Stop wasting your most precious resource: Middle managers: www.mckinsey.com/capabilities/people-and-organizational-performance/our-insights/stop-wasting-your-most-precious-resource-middle-managers, accessed March 10, 2023.
10 Stadler, Hautz, Julia Hautz, Kurt Matzler and Stephan Friedrich von den Eichen. *Open Strategy: Mastering Disruption from Outside the C-Suite*, MIT Press, 2021.
11 McKeown, Max. *The Strategy Book: How to Think and Act Strategically To Deliver Outstanding Results*, Financial Times Series, FT Publishing International, 2024.
12 Christian, Stadler. *Enduring Success: What We Can Learn from the History of Outstanding Corporations*, Stanford University Press, 2011.
13 Rogers, Charlotte. Timpson CEO: Our business shouldn't exist anymore, *Marketing Week*: www.marketingweek.com/timpson-ceo-business, March 18, 2022.
14 Rogers, Charlotte. Timpson CEO: Our business shouldn't exist anymore, *Marketing Week*: www.marketingweek.com/timpson-ceo-business, March 18, 2022.
15 Aristotle. *Metaphysics*, Book I, 982a. Translated by W. D. Ross, Oxford University Press, 1924.
16 Magnuson, William. *For Profit: A History of Corporations*, Basic Books, 2022.
17 Retail Gazette. HMV returns to profit as vinyl overtakes CD sales, 16th January 2023: www.retailgazette.co.uk/blog/2023/01/hmv-profit-vinyl/#:~:text=HMV%20returns%20to%20profit%20as,David%20Bowie%20and%20The%20Beatles, accessed February 16, 2025.
18 Madden, Sophie and Jessica Labhart. HMV Birmingham: Can a record store work in a digital age?, *BBC News*: www.bbc.co.uk/news/uk-england-birmingham-49681272, October 11, 2019, accessed November 16, 2024.
19 Madden, Sophie and Jessica Labhart. HMV Birmingham: Can a record store work in a digital age?, *BBC News*: www.bbc.co.uk/news/uk-england-birmingham-49681272, October 11, 2019, accessed November 16, 2024.
20 Stadler, Hautz, et al. *Open Strategy: Mastering Disruption from Outside the C-Suite*, MIT Press, 2021.
21 Stadler, Hautz, et al. *Open Strategy: Mastering Disruption from Outside the C-Suite*, MIT Press, 2021.
22 Stadler, Hautz, et al. *Open Strategy: Mastering Disruption from Outside the C-Suite*, MIT Press, 2021.

23 Thinkers50. A unique and compelling listing of 50 inspiring leaders drawn from around the world. Leaders50 provides a bridge between thinkers and practitioners: https://thinkers50.com/leaders50, accessed August 28, 2024.
24 Wikipedia. Social architecture: https://en.wikipedia.org/wiki/Social_architecture
25 McKeown, Max. *The Strategy Book: How to Think and Act Strategically to Deliver Outstanding Results*, Financial Times Series, FT Publishing International, 2024.
26 Leinwand, Paul and Cesare R. Mainardi. Creating a strategy that works, *Strategy+ Business*, February 9, 2016: https://www.strategy-business.com/article/00344.
27 Kotter, John P., Vanessa Akhtar and Gaurav Gupta. *Change: How Organizations Achieve Hard-to-Imagine Results in Uncertain and Volatile Times*, John Wiley, 2021, Pgs 6–8.
28 Markides, Constantinos C. and Andrew MacLennan. 3 ways to clearly communicate your company's strategy, *Harvard Business Review*, May 24, 2024: https://hbr.org/2024/05/3-ways-to-clearly-communicate-your-companys-strategy.
29 Christian, Stadler. *Enduring Success: What We Can Learn from the History of Outstanding Corporations*, Stanford University Press, 2011.
30 Senge, Peter. *The Fifth Discipline: The Art and Practice of the Learning Organization*, Second Edition, Random House Business, 2006.

Part III

The Systems of Permanence

Introduction:

Systems of Permanence: Balancing Mindset with the Determinants

In this third part of the book, the idea is how the mindset of Permanence and the dynamic operations combine to form a system:

As the diagram below shows, the determinants have to work together as an integrated system (systems thinking), bearing in mind the scalability strategy of the firm, using the Three Ps of scalability: **Personal, Personnel,** and **Place.** And this is where we start.

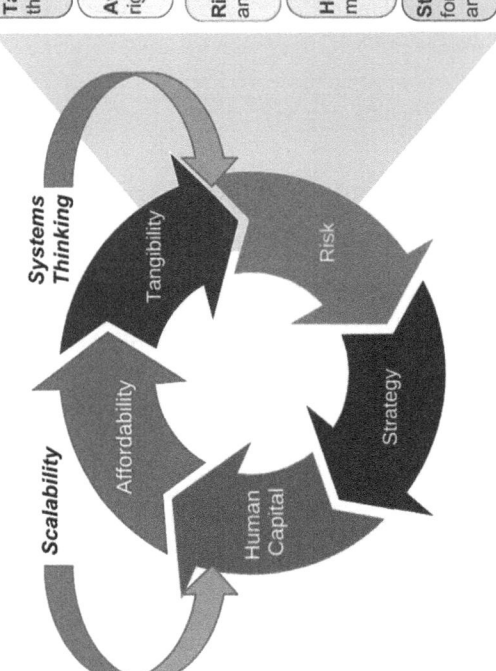

Figure PIII.1 The five determinants model.

Chapter 13

The Three Kinds of Scalability

The most successful businesses (and other businesses, for that matter) on the High Street always go through three phases to scale sustainably correctly.

Most books discuss scalability by increasing the company's geographical reach, such as John A. List's *The Voltage Effect*[1] or Reid Hoffman's *The Masters of Scale*.[2]

However, this book argues that every business needs three kinds of scalability to ensure lasting success: the Three Ps: *Personal, Personnel, and Place*.

In one of his bestselling books, Marshall Goldsmith, arguably the world's number one leadership coach, states, '*What got you here won't get you there*.' [3] He indicates the constant need for evaluation, learning, and an increased mindset, particularly for the CEO/entrepreneur, stressing that increased growth of a company is never achieved without a corresponding growth of the leader.

This is comparable to the 7th Habit in Stephen Covey's classic, *The Seven Habits of Highly Effective People*[4] – 'sharpening the saw' – to start the process of successful scalability.

This personal scalability leads to **Personnel** scalability, where the company culture is continually enhanced. Each organisation member takes responsibility for their learning, and there is an effective feedback loop that ensures best practices are shared. Place (Geographical) scalability, discussed in various business books, can only be achieved after this.

Personal and Personnel scalability involve the intangibles: values, cultures, and learning, while Place scalability involves the tangibles: location, services, and products.

- Personal Scalability
- Personnel Scalability
- Place Scalability

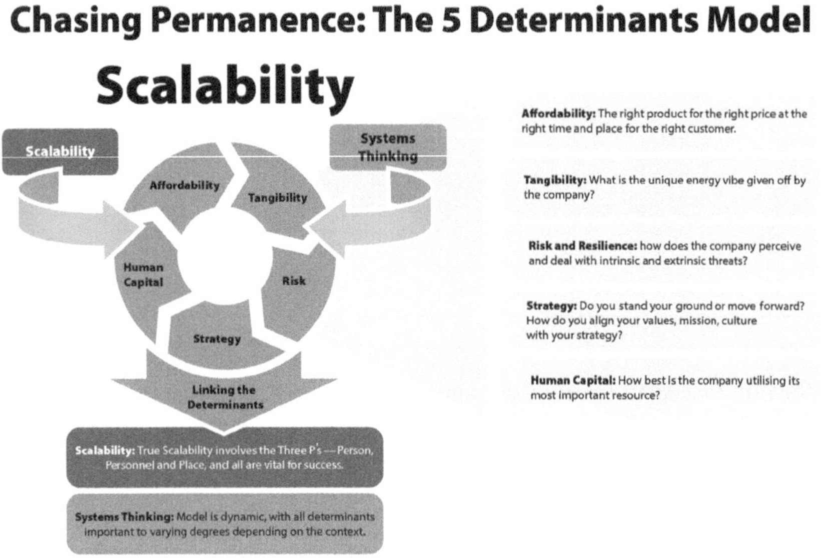

Chasing Permanence: The 5 Determinants Model
Scalability
Scalability
Systems Thinking
Affordability
Tangibility
Human Capital
Risk
Strategy
Linking the Determinants
Scalability: True Scalability involves the Three P's—Person, Personnel and Place, and all are vital for success.
Systems Thinking: Model is dynamic, with all determinants important to varying degrees depending on the context.
Affordability: The right product for the right price at the right time and place for the right customer.
Tangibility: What is the unique energy vibe given off by the company?
Risk and Resilience: how does the company perceive and deal with intrinsic and extrinsic threats?
Strategy: Do you stand your ground or move forward? How do you align your values, mission, culture with your strategy?
Human Capital: How best is the company utilising its most important resource?

Figure 13.1 The Five Determinants Model: Scalability.

CHASING PERMANENCE:
THE SCALABILITY IMPERATIVE PROCESS
01
PERSONAL SCALABILITY:
INCREASING THE LEADERSHIP CAPACITY OF THE LEADER
02
PERSONNEL SCALABILITY:
INCREASING THE LEADERSHIP CAPACITY OF THE TEAM
03
PLACE SCALABILITY:
INCREASING THE CAPACITY OF THE LOCATION(S)
04
CONSOLIDATE OR EXPAND:
THE STAND YOUR GROUND OR MOVE FORWARD STRATEGY
CEO
HOW TO SCALE CORRECTLY

Figure 13.2 The Scalability Imperative Process.

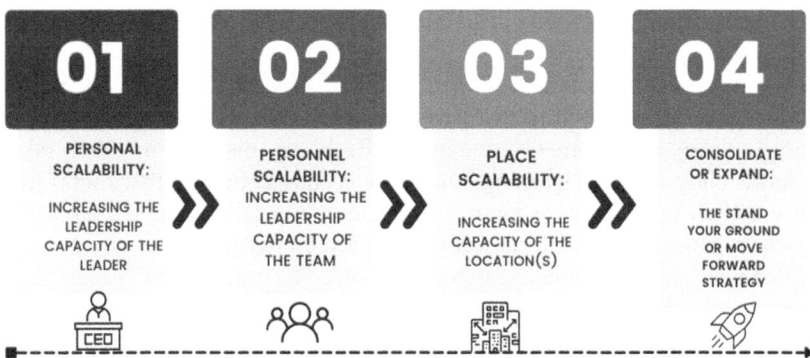

1. Personal Scalability – The Principle of the Notebook

In 1979, Kirit Patel, CEO of HM Patel Chemists, owned just two pharmacies in the UK, both on the High Streets of different London suburbs. He continually used up his time as he dashed between them. Still, he was determined to prioritise learning and development, so a half-day on Wednesdays was set aside for informal CPD – a briefcase, a notebook, and a pen.

In those days, business books, executive education and webinars were not available to the semi-educated immigrant in the UK who had emigrated from Kisumu, Kenya.

So, his personal development consisted mainly of meeting successful businessmen, old civil servants, young entrepreneurs, and anyone and everyone who had something to say, arranging coffee with them and getting out his notebook and pen.

He was not elitist, but he had a burning passion: the desire to learn and be successful at expanding his burgeoning pharmacy retail business.

On one such Wednesday, he met two successful businessmen, Monty Cohen, who had stepped in to mentor and be a friend to another business tycoon, Dadu Patel[5].

'When you go to see a business or to make a deal, always park your Rolls-Royce in the CEO's slot,' Monty was advising Dadu, who had purchased a gleaming 1979 Silver Shadow II, of which he was very proud.

'Really?' Dadu said doubtfully, 'won't that just make him angry?'

'Yes, and that is the point. He will come in and demand to know who has dared to park in his private spot. He'll be angry, but also jealous of the car. Either way, you'll get an audience with the top man – the rest is up to you. If you park around the corner, you'd have to go through the arduous process of meeting lots of gatekeepers before, if ever, you get to meet the MD.'

When he heard this, the young Kirit Patel immediately went on a hunt. Following Monty's advice, he secured a Rolls-Royce. This trick eventually enabled him to partner with Vijay Patel, who co-founded one of the UK's biggest pharmaceutical wholesale companies, Waymade PLC, currently worth over £40 million.

Applying what he learned from his Wednesday learning days, Kirit Patel expanded his family business from HM Patel's Chemist to Day-Lewis Chemist, which has now become the UK's largest independent pharmacy chain with over 250 branches.

Great leaders master themselves before they master the world.

- Sanjiv Patel

Crucially, the current CEO, his son Jay Patel, has continued this same networking and learning – mostly with CEOs and leaders in entirely different sectors. By his admission, this is a big part of Day Lewis' current enduring success.

Any company's ongoing success will only grow if the CEO follows the notebook principle.

This desire for lifelong learning has three crucial advantages: it allows one to be open-minded, avoid blind spots, and build up a reservoir of information.

At the beginning of this book, I laid out seven principles defining a Permanence mindset. These principles are the same and have been for millennia. Still, their application in a constantly evolving culture may change. Using these principles as a personal compass, a fulcrum, means that as a CEO, staying relevant is always a relentless pursuit, a never-ending journey to get better and better and to remain relevant despite the rise in uncertainty – just as the biggest and most successful bands have done over decades.

The more the CEO can scale their mindset and enlarge his vision and perspective, the easier it is to do the next scalability type: scaling people.

As Jim Collins reiterates:

> *As your company grows from 1x to 2x to 10x, are we willing, as leaders, to grow our leadership capacity from 1x to 2x to 10x? Personal scalability is a responsibility, a decision, a wilful action.*[6]

The more you scale personally, the better your view will be. This principle applies equally to scaling a mountain and scaling a business.

This is what I have called **the Notebook Principle.** Kirit Patel's notebook in his pocket at all times was a sign of a deeper meaning – a man who was committed to being a lifelong learner.

Therefore, personal scalability encapsulates a humble personality, a willingness to learn from everything and everyone, and a desire to put what we learn into practice, mainly growing in the seven mindsets of Permanence I wrote about in Part 1 of this book.

Many of the best leaders share this attitude.

Personal scalability also involves values. Although a company's values should remain the same, how they are applied will differ from culture to culture, period to period, and branch to branch.

It involves a deep knowledge of oneself, continually growing, and understanding the actual values that inform leaders and how best to ensure those values remain relevant in a dynamically changing world.

One of the UK's foremost leadership thinkers, John Adair, mentioned the two most cardinal errors of leadership in his 2005 classic, *How to Grow Leaders*[7]:

- *To act is easy; to think is hard:*
- *Top strategic teams' chief error in this field is that they only think and think once it hurts. Lacking clear thinking about leadership and its relation to management means they are at the mercy of the winds.*

What are the winds now?

These are the changes I enumerated earlier in this book: the rapid shift in customer behaviour and the decline of our High Streets. The companies that I have had the advantage of working for, which are struggling on the High Street, have yet to take the time to **think**.

But that's half the problem.

The other half is that the more you scale, the lonelier it becomes. The more challenging it becomes, the harder it becomes to breathe.

Maybe that's where the expression 'scaling a mountain' comes from.

That's why a recent post by renowned leader John C. Maxwell regarding Personal Scalability is so apt:

> *You cannot give what you do not have. We teach what we know, but we reproduce what we are. The only way you can develop better people on your team is for you to get better. The only way you can raise the bar for the next level for your team, which you want to help with, is to raise your bar. You cannot take people where you have not been.*[8]

The only way to improve a business is to improve oneself – accepting critical feedback and listening to learn without judgement are characteristics that help you scale yourself.

As I reiterate later on, James Timpson spends almost a third of his working hours studying other businesses. Sam Patel, the international director of Day Lewis, spends a large chunk of his time looking at different firms on the continent and learning from how improving oneself does not only mean increasing your learning capacity. There is a broader meaning here, as I expand further in my first book, *Pay The Price* – scalable personal success also includes increasing the concept of Personal Capacity:

Personal Capacity = Leadership Ability + Resources + Stewardship

> *Our abilities are not just related to our purposes or vision. They depend on investments in our health, fitness (emotional, mental and spiritual) and our close relationships.... Simply put, we must keep learning.*[9]

Sometimes, visionary leaders' biggest fault is moving too fast, breaking too many things, and leaving their team behind.

If you drive the bus and leave behind the passengers, you'll end up lost, alone and lonely, which is what the next stage of scalability examines.

2. Personnel Scalability

I asked Lynn, a middle manager at a fast-growing healthcare chain, why she wanted to quit.

The SME on the High Street had just expanded into another town, and suddenly, the CEO spent most of his time in this shiny new branch. The other branches spread throughout the South West felt they needed to be addressed.

> *Now that the business has expanded and we have a shiny new branch, we rarely see or hear from him anymore. I have just become a number, another cog in the wheel.*
>
> *I don't know what this company stands for anymore; I just feel like we've become just another business down the street,' she reiterated.*
>
> *The other branches began to suffer, as the staff started to feel neglected.*

Another middle manager, George, in another High Street Business chain, was a rising star who quickly got promoted due to his tremendous potential in leadership and management.

On a hectic day, I caught 15 minutes with him uninterrupted.

A month earlier, he had resigned from area management due to rising mental and physical health issues and had taken a job as a trainer and IT fixer in the same company.

You would never have thought it by looking at him – he seemed incredibly fit, had an upbeat demeanour, and carried a quiet confidence.

Interestingly, George knew the values stuck on the wall that I had seen earlier and could recount them by heart. He was actually at the conference when the values were unveiled with much pomp and pageantry.

I asked him what the values meant to him.

He called them a load of ##@@%!!

He began to tell me a story about how he had also quit – and this was remarkably similar to what I witnessed Anisha do two weeks later.

His potential as a leader was recognised early. He met with top management, who recommended he became a middle manager. It was a moment of pride for him; he travelled across the country, saw things first hand, and met with many members of top management. He was feted.

Then the reality hit. The same issues I had mentioned earlier.
So he quit.
But it wasn't even the quitting that surprised me – it was the fact that all the frontline staff and employees around them had the same reaction:
I could almost read the 'I told you so' in their eyes.
Later, I chatted with one of the longest-serving frontline staff members, who had worked for this company for nearly thirty years.
She summarised the whole experience in an unprintable sentence.

They give you the position, make you feel important; then they sh££## all over you.

None of the staff – not even the lower or middle management – know who their CEO is.
Not one.
Contrast this with James Timpson's approach:

What amazes me when I speak to other retail chief execs is they always say: I don't spend enough time in the shops. They go on Friday afternoon and see a few shops, but I don't think it works well like that.[10]

He spends two days a week visiting shops, not to rap them over their heads by telling them what they were not doing right, but to learn from them and see how what they were doing could be replicated in other branches.
Upside-down management.
Sometimes, the most challenging aspect of scalability for smaller High Street businesses is the CEO's transition from patriarch to leader.
From being a mother hen to being an eagle with a bird's eye view.
This is because many SMEs and, to some extent, more prominent High Street brands still need to practise **Personnel Scalability.**
These conversations brought my mind back to an interview with Rosie, area manager for over 40 Day Lewis stores in the South West. I had also worked for Day Lewis off and on for almost half a decade.
The difference between Rosie of Day Lewis and George and Lynn of the other company was striking.
In the hour we spent together, she rattled off an impressive deep knowledge of the company, their strategy for the year (at the time of the interview, we were coming out of COVID), and how she goes about recruiting staff. She talked about the support she had from Jay, Sam and Rupa Patel and the top leadership; and how Day Lewis even had a Regional Support manager whose sole job was to support the area and store managers in personal and professional training, resilience and growth.

She talked about her direct access to the CEO (actually, she arranged the interview I had with him), her autonomy, and how she could give that same autonomy to the managers below her.

She talked about the learning partnerships, joint ventures and support networks the company had developed with other High Street chains in different sectors, such as Timpson, Medivet, and Cohens Chemists (interestingly, another High Street pharmacy chain), as well as other High Street stores.

She also affirmed the Moving Forward, Stand Your Ground strategy, saying that Day Lewis had paused growth to consolidate its gains after the pandemic and resumed expanding in late 2023.

She touched on the extensive training she had received and how they sought an employee who embodied their values and trained their managers.

I interviewed Jay and one of the pharmacist managers, Melissa, a month later. I had seen the principle of Personnel Scalability in action. Melissa and Jay recounted, almost word for word, what Rosie had told me months earlier.

The Notebook Principle, started by Kirit Patel, had spread to his children, the area managers, retail storefront managers, supervisors, and team leaders.

We Reproduce What We Are

But that's not all,

John Adair reiterates:

> *The basic principle in leadership development is that an organisation should only give a team a leadership role or position to someone trained. A natural starting point is not middle or senior managers but team leaders.*
>
> *Team leaders are at the base of a natural pyramid,* he goes on to say. *The natural window of opportunity for training leaders to become good leaders is when they are on the threshold of becoming leaders for the first time. Miss that opportunity, and you may have already missed the boat.*[11]

If this doesn't happen, he says, the organisation will have to fill slots with poor leaders, if they are leaders at all. This will have an ***inevitable effect on morale.***

The best CEOs spend the latter half of their time mentoring middle management as much as possible, and so on down the pyramid.

Reinforce values – *daily.*

The key to personnel scalability is simple but complex.

> Instil the values you want to teach in your company by instilling a culture of mentorship, starting with the CEO themself.

In turn, they can do what they are best at: inspiring, mentoring, and coaching the management and team leaders below them in the pyramid.

I have seen this in the companies doing well on the High Street: Richer Sounds, Timpson, Waterstones, and Day Lewis. They have all found ways to collapse the traditional hierarchy between senior management and team leaders so that the perceived trappings of seniority are diminished, and training at all levels of the organisation is installed. This shows in morale: the team leaders and lower-level managers feel part and parcel of the organisation, feel that their decisions matter, and are more likely to accept training and mentorship.

This extends not only from the team leaders but also to middle managers.

Another employee experience survey at data company, Percerptyx, conducted a study that showed over 25% of middle managers felt miserable at work.[12]

This is hardly surprising.

Middle management has been criticised in the last five years, especially for adding bureaucracy to the organisation. In 'The Great Unloosing,' entire companies are actively eradicating middle management. Bayer, the pharmaceutical giant, plans to save over $2 billion by doing this.

In a recent interview with Gallup, Novartis CHRO Steven Baert implied that Novartis is also following suit.

Steven Bartlett, author and leading podcaster, recently said on LinkedIn:

> *When you talk to managers, you feel they're important. When you talk to leaders, you get the feeling that you're important – this is what separates managers from leaders.*[13]

Middle management–bashing is the new thing.

Is this the new way to go?

Not so fast.

One thing I have noticed about the companies I surveyed on the High Street is that instead of eliminating middle management, they have found a way to collapse the hierarchy gap by utilising middle management to do what they do best.

Timpson's boss, James Timpson:

> *The company seeks to operate with a flattened hierarchy. While Timpson accepts that the firm needs people to manage, he is adamant that anyone who thinks they are better than anyone else can find a job elsewhere.*[14]

In a recent McKinsey study, it was surprising to note that 59% of middle managers indicated that they wanted more autonomy and agency, rather than pay rises. 44% cite organisational bureaucracy as the most damaging factor affecting their performance.[15]

In one study, organisations whose managers consistently demonstrated key leadership behaviours delivered returns twice as high as those that did not, provided these managers were empowered to perform at their best. This included acting as the critical link between vision, strategy, and execution; receiving clear expectations; having access to targeted training; and operating within well-designed support systems.

A more recent study published by MIT Sloan further underscored the importance of middle management, highlighting its central role in cultivating a healthy and vibrant organisational culture.

The most effective managers excel not only in their own performance but also in identifying, inspiring, and developing the next tier of team leaders and supervisors (leading above), while also translating frontline insights and operational realities to the executive level (leading below). Crucially, they do this while avoiding the drag of bureaucratic, non-managerial tasks that can sap energy and diminish their impact.[16]

Earlier in the book, I spoke about middle manager Kerry, who flourished in her role because she was primarily growing the managers of the teams 'below' her.

And even better, if the pyramid is flatter, as Day Lewis is trying to implement, then it goes without saying that strategy execution and validation is more straightforward to scale than if they have to go through many layers.

In effect, in the stories I have given above, and many others I have encountered as well as many other studies that have been conducted, the most significant factor in middle management – which of course filters down to team leaders, employees and even recruitment – is simple:

It is whether the leaders at the top walk the walk instead of talking the talk.

In light of this, and even though correlation did not necessarily imply causation, I decided to check out the year performance of Day Lewis versus their competitor on the High Street I talked about earlier. Sure enough, their end-of-year financial results suggest confirmation of what I had seen:

Gross profit in Day Lewis 2022 (latest figures available) increased by £4.7m to £115.9 million. At the same time, competitors like Lloyds and Boots Pharmacy were closing down community pharmacies or exiting the sector altogether.

Their main competitor had lost over £30 million over the same period.[17]

The reasons given were also telling. While Day Lewis had increased its profit margin by delivering better professional services (such as blood pressure checks, COVID vaccinations, and flu shots), its competitors had given their reasons for the loss on reduced prescription numbers.

How is this relevant?

Successive UK governments have been trying to shift community pharmacies away from dispensing prescriptions and toward a more clinical role.

This has diverted funds from just reimbursing for dispensing drugs to being more service and community-oriented (such as prescribing, blood pressure monitoring, and vaccinations), which has the added advantage of being impossible to replicate online.

This is combined with the fact that online pharmacies such as Pharmacy2U and Pharmazon Direct are increasingly stealing market share by dispensing over 2 million prescriptions online annually with free delivery as discussed earlier.[18]

The traditional pharmacy model is dying.

Day Lewis had thought through its strategy and delivered it to take advantage of the government's new direction. It tapped into collaboration and community and reaped the rewards where competitors were failing.

To summarise this part of scalability, something happened that summarises it beautifully.

A few months ago, I was contracted to work as a freelancer for a nationwide healthcare chain in one of the UK's major cities.

I noticed an extraordinary phenomenon after working in many of their stores (they had 30 stores scattered on various High Streets in the city).

The stores were divided into sub-areas, each headed by a different manager.

I noticed that one sub-area was consistently performing better than the other: the shops were clean, the staff were hard-working and seemed happier, the shops were managed well by team leaders, and the NHS-commissioned services were consistently delivered better. The other area was almost the opposite: the staff seemed stressed, the stores needed to be appropriately stocked, and customers constantly complained.

I asked for an audience with the manager of the better performing shop and asked her what her secret was. Her five-sentence answer was simple and profound.

'Steven,' she said to me with a smile on her face and a wink in her eye,

I grow my team leaders.

But scaling is not always limited to **Personal** or **Personnel**. Inevitably, companies must decide how to (or not) scale geographically within the store or increase the number of stores/locations within a sensible time frame without over-extending itself.

We can illustrate this using the true but sad story of a woman who racked up a debt of £11,000 (around $15,000) due to the poor scaling strategy of a now-defunct High Street chain.

3. Place Scalability:

Jane (not her real name) was in real trouble.

She had four children, and she was only 33. Having so many children so soon had taken its toll on her emotional and physical health.

She, therefore, decided to take some action to remedy the situation.

On 11 July 2024, she booked into the UK's largest High Street plastic surgery chain, SK:N, and paid £11,000 to finally achieve her dream of looking like her 22-year-old self.

The next day, she took off to her first appointment for abdominal cosmetic surgery and liposuction.

But when she arrived, she had the shock of her life.

Her local SK:N company had closed its doors, and there was a note on the doors of the branch in Essex, near London:

We are sorry this branch has now closed permanently. Please refer to our website for further details.

When Jane checked out the website, there were few details other than that 'its clinics have ceased trading' immediately and that it is doing 'all it can' to address its patients' concerns.

Its website had been taken down. (However, at the time of writing, it was reportedly being taken over by the Optical Express Group).

She tried to call the clinic hotline but got the same message.

She had borrowed the money from her dad and now owed the total amount.

Jane was not alone. Julie had lost £1,300. Mandy, £15,000. And they had little chance of getting their money back.

But it wasn't always like this – the company's original business model was founded on a sound strategy.

The NHS, England's Public Health Service, declined to fund most cosmetic aesthetic treatments, so many people who wanted cosmetic surgery faced huge bills from variable quality across the country or, in some cases, had to travel as far as the Middle East or Turkey to have these treatments done. Only a few could afford to pay; for some, it wasn't an option – until 1990, when entrepreneur John Gill founded the High Street aesthetics chain SK:N in Harrogate.

It was founded to much fanfare, promising to bring aesthetics 'to the mainstream.' It quickly became popular, growing to 51 branches by 2019.

Then, in 2019, it was taken over by the private equity company Tristan. Between 2019 and 2024, Tristan launched a massive scaling initiative, adding 19 more stores in just five years.

Dr. Aenone Harper Machin, a spokeswoman for the British Association of Plastic, Reconstructive, and Aesthetic Surgeons, speculated that it had 'grown too quickly.'

'*Laser kit is costly,*' she said. '*Their rent costs would have been too. I'm not sure, but they probably overextended themselves.*'

SK:N shows companies' mistakes when trying to scale too quickly.

They end up stretching themselves too thin and not having enough to adapt themselves to a rapidly changing market – in this instance, a cutback on cosmetic spending due to the rising cost of living crisis, as well as elegant start-ups and rising business costs, which cut deeply into SK:N's profit margins and eventually leading to its sudden demise.

The company itself acknowledges this:

The company made a £7.2m loss before tax in 2021 and a £4.5m loss in 2022. Many of SK:N's treatments are funded directly by patients, which the company said left it 'exposed to economic cycles.'[19]

For this reason, quick scaling was its downfall and as I indicated earlier, most High Street chains I surveyed limited their place to scalability within that period. Richer Sounds had not expanded into new shops for a long time, preferring to scale their internet operations instead. Day Lewis paused new acquisitions from 2020 to 2022, and HMV had opened just three shops in the past 3 years. Waterstones also opened just three new stores in 2023 and focused on scaling differently, using their existing stores better.

I call this intra-place scaling.

See this statement from Day Lewis in the Group Strategic Report 2022 (as quoted earlier):

*During the financial year, Day Lewis continued its policy by limiting bank debt **by pausing acquisitions,** focusing on enhancing its existing estates, relocating branches to superior locations, **merging multiple pharmacies into more prominent single sights and disposing of pharmacies with exceptional low footfall.***[20]

It is through this that John A List talks about the five main principles of how to scale appropriately:[21]

1. **Beware of false positives:** Trends like market research, polling and repressive samples do not guarantee successful scaling, as the recent poll results between President Trump and Hillary Clinton showed. Samples and market research do not represent an entire population, and what works well in one sample may not work in another. This is another

powerful reason why open strategy is essential: handing power to those on the ground, getting independent verification, and taking steps to avoid confirmation bias.

2. **Know your audience:** In this book, I have spoken about the need for personalisation and how companies in High Street chains have lost millions of pounds by trying to standardise individual branches. In my work with some healthcare High Street chains, one of the first things I have done is synchronise the store with its community. I gave an earlier example of how a particular branch lost hundreds of pounds due to theft because it stocked its high-end products in a poor city suburb.

3. **Know your negotiable and non-negotiables:** Consider the end before trying to Place Scalability. What does good scaling look like to you? Every company's success rests on USPs – the few things that make it stand out, its tangibility. Before scaling, it is imperative to know whether your USP is scalable. Suppose a brand relies heavily on a personal touch, a celebrity chef (consider the failure of Jamie's Italian), or a patriarchal figure. In that case, it is unlikely to be scalable beyond a certain level. As I mentioned before, human beings are not scalable. John List describes this as the "chef" (people) versus "ingredients" (services) principle: chefs cannot scale beyond a specific limit – what Malcolm Gladwell calls the tipping point – whereas ingredients, the services provided, can.

4. **Beware of the cost trap:** The universality of economies of scale is a myth. The key is that economies of scale should achieve greater efficiency as they scale. If the scaling process does not result in greater efficiency and lower costs, it is better to quit (or pivot) when the tipping point is reached rather than keep running to your eventual destruction. Throwing more money and effort at a fundamentally non-scalable business without recognising when to pause or quit (especially during dire economic times) is a major red flag, and this is what happened to SK:N. Their sunk costs, business rates, equipment costs, and trained personnel exceeded the tipping point, but the customer base declined due to squeezed incomes in the post-COVID era (as well as increased competition from other countries in mainland Europe)

5. **Beware of spillovers:** Scaling almost always has unintended consequences, including positive and negative spillovers. I remember the story of local Kenyan entrepreneurs tapping into the city's shortage of mosquito nets. A charity decided to help alleviate the problem and subcontracted a Chinese factory to manufacture these nets at scale. The charity thought they would alleviate the high incidence of malaria in the country. However, there was a spillover: the low prices from China in economies of scale put Kenyan entrepreneurs out of business and caused significant adverse ripple effects such as increased joblessness, poverty, and reduced equality.

Addressing and minimising negative spillovers and exploiting the positives is essential to successful scaling.

However, the operation of Permanence does not primarily depend on Scalability. To succeed, the best companies don't scale. They scale with an adaptable but reproducible system.

To illustrate this, I'll explain how an unintended spillover nearly ruined my career in the next section.

Notes

1 List, John A. *The Voltage Effect: How to Make Good Ideas Great and Great Ideas Scale*, Currency, 2022.
2 Hoffman, Reid, June Cohen, and Deron Triff. *Masters of Scale: Surprising Truths from the World's Most Successful Entrepreneurs*, Penguin, 2023.
3 Marshall, Goldsmith. *What Got You Here Won't Get You There: How Successful People Become Even More Successful*, Profile Books, 2013.
4 Covey, Stephen. *7 Habits of Highly Effective People*, 15th Anniversary Edition, Free Press, 2004.
5 Patel, Sam and Teena Lyons. *Nothing Is Impossible: Kirit's Family Business Adventure*, Rethink Press, 2022.
6 Collins, James C. and William C. Lazier. *Beyond Entrepreneurship 2.0: Turning Your Business into an Enduring Great Company*, Random House Business, 2020.
7 Adair, John. *How to Grow Leaders: The Seven Key Principles of Effective Leadership Development*, Kogan Page, 2009.
8 Maxwell, John, C. Instagram post: www.instagram.com/reel/DBFDW-0BDyk/?igsh=MWl1NWZpbWFwaGE0ag%3D%3D, accessed January 12, 2025.
9 Adjei, Steven, N. Eight ways to successfully unlock diversity potential in your business, *Brainz Magazine*: www.brainzmagazine.com/post/eight-ways-to-successfully-unlock-diversity-potential-in-your-business, August 2022.
10 Rogers, Charlotte. Timpson CEO: Our business shouldn't exist anymore, *Marketing Week*: www.marketingweek.com/timpson-ceo-business/, March 18, 2022.
11 Adair, John. *How to Grow Leaders: The Seven Key Principles of Effective Leadership Development*, Kogan Page, 2009.
12 GlobeNewswire. Perceptyx Report: 1 in 4 Managers Are Flat-Out Miserable Right Now: www.globenewswire.com/news-release/2024/07/16/2913823/0/en/Perceptyx-Report-1-in-4-Managers-Are-Flat-Out-Miserable-Right-Now.html?utm_source=chatgpt.com
13 Bartlett, Steven. When you talk to managers you get the feeling you're important: www.linkedin.com/posts/stevenbartlett-123_when-you-talk-to-managers-you-get-the-feeling-activity-7261075078207913984-cnnM/, accessed August 25, 2025.
14 Timpson Group Services by Great People. Upside-down management: www.timpson-group.co.uk/about-timpson/upside-down-management
15 Field, Emily, Bryan Hancock, Stephanie Smallets, and Brooke Weddle. Investing in middle managers pays off – literally: www.mckinsey.com/capabilities/people-and-organizational-performance/our-insights/investing-in-middle-managers-pays-off-literally?cid=soc-web, June 26, 2023.

16 Field, Emily et al. Investing in middle managers pays off – literally: www.mckinsey.com/capabilities/people-and-organizational-performance/our-insights/investing-in-middle-managers-pays-off-literally, June 26, 2023, accessed June 25, 2025; Harrison, S. and K. Rogers. Building culture from the middle out: Midlevel leaders are critical to fostering an organisational culture that's healthy and vibrant, MIT Sloan Management Review, 22 February, Spring 2024 issue: https://sloanreview.mit.edu/article/building-culture-from-the-middle-out (accessed June 25, 2025).
17 Day Lewis Plc. Annual Report and Financial Statements, for the Year Ending March 2022: https://daylewis.co.uk/wp-content/uploads/2023/01/Day-Lewis-Plc-Annual-Report-Financial-Statements-2022-23.pdf
18 Pharmaceutical Journal. Pharmacy2U facility rejected from pharmaceutical list dispenses more than 1 million NHS prescriptions per month: https://pharmaceutical-journal.com/article/news/pharmacy2u-facility-rejected-from-pharmaceutical-list-dispenses-more-than-1-million-nhs-prescriptions-per-month?utm_source=chatgpt.com
19 Lawson, Eleanor. SK:N cosmetic surgery firm collapses, *BBC News*: www.bbc.co.uk/news/articles/c51yj723r3zo, July 18, 2024.
20 Lawson, Eleanor. SK:N cosmetic surgery firm collapses, *BBC News*: www.bbc.co.uk/news/articles/c51yj723r3zo, July 18, 2024.
21 List, John A. *The Voltage Effect: How to Make Good Ideas Great, and Great Ideas Scale*, Currency, 2022.

Chapter 14

Systems Thinking
Hard Realism or Logical Fallacy?

22 November 2022
This marked a dark day in my life when a patient nearly died on my watch.

It was a hectic sunny day in the aftermath of the pandemic, and I was working in one of the branches of a medium-sized healthcare chain on the High Street with locations all over London and the South of England.

I felt smug; this healthcare branch had been voted the best in my adopted city of Plymouth, England.

However, this success had brought a host of unintended consequences.

A long queue of patients were waiting to receive their medication from the pharmacy.

We were under severe pressure, with nearly an hour's wait for prescriptions.

Some patients were agitated, particularly those who had travelled miles to get here.

And then it happened.

An angry patient stormed to the front of the queue, waving some medication in their hands and screaming some unprintable words in our faces.

Going down to check, I could feel the blood draining from my face.

In a rush, I had made a potentially terrible mistake: giving the patient a blood-thinning medication instead of one for anxiety.

Had he not noticed, the error could have cost him his life.

He reported it, and we had to pay compensation for the error or risk being taken to court to potentially lose my hard-earned professional licence to practice pharmacy here in the United Kingdom.

Now, looking back, I see that the error happened because of a breakdown of our systems.

In this final chapter of the book, we're going to look at the importance of systems in three ways:

1. Systems thinking: Understanding how each determinant functions within systems rather than in isolation and recognising that the

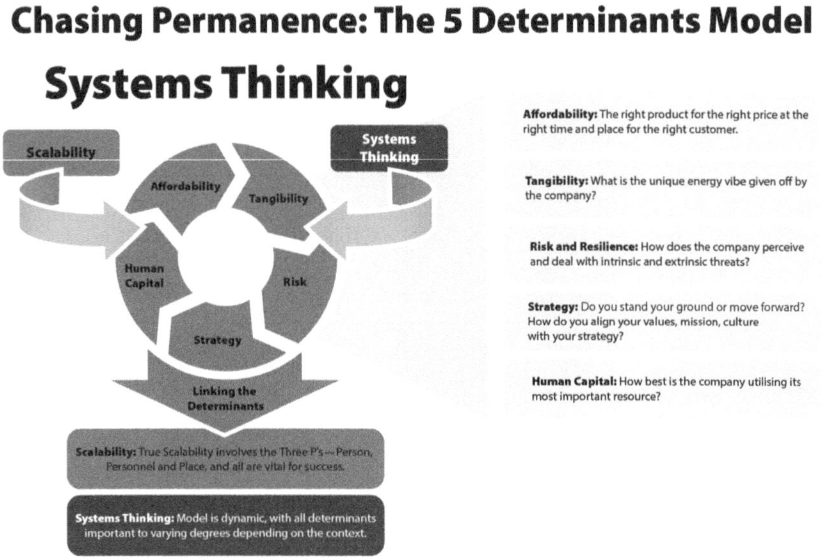
Chasing Permanence: The 5 Determinants Model
Systems Thinking
Scalability
Systems Thinking
Affordability
Tangibility
Human Capital
Risk
Strategy
Linking the Determinants
Affordability: The right product for the right price at the right time and place for the right customer.
Tangibility: What is the unique energy vibe given off by the company?
Risk and Resilience: How does the company perceive and deal with intrinsic and extrinsic threats?
Strategy: Do you stand your ground or move forward? How do you align your values, mission, culture with your strategy?
Human Capital: How best is the company utilising its most important resource?
Scalability: True Scalability involves the Three P's – Person, Personnel and Place, and all are vital for success.
Systems Thinking: Model is dynamic, with all determinants important to varying degrees depending on the context.

Figure 14.1 The Five Determinants Model: Systems Thinking.

significance of each determinant is dependent on the others and the context.

2. The importance of systems: Companies need to establish robust and dependable systems that can guarantee the reproducibility of outcomes and maintain high quality.
3. The fallacy of systems: Paradoxically, in an increasingly dynamic context, over-reliance on systems' rigidity can hinder companies' ability to respond to, anticipate, and stay ahead of the ever-evolving consumer landscape. This is especially pertinent in High Street retail.

The right balance of points 2 and 3 is crucial to maintain the right balance of creativity and rigidity to ensure success, and point 1 is to resist the tendency to put different functions of companies into silos – where one works ignorantly independently of the other. The key is to enable interdependency, where all five determinants work in tandem to create a smooth-functioning, well-oiled machine capable of functioning at high capacity for years.

Different companies do this in various ways, but they all have one thing in common: open communication from the shop floor to top management; the ability to turn the ship around quickly and, as I mentioned earlier, autonomy and the ability to make decisions from the shop floor.

This can be illustrated by how a young CEO with no retail experience rescued one of the UK's biggest High Street Supermarkets when it was **days** away from bankruptcy.

SYSTEMS THINKING – BALANCING THE DETERMINANTS

The concept of Reflective Paranoia

Throughout the book, I have enumerated these five determinants as individual parameters determining Permanence.

Nothing could be further from the truth.

Like all true systems, they are all interconnected, like the systems thinking mentioned by Peter Senge's *The Fifth Discipline*, which states that one determinant inevitably affects the other in any system[1].

In 1991, the High Street supermarket chain, Asda, was days away from bankruptcy. It had overextended its hand in a ferocious expansion drive leveraged with high-interest debt.[2]

In near desperation, they took a significant risk by hiring a relatively unknown 37-year-old named Archie Norman who, at 28, had already become McKinsey's youngest partner, followed at 32 by becoming Chief Finance Officer at Kingfisher plc. He had no experience running a retail group of Asda's size, so this was a big gamble by the supermarket chain[3].

However, it proved to be a stroke of genius.

BALANCING THE DETERMINANTS
The systems balance wheel

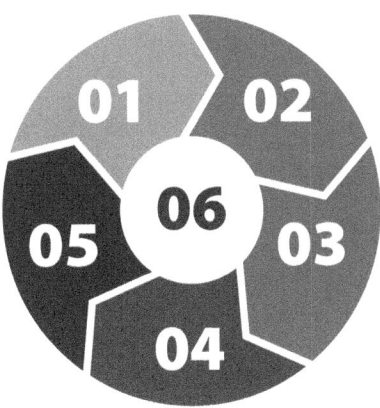

1. TANGIBILITY
The unique 'energy vibe' of the company

2. HUMAN CAPITAL
How best is the company utilising its most important resource?

3. AFFORDABILITY
The right product at the right price at the right time for the right customer

4. RISK
How does the company perceive and deal with intrinsic and extrinsic threats

5. STRATEGY
Moving forward or standing still?

6. THE WHEEL
Permanence is achieved as long as these 5 determinants are balanced dynamically

Figure 14.2 Balancing the Five Determinants: The Systems Balance Wheel.

Archie's turnaround of Asda's fortunes, which led to it becoming Britain's second-biggest supermarket eight years before its $6.7 billion sale to Walmart, is a classic example of balancing the five determinants.

To enhance tangibility, Archie prioritised visiting stores. He toured nearly all of Asda's branches, observing the company culture and actively seeking feedback from customers and frontline staff to ensure that Asda's offerings aligned with customer needs (customer agility and community). As a result of this feedback, he completely revamped the stores. In addition, he assembled a team, including CEO Allan Leighton, to promote team building and collaboration across all levels of the organisation .

For **Human Capital,** Allan Leighton and Archie Norman focused on employee training, empowering them to take the initiative and contribute ideas. They also devolved and dismantled leadership from the central head office and introduced a dynamic and empowering culture that helped them foster a sense of ownership, commitment, collaboration, and belonging. This was almost unheard of in that era.

For **Affordability,** the company's prices were already lower than its competitors, so only minor tweaks were needed.

However, he redefined the company's values to prioritise daily delivery of quality, affordable products. He refocused the business on its core strengths – groceries and essential household items – and eliminated non-core products and services. He also eliminated expensive permanent discounting and offered low prices all year round, positioning Asda as a retailer that directly challenged Tesco and Sainsbury's by providing quality and value at unbeatable prices.

For **Risk and Resilience,** he improved supply chain efficiency and inventory management, ruthlessly eliminating waste and unnecessary costs. He also restructured the company's ballooning debts, eliminated underperforming staff and management, and improved its resilience by partnering with US retail giant Walmart.

For **Strategy,** he paused any further acquisitions using the **Stand Your Ground** strategy. At the same time, he realigned the company to reflect and align the downturn in the economy of 1991, which was linked to high interest rates, falling house prices, less spending, more saving, and less investment. High interest rates led to more saving, less spending, and less investment in the UK's sectors (Christian Stadler's **HOW** framework). An aligned culture, vision and strategy was achieved by bringing in a team that was on board with his plan, as well as getting customers, and staff who successfully executed this strategy.

Only after this did he implement the **Moving Forward Strategy** and begin expanding again.

He balanced the determinants **dynamically.**

By the time Archie resigned in 1999, he had enabled Asda to turn around its fortunes from near bankruptcy to Britain's second biggest supermarket.

It may be ironic that Allan Leighton's previously low-price strategy is now being challenged, resulting in substantial market share losses to the relatively new upstarts ALDI and Lidl, which compete at the same level. Thus, the affordability factor has now become an issue. This is what I call **reflective paranoia:**

Continually scanning the five determinants that threaten to derail the company helps balance the wheel and enables the company to run successfully over an extended period.

This is further emphasised in Peter Senge's landmark book *The Fifth Discipline*. There are always underlying currents, unseen forces, and subtle and significant changes that are shifting beneath an organisation, and they need it to move in tandem, or even better, anticipate these changes and 'turn the ship' to enable the organisation to thrive.

Balancing the wheel will look different for different companies.

Mark Fallick, a Timpson's manager for the South West of England, reiterates this in a personal interview:

Timpson has managers of all the hub stores and our bigger stores. The company also has 'mobile managers,' who cover the store managers' holidays and days off. Above them are the Area Development Managers, whose role is to collate information, support the store managers in their day-to-day tasks, and look at specific areas where the businesses can be developed. Prices are not set but are dynamic according to the area and the manager's discretion.

This year, 55 new stores opened after the opening of stores halted due to COVID-19.

Based on feedback from store managers, we quickly attempt or try new services. Some of these work, in which case they are scaled up quickly, and some don't, which are scaled rapidly down and discarded. This is a dynamic process, so the business constantly changes, adapts, and innovates.[4]

As I mentioned earlier, Jay Patel talks of a 'run team' and a 'change team.' The change team plays a similar role to the ADMs at Timpson, whose job is to continually scan the market, collect feedback from the branches and relay it to senior management so they can decide to adapt. There is also the process of trying and adapting new services and ways of doing things, whilst the 'run team' essentially ensures that the systems, procedures, routines, rituals and SOPs are uniform as far as possible throughout all 250-odd stores. There is always a 'healthy tension' between the change team, who harbour the 'big ideas' of how to disrupt things for the better, and the run team, who emphasise the smooth running of the organisation. I covered this creative tension earlier under the Risk-Resilience Model.

Richer Sounds' recurring Reatiler of the Year awards have been won (in part) by giving store retail managers almost unlimited powers within a well-defined framework. Their management comprises trustees, and middle management deals with functions in a mentoring and support capacity rather than operational – that falls to internal audit inspectors, whose job is to maintain standards.

The Organisational Culture Sweet Spot™ isn't only found in the autonomy-rich blends you see at Timpson or Richer Sounds. Even in a traditional Role Culture business like Day Lewis, it's possible—and that's what makes their story so powerful.

Community pharmacy is one of the most heavily regulated sectors on the High Street. That regulation makes it incredibly hard to break out of the rigidity of Role Culture. Most pharmacy groups remain locked in, running their businesses as if it were still the 1980s.

Day Lewis has however chosen a different path. True to its value of "difference through innovation," it started blending in elements of the other three cultures. The clearest example came in December 2024, when it launched a bold joint-venture scheme. For the first time, internal and external pharmacist managers could own up to 49% of a branch. Nearly 20 branches have already adopted this model – and they're outperforming the rest.

That's the ADD principle from Chapter 10 in action: Autonomy for pharmacist owners, Diversity in how local branches operate, and Dividend in the form of better rewards for everyone involved.

Thus, Day Lewis hasn't abandoned the stability of Role Culture. It has maintained the discipline that regulation demands. But by infusing that stability with innovation from Task, Person, and Power cultures, it has created its own blend—a living example of what the Sweet Spot looks like in arguably one of the toughest sectors of all. They also have the bonus of a feedback loop for what is working and what is not, as well as an unbridled and open commitment to the High Street.

They have also invested heavily in online infrastructure, human capital, and tangibility (even when they have paused physical expansion) while securing reasonable rates by owning their properties or securing great deals.

Whilst Waterstones has minimal leeway with book pricing (affordability), it has invested heavily in tangibility, particularly in community and human capital. It is utilising economies of scale by cautiously opening more branches to offset the risks of brick-and-mortar and spreading risk by running a very efficient online ordering system and diversifying into café, car, and home board games, to name a few.

Melanie Butler, a shop assistant at Waterstones Plymouth, is passionate about books to the point of obsession. Her knowledge of the breadth and length of different genres is outstanding, and meeting her when shopping in Waterstones is genuinely infectious. She represents the brand's strength: the company's investment in **human capital.** I have seen this replicated across the dozens of stores I have visited throughout the country, the passion of the front-row staff to show their love for the one thing that matters in Waterstones: books.

Balancing the determinants also depends on economic headwinds. These are generally out of the business' control, and as I discussed in Risk, all the company can do is detect and respond.

However, as Gerber discussed in his runaway bestseller[5], a business cannot run on balance alone: systems, procedures, and rules must be in place to enable stability.

The new middle manager was upset by the lack of rules in a poorly reforming branch of a multinational company in the north of Devon.

Usually calm and composed, she walked in one day visibly frustrated and agitated. From the sidelines, I observed a side of the manager I had known for over two decades but had never seen before. Why had unsettled her so deeply?

The Importance of Systems

It was an early morning on a lovely summer's day in June 2024 and I had just taken up a new position as a freelance pharmacist in a well-known healthcare chain on the High Street.

It was a position no one wanted and had been available for months.

The shelves were empty as I entered and the branch felt rudderless. Every morning, a queue of disgruntled patients waited at the door. The shop looked tired and pale, and its tangibility was low.

There was a hush in the air, as the shop members came in early and were cleaning frantically.

The hush grew louder as the middle manager walked in.

She said good morning, turned on the company intranet, and pointed to a screen that looked like a dial with many reds.

She began to rattle off some figures – compared to the KPIs set for the other 50-odd branches across the city, this branch was clearly at the bottom of the list.

The figures could have been prettier.

That's why they had so many reds in their chart.

The question was asked in many ways, but boiled down to one:

'*Why has this ... not been done?*' she kept asking.

The branch needed to follow the systems and procedures laid down by management.

It was termed a 'failing' branch and certainly looked very different from the other 'top performing' branches in the same city – some just down the road.

Ayomide, the middle manager in charge of the branch, kept saying that she was 'getting heat from the top' because the branch 'was not performing.'

The branch was deemed to be failing because 'systems and rules were not being followed.'

Ayomide was popular and one of the stars of middle management because she was a stickler for the rules, procedures, and systems. Her job was to ensure that they followed them to the letter; that the managers, supervisors, and line staff who reported to her implemented those systems, and that things ran smoothly, like a well-heeled machine.

Typically, these procedures and systems originate in the original design as the company matures. They are necessary to ensure stability, predictability and uniformity, and these hierarchical roles and procedures are usually the primary source or influence.

The key to seeing if these systems work is simple.

If you are the manager or staff member in a branch of one store, could you go to another store (for example, to cover sickness) in the same chain and immediately fit in if you've been trained?

Many big, mature and successful organisations, both off and on the High Streets, have this culture in place: the key is to provide uniform standards, customer service and operations in all branches.

In his book, *Understanding Organisations*,[6] Charles Handy defines such a company as having a 'role culture.'

Role cultures are coordinated at the top by a narrow band of senior management, the pediment. It is assumed that this should be the only personal coordination needed, for if the separate pillars do their job as laid down by the rules and procedures, the ultimate result will be as planned.

In this culture, the role of a job description is often more important than the individual who fills it.

Individuals are selected for satisfactory role performance, and the role is usually designed to be filled by a range of individuals. Performance beyond the prescription is optional and can be disruptive. Position power is the primary power source in this culture; personal power is frowned upon, and expert power is tolerated only in its proper place.

Rules, roles, formalised hierarchies and procedures are significant methods of influence.

As Jonathan Fields espouses in his 2011 book *Uncertainty: Turning Fear and Doubt into Fuel for Brilliance*:[7]

Routines and rituals create certainty and build consistency. Acting as certainty anchors, they create certainty even in unstable times.

Systems, standardised operation procedures, KPIs, and what I call WGLL (What Good Looks Like – essentially visuals to establish a model store) are crucial to any business' correct functioning, especially chains on the High Street.

I once watched a TV programme where a group of hyenas circled a colossal lion.

The powerful predator had now become prey.
The often-victorious victor had now become a victim.
How?
The hyenas knew the lion was much stronger and could quickly kill them if they confronted it head-on. So, they just circled it, running away when the lion charged at them, but nicking it with their teeth when they could. A little bite on the bum. A clip on the calf. A nick on the neck. A scratch on the side.

Wounds began to open. Blood began to flow. Slowly but surely, the lion started to tire. Multiple wounds let out blood, which exacerbated the fatigue. The hyenas continued to encircle. Gradually, death began to stare the lion in the face.

Then, the inevitable happened. The great lion fell to its knees, let out a great roar, succumbed and gave up the ghost.

The hyenas jumped and began to feast. As the camera started to zoom in on them, I swore I saw a couple of them smile with a twinkle in their eye.

As I mentioned earlier, businesses rarely collapse or go bust instantly. Typically, minor issues, like little hyenas nipping away at parts of the company go unnoticed or ignored, finally leading to a big crash.

This is what happens to businesses when firm systems are not in place.

As W. Edwards Deming says:

A flawed system beats a good employee every time.[8]

Most companies that have existed and thrived over time have these in every part of the organisation. As service standardisation, production, distribution, and administration have become increasingly necessary, managerial rules and procedures have grown in tandem with scale. However, they tend to completely dominate the organisation's entrepreneurial bent as the company matures, forcing it to grow slowly and adapt too late to change.

The Role Culture, which many High Street companies, particularly larger organisations tend to follow, is traditionally well-suited to stable, structured, and predictable environments. However, this culture is increasingly out of step with the dynamic and uncertain realities of today's High Street, and must evolve to remain effective.

Balance is essential. Many books, speakers, and think tanks advocate eliminating Role Culture entirely in the name of 'agility.' Whilst there is some truth in the claim that over-reliance on procedures and systems has contributed to the accelerating decline of our High Streets, that is only part of the story.

Role Culture still plays an important role: it curtails chaos, ensures standardisation, and protects a brand's strength, uniqueness, recognition, economies of scale, and market position.

The problem comes when this becomes either the only culture or, in many cases, the organisation's dominant culture.

In short, the over-reliance on systems that many of these organisations treasure and that are the backbone of their culture may become a fallacy.

Let us explore why, by using a modern perspective on the three other cultures that Charles Handy discussed in his 1976 book, *Understanding Organisations*.

The Fallacy of Systems

At the beginning of this book, I discussed the five main ways our work environment is changing.

Professor Daniel Burrus, in his bestselling book *The Anticipatory Organisation*,[9] has identified complex trends and soft trends that should influence business strategy and which the best High Street companies can manoeuvre well.

Decreased footfall, shifting age demographics, the rise of the hermit consumer, the cost-of-living crisis, pandemics, changes in political power, and emerging soft trends are challenges faced by all High Street businesses. The most successful companies build their long-term strategies on solid, hard data while maintaining flexibility to adapt to softer, more fluid trends.

The Power Culture – The Spider's Web

In 2001, two entrepreneurs – personal friends of mine – met in a small suburb in the South West of England with a bold idea. One was from South Africa, the other was born and raised just three miles from their meeting place. Both had recently left the corporate world, disillusioned by its rigid role culture and frustrated by the lack of personal growth opportunities. One of them had come dangerously close to burnout.

They agreed on one thing: they wanted to build a new chain of High Street community pharmacies – ones that would provide personalised care to underserved communities. They envisioned a business grounded in trust and human connection, stripping away unnecessary rules and cultivating a family-like culture.

In the words of Charles Handy, they built what is known as a **Power Culture**,

Power cultures resemble a spider's web. They rely on a central power source from which strands of influence radiate. Functional or specialist connections weave between them, yet the power rings are hubs of activity and influence.[10]

Such cultures often function like families, with a patriarchal structure that fosters a strong sense of belonging, teamwork, and agility. But there's a downside. Power cultures frequently depend too heavily on the founder or CEO. Though the environment can be warm and welcoming, it can also veer toward paternalism and hero-worship. Without a clear succession plan – what I referred to earlier as transcendence – these cultures rarely endure.

At first, the entrepreneurs succeeded.

Until they didn't.

As the business expanded, tensions emerged between the founders. A feud broke out, and the once-cohesive chain began to stagnate. One founder exited and started a new business. Then, the market took a downturn. Sales dropped. One branch was sold off to a competitor. The remaining founder tried to sell the rest, but weak performance and low staff morale deterred potential buyers. He was left managing stagnating branches – underperforming, under-resourced, and increasingly burdened by external pressures: poor local demograhpics, reduced funding and the rising cost of living.

In an attempt to revive the company, he shifted toward a Role Culture. He hired experienced managers, implemented formal structures, and introduced procedures modelled after larger, more stable firms. But the transition failed. The new managers didn't last, and the cultural shift proved unsustainable – because the business environment hadn't changed to support it. I've seen this pattern repeat more than once. It's a key reason why so many small businesses fail – particularly those on the High Street.

Again, to quote Charles Handy,

A web without a centre has no strength.[11]

Both cultures have existed for millennia. However, another business culture that has emerged in the last two or three decades has seen incredible success – albeit not mainly on our High Streets.

It has proven incredibly agile, adaptable, and flexible with fast, even exponential growth.

And it is to this that we now turn.

The Task Culture: 'Move fast and break things'

Charles Handy could hardly have imagined the era of the new breed of companies when he wrote about 'task culture' in 1976:

> *The task culture is extremely adaptable, able to work quickly, and much of the power and influence is derived from a net-like structure ... Task cultures are most appropriate when flexibility and sensitivity to the market or environment are important. You will find the task culture where the market is competitive, where the product life is short, and the speed of reaction is important.*[12]

In 2005, Facebook heralded the initiation of a significant transformation in the organisation's history, commonly referred to as a start-up.

In a sense, start-ups are as old as the term itself; every corporation, organisation, or company has had to start from somewhere.

We sometimes confuse entrepreneurship with start-ups, but by definition, a start-up is a different kind of organisation.

As William Magnusson explains, start-ups are all about growth – the internet, mobile phones, platforms and hiring. They aim to grow fast and dominate their markets, usually by going all out to acquire new users through free or low prices and gaining a reputation as the latest thing, with a typical employee: young, hippy, cool, and probably bankrolled by a venture firm.

As he explains:

> *Start-ups all share a similar model: they take the internet, add some proprietary technology, and then let users take control. They are platforms. Their sole aim is to grow fast, dominate their markets, and gain a reputation as the 'new cool app' trendy, pretty and practical.*
>
> *Their value lies in their ability to create networks – friends, coworkers, drivers, and music listeners – which drives the growth effect.*

With the advent of artificial intelligence, the start-up era has barely begun.

And yes, they have transformed our lives. With the click of a mouse, you can book a room, board a train, buy virtually anything, get a taxi, or combat loneliness.

Spotify. Facebook. Instagram. Airbnb. Uber. X. Google. Amazon. Temu. LinkedIn. TikTok.

Its value lies in its ability to create networks, which beget growth and profits. That is why Elon Musk was prepared to pay $44 billion for Twitter.

And yes, start-ups present the greatest threat to our High Streets.

They have decreased footfall and can adapt quickly (or even drive) customer behaviour, increase convenience, and have a seemingly endless capacity to drive innovation. They have shaken and broken the old companies as we know them and even invented new ones we couldn't even dream about 25 years ago.

They typify a *'task culture'* – they can move fast and break things.

But it's not all rosy; we are just beginning to realise their pitfalls. For all their good, start-ups have also caused problems.

And this is where Charles Handy got it wrong:

> *...the task culture finds it hard to produce economies of scale or great depth of expertise.*

Exponential scalability and growth, sometimes at any cost; excessive risk-taking; taking customers for granted and manipulating them; ignoring, or in some cases facilitating, hate speech; entrenched divisions; silo mentality; questionable ethics. As Mark Zuckerberg said, somewhat regretfully in 2018 before the US Congress:

> *We didn't take a broad enough view of our responsibility. Connecting people is not enough – we must ensure those connections are positive. It's not enough to give people a voice; we have to make sure people aren't using it to hurt each other or spread misinformation. Across the board, we have a responsibility not just to build tools but to make sure these tools are used for good.*[13]

Start-ups are typically agile – they can 'move fast and break things,' operating almost as the antithesis of a role culture. Yet that very speed can become a liability when clear procedures, robust systems, and well-defined roles are lacking. Commitment to the greater good does not always come first – external pressure is sometimes required to ensure responsible behaviour. Amazon and Uber, for example, have faced strikes and protests over alleged unfair pay and poor working conditions and a recent TUC report sharply criticised Amazon's treatment of its workforce. Governments are increasingly concerned about the broader implications of such practices, particularly where security is involved.

An example in the Guardian:

> *The US's top workplace safety regulator and the justice department are pressuring Amazon to explain safety practices that have led to injury rates for warehouse workers that are on average close to twice as high as the company's competitors and in one case five times higher.*[14]

So, in short, the growth, innovation, networking, and endless capacity for the creativity of start-ups is mind-boggling and sometimes to be envied. It has improved our lives immensely in almost every sector.

But sometimes, this growth comes at the cost of breaking laws, ignoring red tape, and sometimes not caring enough about the consequences.

Start-ups have also encouraged the rise of another form of culture in which the individual is the hero, to which we now turn.

The Person Culture: The Rise of the Thought Leader

Born in Cleveland, Ohio in 1997, Jake Paul is no ordinary man with a camera and a microphone. One day in early September 2013, Jake began posting videos and content on an app called Vine, founded by Twitter, a predecessor of TikTok. He amassed over 5 million followers and 2 billion streams before Vine was bought out in 2014. He then turned his attention to YouTube.[15]

At last count, he had almost 21 million followers. Through this, he has developed a venture capital fund, released platinum singles and, probably what he is best known for, entered the world of professional boxing. His recent fight with former world champion Mike Tyson was the most streamed sporting event in history, peaking at 65 million concurrent streams, earning over 1.4 billion impressions, and being the number one event in 78 countries.[16]

Joe Rogan, the world's leading podcaster, once again claimed Spotify's top show for 2023. He entered a $200 million deal with the platform over two years ago. Notable guests like Elon Musk, Donald Trump, and Edward Snowden have featured on the show, with his top 10 episodes amassing an impressive 410 million views.[17]

Writing in 1976, Charles Handy could hardly have forseen this recent type of culture times when he wrote,

In this culture, the individual is the central figure. If there is a structure or organisation, it exists only to serve and assist the individuals within it ... Dionysus (the Greek god of wine, fantasy, partying, and fertility) is the patron deity of this culture. He is the god of the self-oriented individual, the first existentialist.[18]

Examples of person cultures include independent knowledge workers, coaches, mentors, thought leaders, and authors.

This culture type has grown significantly in the last decade, particularly after COVID-19. For example, a study by the International Coaching Federation indicates that there has been a 54% increase in coaches since 2019, with the number of coaches surpassing 100,000 for the first time. Thanks to the start-up, it is now easier than ever for everyone to have a voice. You only need a microphone, mobile or laptop, space, and the internet. For instance, LinkedIn, the world's premier business networking site, is closing in on 1 billion members and has a whopping 17 million 'thought and opinion' leaders, which the site appropriately calls **influencers**.

The danger is a constant clamour for attention and an inexhaustible plethora of advice and recommendations, ranging from professional and reliable, to ludicrous and even dangerous.

As a trained pharmacist and an expert on medicines, I find it amazing how many patients come in requesting a particular therapy or treatment for a specific ailment or rejecting a recommended treatment regime because they 'listened to a particular podcast,' read it 'online,' or watched an 'expert on TikTok,' which I know to be wrong, or even potentially harmful.

The obvious question is: how does this apply to our High Street businesses?

The key takeaway:

The era where Charles Handy segregated these cultures into four distinct types is over.

Though many High Street businesses may inherently have to adopt a dominant culture to survive, thrive, and adapt, they must embrace the best practices of all four cultures and discard the worst practices as appropriate to their sector (see Table 14.1)

Let's use Timpson and Day Lewis as examples:

An excerpt from Marketing Week:

James Timpson admits his business shouldn't exist any more. The company, which spans Timpson, Snappy Snaps, Max Spielmann and Johnsons The Cleaners, has seen virtually all its competitors go bust.[19]

Timpson, founded in 1865, has a staggering network of over 2,000 owned stores throughout the UK, with 559 on the High Street.

Timpson Ltd, its largest subsidiary, is now the largest service retailer in the UK with 1300 shops.

Timpson probably leans towards a task culture in the way the company is set up: James Timpson says in the same article:

When we make a mistake, I'm happy to fail fast, and if it doesn't work, don't keep trying to put lipstick on a pig, as they say.

The business celebrates failure because it means the team knows what won't work. However, when a new idea succeeds, they pursue it full throttle.

But it has proven stable, resilient and adaptable by embracing the good and relevant bits of all four:

Role Culture: Timpson House's head office is in Wythenshawe, Manchester, where it oversees all its shops and franchises. Standards are maintained, procedures and systems are implemented, and new acquisitions are made. Rather than being called the HQ or head office, Timpson House is known as Timpson House. Though its primary aim is to support its branches, the **role culture is** developed here, where best practices, training, procedures, etc., are implemented. Timpson does not delegate three areas of the business: the shops the company opens, capital expenditure, and strategy. And there are still rules: new products must be given high margins, push the brand, and be approved by staff. They have strict criteria of standards and

Table 14.1 Dominant Organisational Cultures of Selected High Street Companies

	Organisation Type	Advantages	Disadvantages	Culture	Orientation focus	Company default
Role	Mature multinational	Uniformity, Stability, Predictability	Slow response to market trends	Formal, Hierarchical	How (processes and systems)	Day Lewis/ Waterstones/
Task	Start-up	Agile, Adaptable innovative, entrepreneurial,	Erratic standardisation of processes and services, competition for power	Informal, relaxed	What (Delivery of outcomes)	Timpson
Power	Small Business	Welcoming culture, entrepreneurial, great customer service and agility	Inherently unstable and unscalable, succession issues, too dependent on founder or CEO	Family/ Community	Why	Richer Sounds
Person	Thought leaders and inflluencers	Agile, influential, respected	Difficult to scale, Potential to self-aggrandize	Existential	Who (the individual)	Timpson

how good their staff are (rated up to a 'ten'), and staff who consistently fall below their high standards are 'managed out' of the company.

These are run directly from Timpson House.

Task Culture: I thought I'd illustrate these quotes from James Timpson's interview with Market Week in 2022[20]:

> *'All the time, we're breaking down the bits of the business to see what we can do to increase while understanding that there are certain bits that are always doing rubbish.'*
>
> *'There are only two rules for staff: to put money in the till and to look the part while upholding standards.'*
>
> *'It meant all the really good people, the vast majority, had to restrict what they could do because of all these stupid rules. Because I was the boss' son, I could get away with it, give discounts and promotions, and do whatever I wanted. This informed my style when I became CEO.'*
>
> *'The rest, anyone can do whatever they want; there are no rules. All our training concerns the technical skills you need to do the job and the culture and how we do it. This is where the trust and the no rules come in.'*
>
> *'The in-store colleagues have complete authority to do whatever they think is right to offer a fantastic service, from coming up with new ideas to offering discounts. Timpson's first experiences working in a store informed this mentality.'*
>
> *'When I first joined the business properly after university, I could put 50% on the sales in every shop I worked in. The reason wasn't because I was a good shoe repairer or key cutter; it's because I could break all these rules that had been put in place,' he explained.*

Again, from the Marketing Week interview:

> *There is an ambition to trial new ideas and not get hung up on costs in the initial phase. Starting small is crucial, said Timpson, who is wary of companies launching new products or services at scale without proper testing. In his experience, it takes three years to get a concept right.*

When I read these quotes in the Marketing Week online blog, I set myself on a mission to verify this. In this book, I have given several examples where I spoke with store managers from the companies I have used as case studies and who have been given, and have shown, incredible autonomy, unheard of in many other High Street stores.

From barber shops to cleaners, supermarket openings to Airbnb experiments, and 24-hour locksmith callouts to shop repair, Timpson resembles a start-up. It continually expands, innovates, and experiments while focusing on high-level margins that cannot be replicated online.

Power Culture: Timpson has been a family business for over a century. As I discussed earlier, the key to a power culture is that it should not *'die in the centre,'* as Charles Handy puts it. The Timpsons have not been afraid to preach their doctrine of upside-down management to anyone who will listen – in interviews, books, newspaper articles. Even more importantly, they have striven to make each business autonomous in its own right.

Charles Handy says it best:

> *The Power Culture and organisations based on them are proud and strong. They have the ability to move quickly and can react well to threats or danger. Whether they do move in the right direction will, however, depend on the persons in the centre, for the quality of these individuals is of paramount importance, and the succession issue is key to their continued success.*[21]

Returning to Part One of this book, The Mindset of Permanence, it is easy to see why the Timpsons have remained successful for so long. The leadership consistently ranks high in all seven mindsets discussed.

Person Culture: In the interview, James Timpson recalled touring an open prison and being approached by a prisoner with a *'buzzy personality'* who asked if the chain had any jobs available. Timpson gave the man his card and promised to give him a job upon release. The ex-offender still works for the business today.

He says:

> *For about six months, I'd go around the local prisons in the North West, walking the wings, looking for 'sparky' prisoners. I chatted with them and gave them my business card. I ended up getting about 20 ex-offenders – or, as we call them, foundation colleagues – and went from there.*

Timpson's entrepreneurial spirit is fed by a strange source: Prisons.

Why this approach?

Most prisoners do have this streak of being 'rebels' (or mavericks) – the bad side of which ends them up being on the wrong side of the law, but the flip side is that they are more willing to be 'intrapreneurs' – loyal employees who are grateful to have been given a second chance, but also who are not afraid to take sensible risks to try new ways of doing things. And it is this which fits in perfectly with the company's ethos, yet at the same time *fulfilling a crucial tenet of today's business: doing well and doing good.*

I talked about the thought leader and influencer in the Person's Culture. An intensive 16-week training course in Timpson House and a kind, but with high standards, manager is required. Each Timpson manager is a 'thought leader' in their field, a centre of the community who customers can rely on for professional, reliable recommendations and advice – from key cutting, shoe repair, and haircuts, to dry cleaning. The managers are trained to such a high standard, and 'culture indoctrinated' with the principle of the trail: a balance of competence and compassion.

Again, Charles Handy:

> *Individuals employed in these organisations will prosper and be satisfied to the extent that they are power-orientated, politically minded, risk-taking and rate security as a minor element in their psychological contract.*[22]

Sparky. Buzzy. Power-orientated. Rebels. These are the tenets of a Power Culture.

A striking resemblance to either Joe Rogan or Jake Paul.

However, it should be noted that although James Timpson's 'no rules' tenet may not work for every organisation, the same principles apply.

Let's look, for instance at Day Lewis Pharmacies:

Role Culture: Community pharmacy is very heavily regulated by the government and must operate within stringent rules. Pharmacists and their technicians must have specific qualifications, be members of a professional body, and adhere to a professional code of conduct. By law, every pharmacy chain must employ a 'superintendent pharmacist' responsible for upholding standards and ensuring the company's employees work within the confines of the law. Such regulations lend itself to a hierarchical structure, and consequently, role culture

But even within this 'rigid' confines, Day Lewis has found ways to incorporate the other three kinds of cultures:

Person/Task Culture: Day Lewis, probably more so than other pharmacy chains, has been able to put the pharmacist at the centre of the community by giving them the freedom, within the law, to do whatever it takes to drive the business forward.

Melissa Baidoo, for example, is a pharmacist store manager in Keyham, South West England. She took the very unusual initiative of setting up a shop in a supermarket, where she was able to take the blood pressure of many people. This brought healthcare out of the pharmacy into the community, fostering relationships, and driving footfall to her pharmacy. She also visits schools and communities in the city to deliver talks, administer COVID and flu jabs, and participate in community events. According to

Google, this and other initiatives has resulted in the pharmacy having the highest rating in the city of Plymouth at 4.3.

Power Culture: Even though the role culture predominates, the branches are given the freedom to find the best way they can to drive customer engagement and instigate collaboration. Each branch functions semi-autonomously as much as possible and unlike many other pharmacy High Street chains, the directors, Sam, Jay and Rupa still like to keep the small business feel:

In an interview with the community pharmacy business magazine P3, Rupa says:

> *Pre-pandemic, the three [directors] would aim to visit every pharmacy in the group over 18 months, continuing their father's practice of regular in-person visits focused on meeting teams and being visible, rather than on operational performance. We call them family visits. It's a chance to connect with a team and ask them how things are going.*
>
> *There is a challenge to maintaining our family values as the business has grown, but we might send chocolates out when kids are born, or we might do ice cream to recognise a hot day. And we always celebrate Dad's anniversary on 16 July.*
>
> *Growth for us will be defined by the impact we can make on people. We're not just a pharmacy – we like to call ourselves a family.*[23]

The only drawback of pharmacies is the chronic shortage of pharmacists in the country, who are now required to perform more and more of a clinical role than just five years ago. Again, Day Lewis is adapting quickly to these changes by state-of-the-art innovation:

Danny McNally, Pharmacy Process Improvement Manager, at Day Lewis Pharmacy, discusses the group's journey to a hub and spoke model of pharmacy dispensing, speaking in October 2024:

> *This simplified model of hub-and-spoke dispensing, starts with the store pharmacist performing the clinical and accuracy check upfront. The software then transmits patient orders to the hub and after that the pharmacist is not required in the process unless there is an anomaly.*
>
> *This concentrated approach is far more efficient, as it means the pharmacist doesn't spend the entire day checking medication.*[24]

Innovation using this hub-and-spoke system, powered by AI, is helping relieve pharmacists' pressure, freeing them to be the healthcare influencers and thought leaders of the community – the Day Lewis version of the Person Culture, whilst also fulfilling its value of Innovation.

And in keeping with its values, Day Lewis keeps finding new ways to run its business – setting it apart from competitors still stuck in a pure

Role culture. It's proof that even a traditional Role business can hit the Organisational Culture Sweet Spot™ while delivering on the ADD principle we saw in Chapter 10.

This same balancing is seen in Waterstones and HMV.

According to an article in 2023 on the business website Fast Company[25] (as I highlighted earlier)

> *James Daunt (CEO of Waterstones and Barnes and Noble) has applied the lessons he's learned over thirty years as an indie seller to Waterstones. He **empowers** booksellers at each location to curate books based on their quirky, idiosyncratic tastes. This strategy leads to more engaged workers and more exciting stores.*[26]

Amazon has been unable to replicate this and, in a queer twist of fate, Barnes & Noble – often called the American equivalent of Waterstones – has moved into two failed Amazon Book locations in Boston, which the company says are doing 'very well.'

To illustrate:

Figure 14.3 (Diagram adapted and used with permission from Dan Underwood Coaching, www.danunderwood.me). The circle in the middle depicts how an intersection of all four cultures would look for each organisation.

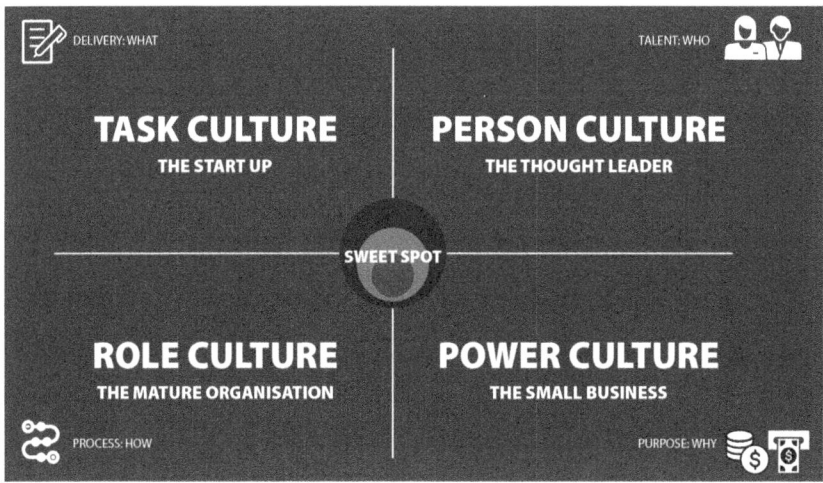

Figure 14.3 Role, Task, Power, and Person cultures meet, balancing creativity with stability, autonomy with structure, and agility with consistency.[27]

Adapted by Steven N. Adjei from Charles Handy; diagram styling by Dan Underwood Coaching, used with permission.™

This ability to collapse the distance between shop-floor colleagues and top management has been a central tenet of these high street chains, enabling agility whilst still maintaining stability.

As the managing secretary of an NGO in Accra, Ghana – an organisation with 15,000 branches worldwide and approaching its centenary anniversary – recently said to me in a conversation:

We believe in one tenet: This organisation is a living organism. But every organism needs organisation to succeed.

He continued:

In other words, the creativity, autonomy, and growth of the business (organism) must be balanced by the structure and procedures (organisation) needed to succeed. The key to our success is balancing the two: the ability to allow the organism to live and thrive whilst making sure the structures and procedures (systems) regulate its survival and growth, both internally and externally.[28]

However, one final determinant is crucial to the success of our High Streets. I have saved this one for reasons I will explain later.

It is this final cog in the wheel to which we now turn.

Notes

1 Senge, Peter. *The Fifth Discipline: The Art and Practice of the Learning Organization*, Random House Publishers, 2006.
2 Beer, Michael and James Weber. Asda (A1), Harvard Business School Case 498-039, Boston, Harvard Business School Publishing, October 1997, revised May 1998.
3 Tomlinson, Heather. Asda's secret success story leaks out. *The Guardian*: www.theguardian.com/business/2003/dec/01/supermarkets#:~:text=Asda%20increased%20its%20profits%20by,Wal%2DMart%2C%20in%201999, December 1, 2003, accessed November 15, 2024.
4 Interview with Mark Fallick, July 8, 2024, reproduced by permission: www.theguardian.com/business/2003/dec/01/supermarkets
5 Gerber, Michael. *The E-Myth Revisited: Why Most Small Businesses Don't Work and What to Do About It*, Harper Business, 2001.
6 Handy, Charles. *Understanding Organizations*, Fourth Edition, Penguin Business, 2004.
7 Fields, Jonathan. *Uncertainty: Turning Fear and Doubt into Fuel for Brilliance*, Penguin, 2011.
8 Goodreads. Quote from Goodreads: www.goodreads.com/quotes/6513250-a-bad-system-will-beat-a-good-person-every-time, accessed February 19, 2025.

9 Burrus, Daniel. *The Anticipatory Organization: Turn Disruption and Change into Opportunity and Advantage* (Kindle Edition) Chapter 2, Greenleaf Book Press, 2017.
10 Handy, Charles. *Understanding Organizations*, Fourth Edition, Penguin Business, 2004.
11 Handy, Charles. *Understanding Organizations*, Fourth Edition, Penguin Business, 2004.
12 Handy, Charles. *Understanding Organizations*, Fourth Edition, Penguin Business, 2004.
13 Zuckerberg, Mark. Facebook CEO in his testimony before the US congress in April 2018.
14 Sainato, Michael. They're more concerned about profit: OSHA, DOJ take on Amazon's gruelling working conditions," *The Guardian*, March 2, 2023: https://www.theguardian.com/us-news/2023/mar/02/amazon-working-conditions-osha-doj-investigation.
15 Wikipedia. Jake Paul: https://en.wikipedia.org/wiki/Jake_Paul
16 Netflix and Most Valuable Promotions. Jake Paul vs Mike Tyson mega-event makes history with over 108 million live global viewers, Netflix (press release/news), November 19, 2024: https://about.netflix.com/news/jake-paul-vs-mike-tyson-over-108-million-live-global-viewers.
17 Bloomberg. Joe Rogan Experience Podcast Stats: www.bloomberg.com/news/newsletters/2024-03-21/spotify-reveals-podcast-numbers-for-joe-rogan-alex-cooper-travis-kelce
18 Handy, Charles. *Understanding Organizations*, Fourth Edition, Penguin Business, 2004.
19 Timpson, James. Timpson shouldn't exist anymore, *Marketing Week*, March 18, 2022: https://www.marketingweek.com/timpson-ceo-business/, accessed October 7, 2025; Handy, Charles. *Understanding Organizations*, Fourth Edition, Penguin Business, 2004.
20 Rogers, Charlotte. Timpson CEO: Our business shouldn't exist anymore, 18 March 2022: www.marketingweek.com/timpson-ceo-business, March 18, 2022. accessed December 7, 2024.
21 Handy, Charles. *Understanding Organizations*, Fourth Edition, Penguin Business, 2004.
22 Handy, Charles. *Understanding Organizations*, Fourth Edition, Penguin Business, 2004.
23 P3 Pharmacy. The Business of Family: www.p3pharmacy.co.uk/insight/the-power-of-three, March 18, 2022, accessed November 11, 2024.
24 Centred Solutions. Day Lewis Pharmacy: The Journey to Hub and Spoke, October 3, 2024: www.centredsolutions.co.uk/blogs/day-lewis-pharmacy-the-journey-to-hub-and-spoke, accessed December 7, 2024.
25 Fast Company. Barnes & Noble is stealing the indie shop playbook, and it's working: www.fastcompany.com/90854345/barnes-noble-stealing-the-indie-shop-playbook-and-its-working, February 28, 2023, accessed December 7, 2024.
26 See also his podcast interview with 3books: www.3books.co/transcripts/141
27 Dan Underwood. www.danunderwood.me, used with permission.
28 Obuobi, Samuel. General Secretary, Church of Pentecost, interview with the author, September 23, 2024.

Chapter 15

The Final Determinant

The Importance of Local and Federal Government

Just as I wrote this, on December 2, 2024, a borough took over a shopping centre on the brink of collapse.

Tamworth Borough Council completed a mutual agreement to take over and rejuvenate the Ankerside Shopping Centre. Councillor Nova Arkney said,

> *We're committed to seeing a town centre fit for the future, and this move seeks to provide stability and reassurance to Ankerside tenants and shoppers to secure the long-term future of the shopping centre in the heart of our town centre.*[1]

It showcases the problematic and sometimes crucial decisions that the government (nationally) and local administrations must make to ensure the success of our High Streets.

As Daniel Burus said in his book *The Anticipatory Organisation*:

> *No matter what any politician of any philosophical persuasion might argue, there will be more government regulation in the future, not less. This is true for every country.*[2]

Yes, local and national governments have a crucial role to play in the success of our High Streets.

Why is this crucial element not emphasised further in this book?

1. It is mainly outside the control of High Street businesses (though lobbying can certainly help) and, therefore, outside the scope of this book.
2. There are no guarantees that the concerned government party will implement this.

DOI: 10.4324/9781003569527-18

3. Frequent changes to policymakers (either by election or appointment) create an unpredictable and unstable environment, making long-term planning for sustained investments almost impossible. Efforts to elect mayors may help (currently underway in many UK cities).
4. Numerous studies, articles and reports on this topic undertaken by far more competent experts abound in the media and on the websites of interested parties and are readily available. I have quoted widely from these sources.

In August 2024, the Federation of Small Businesses conducted an in-depth and extensive report into the future of the High Street.[3] Most of the problems they discovered are primarily in sync and have been addressed previously **with an emphasis on the firm itself.** However, there is no doubt that to ensure the success of the High Street, both local and national governments need to play a crucial role. The report highlighted five key areas where the government's help was essential:

- **Destination**: Getting more footfall to the High Street
- **Transformation**: Easier funding and business support
- **Experience:** Providing a better experience for customers who visit the High Street
- **Infrastructure:** Easy transport links, transforming the High Street to a more liveable and family-friendly area, with spaces for targeted events, easy parking and transport access
- **Competitiveness:** Reduce business and tenancy rates, provide easier access to finance, and lower taxes for High Street businesses so they can compete better and more fairly with their online and retail park counterparts

The House of Lords also researched the same theme and came up with the following recommendations:

1. High Streets function in collaboration, and the introduction of new out-of-town retail and leisure centres can significantly negatively impact the vitality of a local High Stre
2. The government should introduce a 'town centre first' policy to ensure new public services, including libraries, diagnostic centres and local government buildings, are opened on our High Streets.
3. Each local authority should have an active town centre manager to support the development of their High Streets and town centres. Town centre managers nationwide should share experiences and best practices to benefit from cohort-based learning[4]
4. Young people, especially young women, told the committee that they often feel unsafe on their local High Street. Adequate street lighting,

clear sightlines, 'eyes on the street,' and a mix of uses, including residential and those open at night, can help contribute to safer-feeling spaces.
5. Access to public toilets is essential for older people and families with young children. They may visit their local High Street but spend less time there if they are unavailable. Local authorities must be proactive in using the many ways to provide decent public toilets.
6. Local markets can boost footfall on High Streets and contribute to the unique character of towns and small cities nationwide. Markets contribute to local economies and can act as catalysts for the High Street brands of tomorrow. Local authorities and other market operators should continue to support market traders.

However, security is probably the most significant improvement governments and local councils could make in securing the future of our High Streets. Business Improvement Districts (BID) are doing their best to help, but more investment should be made in High Retail crime prevention.

The British Retail Consortium boss, Helen Dickinson, said in the report:

The pandemic has normalised appalling levels of violent and abusive behaviour against retail workers. While a confrontation may be over in minutes, for many victims, their families and colleagues, the physical and emotional impact can last a lifetime. To make the UK a safer workplace, the Home Office must improve its reporting regarding the amendment to the Police, Crime, Sentencing and Courts Act, and the police must prioritise adequately resourcing retail crime. Surely everyone deserves the right to go to work without fear.[5]

Again, proactive High Street retailers have taken the matter into their own hands, funding an operation – around £1 billion in 2021 –to augment the police efforts.

Ten retailers will spend about £600,000 on the project, using CCTV pictures and data provided by the shops to understand shoplifters' operations better.

Analysts and intelligence officers will collect and examine data on shoplifting incidents from various retailers.

According to the British Retail Consortium report in 2023, the security issues went beyond just shoplifting:

- Retailers spent £715million in 2021 on crime prevention
- There are 850 serious issues of retail violence and abuse at over 850 incidents daily
- Shoplifting is up 22% year on year since 2021[6]

Multiple studies by many organisations, such as the Centre for Research in Ethnic Minority Entrepreneurship (CREME), the Federation of Small Businesses (FSB), and many others, have reached the same conclusions. The appendix of this book contains links to a few of these studies.

Government and policymakers have a massive role in supporting High Street businesses and making the continually evolving High Street a success for many years.

For this to work, we must have a pro-growth government that sees as of paramount importance, the sustainability of entrepreneurship and business and its power to create jobs and wealth.

But as I said before, any local government's policies are mainly outside High Street businesses' control.

However, businesses can still decide the future of their High Streets.

For instance, I use my adopted city of Plymouth as an example of how business collaboration can help create a bustling High Street and city centre.

Today, just before I sat down to write this part of the book, I met Steve Hughes, CEO of Plymouth City Centre Company, for a coffee.

He was beaming with pride. PwC had just voted Plymouth the most liveable city in the UK.[7]

The Plymouth City Centre Company was established 20 years ago, in 2005, and runs the city centre BID over 350 districts in the UK.

BIDs are not-for-profit, independent, business-led organisations supported by government legislation with the power to raise funds locally to be invested in projects and services to improve the trading environment. Local businesses vote for a 5-year term and are accountable to these businesses.

The 2024 House of Lords report on the High Street highlights the importance of BIDs:

> *Business Improvement Districts are a valuable tool for coordinating business involvement in their local areas. The government should support Business*
> *Improvement Districts, but they should not be mandated.*[8]

2024 marks the 20th anniversary of BIDs in the UK. They invest over £1 billion in local services and events to improve towns and cities nationwide.

A BID is created when most business ratepayers in the area vote to support the business plan and actively invest collectively through a levy based on the rateable value of the business premises.

In return, BIDs advocate for High Street and city centre businesses, direct investing, lobbying for better business rates, and creating events, branding, and marketing, such as Christmas markets and carnivals, to increase footfall on the High Street. They also grant small loans, improve security, cleanliness, and promotion, and offer business support.

For instance, in Plymouth, the BID lobbied and actively supported the creation of the UK's most significant new cultural attraction, The Box, and a new restaurant, cinema, and leisure complex called The Barcode. The Box, a brand new cultural museum, has attracted over 800,000 visitors since its opening in September 2020.

This collaboration has achieved remarkable results:

- Plymouth has been named the second-best holiday destination in the world by Condé Nast Traveller magazine for 2020[9]
- It has been voted the most liveable city in the UK for 2024
- It has been one of the fastest-recovering High Streets in the UK since the COVID-19 epidemic, with a 20% year-on-year increase[10]
- The BID has also secured strong support from the local city council and the Devon Business Chamber, and it is well on its way to attracting a further £250 million in investment by 2030

Other BIDs, such as Falmouth and Sutton have delivered outstanding results. Falmouth's BID, for instance, invested in a public WiFi network, which drove footfall to the High Street and resulted in it winning the UK's best digital High Street award in 2020.[11]

In 2018, the Conservative Party nominated Sir John Timpson to head an expert panel to look at practical ways the government could support the regeneration of High Streets. One of the key recommendations they made was to establish a High Street Taskforce (HSTF) which, in the words of Sir John Timpson, was tasked to:

support inspirational local leaders, working with all sections of their community who could put the buzz back into their town centre.

After six years, the HSTF, based in the Manchester Metropolitan University and with support from Cardiff University, has achieved some impressive successes[12]:

- 79% of councils acted on HSTF recommendations, and 69% increased their capacity for High Street transformation through improved collaboration.
- The HSTF trained nearly 1,000 place makers, of whom 90% reported enhanced skills and 97% felt encouraged to continue collaborating to improve their High Streets.

- The HSTF created the most comprehensive online resource library for High Streets globally, featuring over 1,000 items. The library received over 250,000 views and 45,000 unique visitors. The HSTF website and resource repository have been saved through the National Archives.
- Over 100 experts were recruited from professional bodies, providing 300 days of expert support and 2,700 hours of local analysis.
- 90% of media mentions about the HSTF were positive, highlighting success stories and outcomes. The HSTF challenged the 'death of the High Street' narrative by showcasing stories of hope and renewal.

The HSTF's mandate ended in 2024, with a future mandate uncertain (which, in my view, again highlights the risks of relying solely on the government for High Street improvements).

So, what does all this mean? Let's end with one of Netflix's most popular shows as an illustration.[13]

Notes

1. Price, Richards. Council takes ownership of town's shopping centre, *BBC News*: www.bbc.co.uk/news/articles/c791wrnn9vro.amp
2. Burus, Daniel: *The Anticipatory Organisation*, Greenleaf Books, 2017.
3. Federation of Small Businesses. The Future of the High Street: www.fsb.org.uk/resource-report/the-future-of-the-high-street.html
4. UK Parliament. UK parliament report: Look beyond retail to reverse High Street decline, says new Lords report: www.parliament.uk/business/lords/media-centre/house-of-lords-media-notices/2024/november-2024/look-beyond-retail-to-reverse-high-street-decline-says-new-lords-report/#:~:text=In%202023%20there%20were%20over,is%20something%20of%20the%20past.
5. British Retail Consortium. BRC Crime Survey 2023: https://brc.org.uk/news-and-events/news/corporate-affairs/2025/ungated/retail-crime-spiralling-out-of-control/#:~:text=The%20survey%20reveals%20incidents%20of,assault%20or%20threats%20with%20weapons
6. British Retail Consortium. BRC Crime Survey 2023: https://brc.org.uk/news-and-events/news/corporate-affairs/2025/ungated/retail-crime-spiralling-out-of-control/#:~:text=The%20survey%20reveals%20incidents%20of,assault%20or%20threats%20with%20weapons
7. McNamee, Annie. This underrated English seaside city is officially the UK's best place to live, *Time Out*: www.timeout.com/uk/news/this-underrated-english-seaside-city-is-officially-the-uks-best-place-to-live-091124#google_vignette, September 11, 2024.
8. McNamee, Annie. This underrated English seaside city is officially the UK's best place to live, *Time Out*: www.timeout.com/uk/news/this-underrated-english-seaside-city-is-officially-the-uks-best-place-to-live-091124#google_vignette, September 11, 2024.
9. Plymouth Live. Plymouth rated top destination for travel by luxury travel magazine: www.plymouthherald.co.uk/news/plymouth-news/plymouth-rated-top-destination-2020-3383571, accessed 2024.

10 Plymouth City Centre Company. Plymouth has the strongest High Street in the UK post-lockdown: www.citycentrebid.co.uk/news/2024/02/01/plymouth-has-the-strongest-high-street-in-the-uk-post-lockdown
11 Spark TSL. 2019. Recent win by Falmouth for the UK's best digital high street award. *Spark TSL*, September 2: https://www.sparktsl.com/blog/recent-win-by-falmouth-for-the-uks-best-digital-high-street-award, accessed December 15, 2024.
12 Institute of Place Management at Manchester Metropolitan University. IPM Reflects on Five Years of Revitalising England's High Streets: www.placemanagement.org/news/posts/2024/november/high-streets-task-force-ipm-reflects-on-five-years-of-revitalising-england-s-high-streets
13 Netflix. *Breaking Bad*, 2013: www.netflix.com/title/70143836

Epilogue
The Transformation of Our High Streets

In the TV series *Breaking Bad*, Walter White, a good but overlooked chemistry teacher, gets the worst news: late-stage cancer, not long to live. To provide for his family, he makes a decision. At first, it feels small, maybe even justified. But step by step, the compromises grow. The teacher becomes the dealer. The provider becomes the destroyer. What started with good intentions ends with nothing left.

In one lesson, Walter told his class that chemistry is the study of change – combining, dissolving, decaying, transforming. That became his story. And it is also the story of our High Streets.

This book, though, began with my mother's story – a woman who started with nothing and built a life with grit and grace. Her life showed me that endurance, even in the toughest conditions, is possible.

On our High Streets, we've seen echoes of that same spirit. Some names have endured for over a century, reinventing themselves again and again. Selfridges, still reinventing, is chasing permanence in a changing retail world. Others, like Debenhams, BHS, and Woolworths, chose too late – and are now only memories.

Change will come. The only question is which way it goes.

Some businesses cling to the past. They keep chasing discounts. They let their shops get tired. They believe what worked yesterday will work tomorrow. And they vanish.

Others take another path, like the companies we've talked about in this book. They learn faster, adapt sooner, care more. They don't just write values on the wall, they live them. They try new things, make mistakes, and keep going until it sticks. As the World Economic Forum keeps reminding us, the future belongs to those who innovate and then make those innovations part of everyday life. You can feel it when it happens. The questions get sharper. The shelves make sense. The service has life again.

The High Street still has what online never will: presence, community, human connection. When businesses lean into that, the lights come back on. Currys showed this in its Beyond Techspectations campaign – proving what only a real store can do: let people see, feel, and try.[1]

Walter White's story ended in loss. My mother's ended in triumph. Our High Streets stand between the two.

Chasing Permanence is not about luck. It is a decision – made every day, in full view, on our High Streets.

The choice is ours.

Note

1 Currys. Currys | Beyond Techspectations: IRL – Extended Cut. YouTube video, 1:11. March 22, 2023: https://youtu.be/Ri4qimJbi04?si=zslGjW8BJsX1ZDCm

Acknowledgements

Every author more or less says the same thing: they could not have written the book without an army of supporters, fans and friends. This support was crucial for me while taking on such a vast topic.

My family – Dela, Nshira and Nana – have been massive supporters of this book, creating the time and space, giving valuable feedback and drawing my attention to various trends and articles that I have found tremendously helpful.

My cherished friend Charles Lartey spent hours poring over this book's design, style and content details.

My core gang, Jabo Butera, Steven Bell, Liliane Uwimana, Tendai Mudame, Coach Dan Underwood, Coach Kate Wright, and Anthony Thompson – always had my back, encouraged and cheered me on.

My beta readers: Melanie Butler, Akofa Wallace, Bernice Atubra, Emmanuel Anderson, Karen Turvey and my brother Michael Adjei, who read the book in its rough form and offered valuable feedback.

My business partners of over a decade, Abhinav Srivastava and Robert Smith.

My mother, Rose, and my dad, Nana, have been a continual source of encouragement, support, and love.

My friends Paul Wright, Mike Smith, Julie Nash, Gordon Field, Chris Oppong, and Chris Clewer, for their continual chauffeuring, support, prayers, and belief.

Thank you to all the incredible experts who took the time to read my book and offered such glowing endorsements. Your faith in me spurred on me to make all this happen, and I'll never forget your kindness.

I am grateful to the invaluable staff and management of Waterstones, Richer Sounds, HMV, Day Lewis, and Timpson, as well as to all the small businesses that supported and helped me along the way.

And to all the numerous podcasters who gave (and continue to give) me a platform to express and test these ideas publicly, a shout-out to Ninder

Johal and the team at Nachural, Sanjiv Patel, Daniel Coker, and Emmanuel Anderson.

And to all the readers of my first book, **Pay The Price,** who gave me the angelic confidence I needed to believe I could take on such a massive task for this second book. I hope I have done you proud.

Finally, I thank the heroic team at Routledge, especially Meredith Norwich and Bethany Nelson, who believed in me and made me think.

I hope I've done you all proud.

Appendix
For Further Reading

Books:
For further reading:
1. Bersin, Josh. *Irresistible: The Seven Secrets of the World's Most Enduring, Employee-Focused Organizations*, IdeaPress Publishing, 2022.
2. Stadler, Christian. *Enduring Success: What We Can Learn from the History of Outstanding Corporations*, Stanford Business Books, 2011.
3. Collins, James C. and Jerry I. Porras. *Built to Last: Successful Habits of Visionary Companies*, Harper Business, 1994.
4. Magnusson, William: *For Profit: A History of Corporations*, Basic Books, 2022.
5. Hill, Alex. *Centennials: The 12 Habits of Great, Enduring Organisations*, Penguin Books, 2024.
6. Gerber, Michael. *The E- Myth Revisited: Why Most Small Businesses Don't Work and What to Do About It*, Harper Business, 2001.
7. Collins, James C. and Lazier, William C. *Beyond Entrepreneurship 2.0: Turning Your Business into an Enduring Great Company*, London: Random House Business, 2020.
8. Covey, Stephen M. R. *Trust and Inspire: How Truly Great Leaders Unleash Greatness in Others*, Simon and Schuster, 2022.
9. Senge, Peter. *The Fifth Discipline: The Art and Practice of the Learning Organisation*, Second Edition, Random House Publishers, 2006.
10. Kotter, John P., Vanessa Akhtar and Gaurav Gupta. *Change: How Organizations Achieve Hard-to-Imagine Results in Uncertain and Volatile Times*, John Wiley, 2021.

Reports: These are the major accessible studies on the High Street by CREME, the FSB and the High Street Expert Panel.

Appendix

1. Time to Change: A blueprint for advancing the UK's ethnic minotiry businesses: www.aston.ac.uk/latest-news/new-aston-university-report-sets-out-blueprint-advancing-growth-potential-ethnic
2. The Future of the High Street: www.fsb.org.uk/resource-report/the-future-of-the-high-street.html
3. High Street 2030: Achieving Change: https://assets.publishing.service.gov.uk/media/5c1cbfee40f0b66cfcc90e3e/High_Street_2030-Achieving_Change.pdf
4. The High Street Report: https://assets.publishing.service.gov.uk/media/5c1a7322e5274a4685bfbb28/The_High_Street_Report.pdf
5. High Streets: Life: beyond retail? https://publications.parliament.uk/pa/ld5901/ldselect/ldbuiltenv/42/42.pdf, 28 November 2024
6. The High Street Task Force framework for restructuring England's High Streets:

    https://webarchive.nationalarchives.gov.uk/ukgwa/20241004153257/https://www.highstreetstaskforce.org.uk/news/high-streets-task-force-frameworks-for-high-street-and-town-centre-action-and-renewal

7. To read positive news on the High Street every month, subscribe to my friend and consultant Laura Harris' newsletter High Street Positives: https://highstreetpositives.beehiiv.com/p/high-street-positives-newsletter

Index

2Pac 40
4P's of marketing 69
7 Habits of Highly Effective People, The (Stephen Covey) xxxvii
7P's of marketing 69

accountability, notion of 117
Accra, Ghana xvii
act and adapt, principle of 125
acts of service 107
Adair, John 24, 152, 156
ADD (Autonomy, Diversity, Dividend) principle 89, 92
adjacency, principle of 135
aesthetic intelligence 32
affordability: components of 60–1; notion of xxxvii, 168
Ali, Hira 98
Amazon xxiv, xxx, xxxv, 51, 55, 70, 119, 176–7, 185
Amazon Prime xxvi, 50
Ansoff Matrix 132, 134
Anticipatory Organisation, The (Daniel Burus) 174
Apple Watch 117
appreciation, words of 106–7
artificial intelligence (AI) 176, 184; rise of 117, 123
Aspergers' syndrome 41
attunement, attribute of 41
authenticity: adjustments to foster 98–9; Authenticity Framework® 78
authentic leadership, by autonomy 92
autism 41
autonomy, principle of 90; authentic leadership and 92

Baert, Steven 157
Baidoo, Melissa 183
BAME pharmacists 95
bankruptcy 47, 66, 167
Barcode, The 192
Bartlett, Steven 45, 60, 157
Beacon Electricals 32–3, 40–1, 64
Bersin, Josh 74, 78, 80
Best Before Date 10–11
Best Before End (BBE) 8, 10
Billboard Charts 18
Black History Month 66, 96
BlueCloud Health 8
books xxix
Booths 50
Boyatzis, Richard 40
brain intelligence 13
brain interconnectedness, system of 40–1
brainstorming 34
Branson, Richard 34–5
Bregman, Peter 92
Brexit 122
brick-and-mortar stores 29–30
British ghost xviii
British Red Cross 45, 50
British Retail Consortium 190
bubonic plague of 1348 xxiv
bucket, principle of 85; primary bucket 87; secondary bucket 87; third bucket 88
Buffett, Warren 65
Build for Tomorrow (Jason Feifer) 119
burnout 174
Burrus, David 188
Burrus, Daniel 174

Business Improvement District (BID) 42, 190–1
business insurance 124
business's cash flow 66
Butera, Jabo 93
Butler, Melanie 170
buzzy personality 182

Candle In The Wind (1997) 9
capabilities 37
career development 92
catastrophes, quadrants of 111
Centennials, the 12 Habits of Great, Enduring Organisations (Alex Hill) 11
Centre for Research in Ethnic Minority Entrepreneurship (CREME) 190–1
change and uncertainty, rapid acceleration of xxv–xxxii
changing habits of customers xxix
Chapman, Gary 104
"Cheat Sheets" program 20
Clark, Dorie xv
Clinton, Hillary 161
Cloud, Henry 11, 24
Cohen, Monty 151
Coldplay 12, 39, 54
Coleman, Daniel 41
collaboration: art of 39–43; symbol group model 64
collaborative behaviour 16
Collins, Jim 63, 80, 100, 152
colonial enslavers, revolt against 82–3
community-based programmes 48
community pharmacy xxix, 43–56, 63, 183–4
Community Pharmacy England 122
community, sense of 48, 56
connections 37
Constantine, Mark 11
consumer behaviour 43–4
cooperation 37
co-ordination 37
correlation and causality, delusion of xxviii
cost-of-living crisis 174
cost trap, beware of 162
Cotter, John 125
Covey, Stephen 149
COVID epidemic 83, 85–6, 106, 115, 123, 132, 169, 178, 192

Crystallised Intelligence 12–13
cultural misfit 85
customer agility 37–8
Customer Agility under Tangibility 137
customer-focused collaboration 37
customer service 33–5, 62, 65, 120, 138, 172
cybercrime 112, 120

Dashti, Shideh 31
Daunt, James 19, 36, 48, 91, 138, 185
Day Lewis Chemists xxxiv, 10, 19, 22, 32, 36, 52, 76, 79; values 80, 87
Day Lewis Pharmacies 48
Death Row Records 3
Debenham, Neil 34
decision-making 37
detect, principle of 123–4
developing others, attribute of 41
Diary of a CEO, the 33 Laws of Business and Life (Steven Bartlett) 60–1
Dickinson, Helen 190
Differentiation Strategy (Kevin Holt) 60
Dion, Celine 2
Diversity Training Doesn't Work (Peter Bregman) 93
division of labour 37
Dogg, Snoop 3, 16
"Done for You" program 20
Do Penguins Eat Peaches? (Katie Tucker) 38
drug addiction 62; proliferation of 62
drumbeat of panic, phenomenon of 119

economies of scale xxxvii, 162, 170, 173, 176
Eddie, Joff 51
Eminem (hip-hop artist) 40
empathy, attribute of 41
employee benefits, era of 83
employee personalisation, era of 83
employee power, wheels of 82
employee revolt, era of 82–3
energy efficiency 112
Entrepreneur magazine 119
Erdly, Catherine 65
Euronics xxxv, 16, 64
Evans, Morris S. 48, 56, 91

Facebook 12, 19, 119, 176
Fallick, Mark 82, 90, 169

Federation of Small Businesses (FSB) xx, 189, 191
FedEx 9
Ferguson, Alex 8, 11–12
Fields, Jonathan 172
Fifth Discipline, The (Peter Senge) 167, 169
financial crash of the 1930s 82, 115
fire drill 124
Five Love Languages, for romantic relationships 104
Flag Response System 115–16
flexibility, notion of 122
Floyd, George 83
fluid intelligence 12–13
Folkestone 50
Ford, Henry 34–5
Ford Motor Company xxiii
From Strength to Strength, Finding Happiness and Deep Purpose in the Second Half of Life (Arthur C. Brooks) 12
front-of-the-queue service 48

Gadkari, Nupur 69
Game 50
Garrod, Catherine 95
Gennette, Jeff 100
Gen Zs 45
gifts 106
Gill, John 160
Gladwell, Malcolm 15, 162
Glastonbury festival 9, 18, 38–9
Go-Compare.com 50
Goldsmith, Marshall 19, 99, 135, 149
good citizen, notion of 122
Google 12, 119, 183–4
Google Reviews 52
Grant, Adam xxv
gratitude gap 107
Great Depression 82
Great Good Places, The (Ray Oldenburg) 46
Great Resignation xxiv, 19, 75, 104–5
Guardian newspaper 39, 70
Gulati, Ranjay 36
GymShark 34

Hackney Diamonds 12
Halo Effect delusion xxviii
Handy, Charles 172, 174–5, 182

Happy Index, The (James Timpson) 7
Harvard Business Review xxiv–xxv, 16, 40, 93, 98, 131, 133
hate speech 176–7
Hewitt, Steve 34
HHCL 34
Hien, Piet 4
Higgins, Mark 16
High Street Businesses 73, 108, 133, 140; decline of 196
high-street chains 62, 162
High Street Companies xxvi, xxxii, 19, 32, 37–8, 40–3, 47–8, 51–2, 60, 63, 85, 173, 196
High Street Taskforce (HSTF) 192, 193
Hill, Alex 125
Hirst, Anderson 65
Hirst, John 49
HMV xxxiv–xxxv, 19, 32, 44, 47–9, 51–2, 76
HMV Vault, in Birmingham 136
Housel, Morgan 20
How to Better Support Muslim Women at Work (Hira Ali) 98
How to Grow Leaders (John Adair, 2005) 152–3
how to scale appropriately, principles of 161–2
hub-and-spoke system 184
human capital 139, 143, 168, 170; as appreciating assets 78; authenticity and values framework 79; and era of employee revolt 82–3; five determinants model of 73; hiring bias 81; labour turnover 77; person, purpose, and passion 81; *see also* people, kinds of
human interaction, between staff and customers 50
humility, principle of 4, 15, 17, 40

identity and core values, sense of 7
Iger, Bob 9
individualism, rise of xxvii, 40, 51
Industrial Age xxv–xxvi
influence, attribute of 41
Information Age xxvi
information sharing 37
inspiration 41
Instagram xix, 19, 176
intellectual capacity xxxvii, 140

intellectual capital 140, 142
inter-collaboration 41–2
International Coaching Federation 178
International Women's Day 96
intrapreneurs 100, 182
intra-shopping 43

James, Sebastian 34
JD Sports 135
job description 172
job satisfaction 88–9
job security 82
Jobs, Steve 34–5, 118
job vacancy 81
John, Elton 9, 18, 40, 55; Farewell Yellow Brick Road tour 18

key performance indicators (KPIs) 171
Kindle e-books xxxv
King, Martin Luther 82
know your audience 162
Kotter, John xxv–xxvi, 126, 141
Kurzweil, Ray xxv

labour effectiveness, decline in 83
labour turnover 77
Lambert, Adam 12–13
lasting success, delusion of xxix
leaders, attributes that foster collaboration 40–1
leadership development 156
Lee, Kerry 29, 30
Leighton, Allan 168
Leinwand, Paul 140
LGBTQ community 95, 97
lifelong learning 152
likelihood, principle of 122
likelihood vs impact 112; high likelihood and high impact 114; high likelihood and low impact 114–15; low likelihood and high impact 115; low likelihood and low impact 113–14
LinkedIn xxv, 104, 157, 176, 178
Lipa, Dua 40
Lloyds Pharmacies xxxiv
loneliness, attribute of 45–7
Lynskey, Dorian 40

MacDonald, Gordon 11
Machin, Aenone Harper 160

Magnussen, William xx
Magnusson, William 176
Mainardi, Cesare 140
Manor Park, East London xvi–xvii
marketing mix 69
Marley, Bob 13, 40
Martin, Chris 6, 39–40, 51
Maxwell, John C 8, 153
McCartney, Paul xxviii, xxxvi
McDonald's 118
McElhennyy, Rob xviii
Mckenzie, Tina xxii
McKeown, Max 130–1
McNally, Danny 184
Medici Bank xx, xxiii
messianic fantasy 6, 9
Me Too movement xxiv
Miyazaki, Hayao 10
modern societies, suburbanisation of 47
mood contagion 41
Moon Music (music album) 39
Moyes, David 11–12
Murdoch, Rupert 9
Murthy, Vivek 45
Musk, Elon 176, 178

'negative energy and vibe' customers 41
Netflix 50, 66
Nieuwholf, Carey 45
Norman, Archie 167, 168

O'Brien, Conan 39
Oldenburg, Ray 46, 47
oligopoly 38
online community 44, 48
Optical Express Group 160
Orben, Amy 119
Ordering Your Private World (Gordon MacDonald) 11
O'Reilly, Charles 133
organisational awareness 41
Owuo Junior, Michael Ebenezer Kwadjo Omari 38
Oxford Street, London xiv–xvi

Pareto rule 112
Parker, Louise 47
Patel, Dadu 151
Patel, Jay 10, 15, 19, 22, 25, 40, 151–2, 169
Patel, Kirit xxxiv, 10–11, 19, 151–2

Patel, Priti 33
Patel, Sam 7
Patel, Vijay 151
Paul, Jake 177, 183
Peloton xxix
people, kinds of: gatherer 100–1; hunter 100; people-gatherer 102; people hunter 101–2; people-oriented 101; process gatherer 102–3; process hunter 102; task-oriented 101
Percerptyx (data company) 157
permanence: about scaling xxvi–xxvii; about surviving xxviii–xxxii; about thriving xxvii–xxviii; mindset of xxxvi, 2; not always about scaling xxvi–xxvii; operation of xxvi–xxvii, 16, 26, 140, 163; systems of xxxvii, 86
personal and personnel scalability 149
personal capacity, concept of 153–4
personal development 151
personalisation, concept of 70, 107–8
personal scalability, principle of xxvii, 23, 151–3, 154–6
person culture, principle of 177–86
personnel scalability, concept of xxvii, 20, 149, 154–6
Pharmacy2U 159
pharmacy retail business 54, 151
Pharmazon xxix, 36, 159
Phoenix 64
physical music xxx
physical touch 107
Pie, principle of 23
place scalability, principle of 159–63
planned obsolescence xxix–xxx
Plymouth 66
polycrisis 120
Poundland (British discount chain) 60
power culture 174–5, 182, 183–6
The Power of Resilience: How the Best Companies Manage the Unexpected (Yossi Sheffi) 4
practice training, issue of 142
primary customers 53–4
professional code of conduct 183
Public Health Service (England) 160
Putman, Doug 19, 44–5, 49–51

QR codes 36
Quiet Quitting, phenomenon of xxiv

racial bigotry 99
Rai, Mandeep 29
redundancy, principle of 122–3
reflective paranoia 169; concept of 167–86
remuneration 113
reserve, principle of 121–3
resilience, findings for maintaining 4–5; detect 4–5; five determinants model 112; prevent 5; respond 5
Retail Gazette xxxv, 19, 34, 49
Reynolds, Ryan xviii
Richer, Julian 7, 15, 19, 22, 25, 36, 77, 82, 108
Richer Sounds xxxv–xxxvii, 11, 22, 32, 36, 47–8, 67, 70, 82, 108, 135, 161
Richer Unsigned 48
Ride of a Lifetime, The (Bob Iger) 9
right customer 60, 62, 68–70
right people 81
right place 66–8
right price 64–5
right product 62–4, 67
right time xxxvii, 60, 62, 65–6
risk xxxvii; amber flag of 117; five determinants model 112; flag response model of 116; green flag of 118–19; kinds of 113–21; red flag of 116–17; of self-sabotage 116; white flag of 118
risk development 120
risk-resilience cycle 121–25, 169–70; act and adapt 125; detect 124; integrate 125–7; reserve 121–3
Rogan, Joe 178, 183
Rogers, Charlotte 25
role cultures, of an organisations 170, 172, 179, 183
Rolls-Royce 143
Roman Empire, collapse of 4
Romo, Melissa 106
Ronseal (UK DIY company) 34
Roosevelt, President 83
Rothbard, Nancy 19
Rumsfeld, Donald 111

scalability: imperative process 150; principle of 151
Schultz, Howard 9
secondary customers 53–4
self-awareness, principle of 4

self-sabotage, risk of 116
Senge, Peter 125, 143
Sheffi, Yossi 4, 112, 118, 122
Silo Busting: How to Execute on the Promise of Customer Focus (Ranjay Gulati) 36–7
Sisyphean Cycle 119
Skills4Pharmacy 40
Skipper, Kate 130
Sky TV 50
Smith, Emily 105
Smith, Fred 9
Snowden, Edward 178
social architecture 138
social behaviours 138
social cohesion 120
social disorders 40–1
social equality 47
Social Intelligence and the Biology of Leadership (Daniel Coleman and Richard Boyartzis) 40
social interactions, brain associated with 41
societal polarisation 120
Sogakope, Ghana xvii–xviii
Soult, Graham 19
Spider's Web, The 174
spillovers, beware of 162–3
Spirited Away (2020) 9
Sports Direct 50
Spotify 39, 66
Stadler, Christian 15, 35, 137, 199; HOW Framework 133, 137, 168, 195
Standard Operating Procedures (SOPs) 101, 114, 122, 169
start-ups 176, 177; creativity of 177; rise of xxvi
stereotyping 98
Stiff Person Syndrome 3
Stobbart, Eddie 19
strategic decisions 141
strategy xxxvii; 3 Ways to Communicate Your Company's Strategy 141; corporate strategy 141; decisions in action 141–3; eight points for executing 129; futuristic framework for planning of 131; harmony with the environment 137–9; Minding the Gap strategy 139–41; Moving Forward strategy 133–7, 168; open strategy 142; Seven Habits of Highly Effective People 149; Stand Your Ground strategy 133, 168; We Reproduce What We Are strategy 156–9
Strategy Book, The (Max McKeown, 2024) 133
Suez Canal crisis 122
superintendent pharmacist 183
supply chain management 111
Swift, Taylor 54–5
SWOT analysis 143
symbol group model 64
systems balance wheel 167
systems thinking: fallacy of 166, 174–5; five determinants model of 166; importance of 171–4; person culture 177–86; right balance of creativity and rigidity 166; task culture 175–7

Talk Retail blog 34
tangible factor for businesses 29–57; essence of 29
task culture 175–7, 179, 183
team leaders 142, 156–9
teamwork facilitation 41
tertiary customers 53–4
Thatcher, Margaret 33
'The law of Accelerating Returns' theory xxv
Third Web 12
thought leader, rise of 177–86
TikTok xix, 67, 176, 177–8
time, significance of 105–6
Timpson, James xxxv, 15, 36, 90–1, 136, 153, 157
Timpson, John xxxv, 7, 19–20, 192; "Upside Down Management" theory 138
Timpson Ltd xxxv, 16, 32, 40, 107, 179
Timpson, William 179
tolerance, principle of 93–6
'town centre first' policy 189
trail, principle of 24
transcendence, principle of 9–11
Trump, Donald 161, 178
Trustpilot 52, 70, 119
Tucker, Katie 38
Tushman, Michale 133
Twitter 12, 67, 176, 177

uncertainty, sense of xxvi
Understanding Organisations (Charles Handy) 172
Upside-down Management, doctrine of 182
use by date 10
use by phase 10

value-add model 64–5
video games 50
virtual chain model 64
Vitality Health Insurance 50
VUE (high-street cinema chain) 50

Warhammer (proprietary fantasy game) 49
Waterstones xxxv, 32, 36, 47–8
Waymade PLC 151

Webb, Amy 131
Welch, Jack 9
what good looks like (WGLL) 172
White, Paul 104
Why Diversity Programs Fail (Frank Dobben and Alexandra Kalev) 93
Wind Rises, The (2013) 9
World Economic Forum 92, 194; Global Risks Report 2023 120
World Kindness Day 66

Yoga Sutras, of Patanjali 92
Your Resource is Human (Melissa Romo) xxiv, 106

Zoom xxix, 106, 173
Zuckerberg, Mark 177

For Product Safety Concerns and Information please contact our
EU representative GPSR@taylorandfrancis.com Taylor & Francis
Verlag GmbH, Kaufingerstraße 24, 80331 München, Germany